THE ART OF STRATEGIC PLANNING FOR INFORMATION TECHNOLOGY

Crafting Strategy for the 90s

Bernard H. Boar
American Telephone and Telegraph Company

John Wiley & Sons, Inc.
New York • Chichester • Brisbane • Toronto • Singapore

Associate Publisher: Katherine Schowalter
Senior Acquisitions Editor: Diane Cerra
Managing Editor: Jacqueline A. Martin
Composition: Electric Ink, Ltd.

This text is printed on acid-free paper.

Designations used by companies to distinguish their products are often claimed as trademarks. In all instances where John Wiley & Sons, Inc. is aware of a claim, the product names appear in Initial Capital or all capital letters. Readers, however, should contact the appropriate companies for more complete information regarding trademarks and registration.

This publication is designed to provide accurate and authoritative information in regard to the subject matter covered. It is sold with the understanding that the publisher is not engaged in rendering legal, accounting, or other professional services. If legal advice or other expert assistance is required, the services of a competent professional person should be sought. FROM A DECLARATION OF PRINCIPLES JOINTLY ADOPTED BY A COMMITTEE OF THE AMERICAN BAR ASSOCIATION AND A COMMITTEE OF PUBLISHERS.

The opinions expressed in this book are those of the author and do not necessarily represent those of the American Telephone & Telegraph Company.

Library of Congress Cataloging-in-Publication Data:

Boar, Bernard H.
    The art of strategic planning for information technology: crafting strategy for the 90s
    / Benard H. Boar.
        p.   cm.
    Includes index.
    ISBN 0–471–59918–2   (cloth: alk. paper)
    1. Strategic planning—Data processing.   2. Information technology—Management.
3. Management information systems.   I. Title.
HD30.28.863   1993
658.4′012—dc20   93–9880
                                                                                CIP

Printed in the United States of America

10 9 8 7 6 5 4 3 2

To Diane, Jessica and Debbie
With Love Always

Contents

Other Books by the Author

Abend Debugging for Cobol Programmers

Application Prototyping: A Requirements Definition Strategy for the 80s

Implementing Client/Server Computing: A Strategic Perspective

Author's Note

Throughout this book two terms, Information Technology (I/T) and Information Movement and Management (IM&M) are used interchangeably to refer to those technologies used to access, move, store, and manage information in all its forms. While I/T is the generally accepted industry label for such technology, IM&M is the term we use at AT&T and the one I believe more robustly communicates the purpose of information technology. Please read them as synonyms.

On Strategy

"In ancient times, those known as great warriors prevailed when it was easy to prevail. Their victories in battle were not flukes. Their victories were not flukes because they positioned themselves so that they would surely win, prevailing over those who had already lost. So it is said that great warriors take their stand on ground where they cannot lose. Therefore a victorious army first wins and then seeks battle; a defeated army first battles and then seeks victory."

The Art of War—Sun Tzu

Foreword

The struggle of business has always been and remains a struggle for advantage. Those who build, compound, and sustain competitive advantage win; those who do not lose. Competition is all about advantage. It really is that simple, yet at the same time, so complicated.

There is much confusion and misunderstanding in the Information Movement and Management (IM&M) community. Many do not understand the purpose of the technologies that they deploy daily; they proceed in a fog. They do not understand why the IM&M industry is a $.9 trillion world-wide industry growing at over ten percent per year. Some think the purpose is to "save money," some think it is to "help in making better and faster decisions," and others think it is to improve productivity. This understanding is very near-sighted and shallow; they have entirely missed the deeper point.

The purpose of IM&M is competitiveness. The purpose of IM&M is to provide a robust resource for the building, compounding, and sustaining of competitive advantage for the enterprise. Cost reduction, expedited decision making, and improved productivity, while of course important, are but specific instances of this greater purpose. In the 1990s and onward, the purpose of IM&M is to be the foundation of competitive advantage for the business. How else could one justify an industry growing to $1.6 trillion by 1995?

At the Information Management Services (IMS) Division of the American Telegraph and Telephone Company (AT&T), we fully understand this mission and collaborate daily with the other AT&T business units to fulfill this purpose. To compete and succeed globally, one cannot be confused about the purpose of such a valuable resource. We are in the business of developing, provisioning, operating, and selling competitiveness.

We manage our services strategically. While one of the country's largest suppliers of IM&M services, i.e., voice services, data connectivity services, processing services, and desktop services, we never forget that we are managers of a business, not managers of technologies. We have demanding customers, a robust supplier chain, hungry competitors, and the opportunity to add incredible value through our services.

The strategic planning methods presented in this book contribute significantly to our success. By applying concepts such as core competencies, critical success factors, five forces, driving force, strategic intent, scenario analysis, benchmarking value chain analysis, and product maps to our strategic planning efforts, we are better able to master the possibilities of technology and position chosen technologies for maximum leverage.

The business model of the 1990s is in significant transition. The "command and control" model of management, the "order-chain," is dying and being replaced by a team model in which professionals are engaged, enrolled, and challenged to innovate. The resulting business structure more resembles an orchestra of skilled musicians than a traditional, hierarchical military command structure.

But even an orchestra needs a score. Our strategic plans provide the required score to enable our staff to craft evermore powerful solutions for our customers while maintaining harmony across the multitude of efforts. Agile employees working in an empowered environment require an anchor. The strategic plan provides that point of common reference; "superglue" for direction and purpose.

We strongly urge you to study and apply the methods presented in this book. We are confident of continued future success and believe it is neither an accident nor simply good fortune, rather, it is the result of the stimulating, challenging, and exciting insights derived from careful planning. Though not at your command, the future is not a totally impenetrable mystery. Sun Tzu, the master of strategy, said " . . . much strategy prevails over little strategy, so those with no strategy cannot but be defeated." We concur completely; how else could it be?

Bart P. Donohue III
Vice President,
Product Management & Engineering
Information Management Services
AT&T

Sam S. Coursen
Division Manager,
Processing Product Line
Information Management Services
AT&T

Ben Doyle
Division Manager,
Product Engineering
Information Management Services
AT&T

Preface

The word and its derivatives are everywhere. Its presence creates an aura of importance, commands respect and demands attention. The word is, of course, "strategy." The variations are "strategic," "strategically," "strategize," "strategist," "stratagem," and "strategies." The word is pervasive.

Vendors announce their new "strategic alliance." The industry pundit predicts "Successful Strategies for the 90s." Your account executive assures you that the product you are considering purchasing is "strategic." We are reminded by our management team to align our actions to support and enable the "Corporate Business Strategy." The weekly industry newsletter applauds the "stratagems" used by the upstart vendor to surpass the industry leader in price/performance. The year end magazine issue contains a round-table of industry "strategists" who confidently foretell the future without reservation. Strategy is not tangential to the debate, it is the debate.

But what are they all talking about? What is strategy? How does one create winning strategies? Why do some succeed and others fail? How do strategists think? Why does strategy command such respect? Why does it deserve such an aura of importance? What are these people really saying with all this talk about strategy?

The purpose of this book is to answer these questions as well as many others about "the word." If you are like myself, a manager in the Information Movement and Management (IM&M) industry, understanding, influencing, developing, and executing strategy is growing in importance. Historically, IM&M strategy has focused on technology, often technology for technology's sake. While understanding the bits, bytes, mips, pixels, and packets remains important, it is simply an inadequate response to the demands of the 1990s.

As the 1990s unfold, the IM&M function finds itself caught in a three way pincer squeeze:

1. The business is exerting tremendous pressure on the IM&M function to add-value—to enable the building and maintenance of competitive advantage through information technology.

2. The IM&M industry is in a period of unparalleled change. The computing paradigm, host-centered computing, which has dominated computing for the last thirty years, is in decline and being replaced by a new paradigm, network computing (also called client/server computing). Coupled with this paradigm shift is a whole range of emerging and opportunistic IM&M technologies.

3. There exists growing competition to in-house IM&M services. Outsourcers, systems integrators, facility managers, and consultants all assert that they are better equipped to meet the needs of the users of information technology.

The mission of the IM&M function is being re-defined from application provider to being the basis of competitiveness for the enterprise.

To succeed in this mission, IM&M management requires the skills to develop and execute rich business strategies. They need to view the IM&M organization as a logical strategic business unit (an entity with a distinct mission, well defined markets and competitors, and a robust set of products to provide value to its customers) and develop comprehensive business strategies to guide its actions. Unfortunately, most IM&M professionals are ill-equipped for this challenge. Their backgrounds are usually technical (engineering, mathematics, computer science, systems engineering, etc.) and their experience and perspectives reflect this. They simply lack expertise and experience in the sophisticated discipline of formal business strategy development. While they may have developed technology strategies, such an effort is but a small subset of a properly developed strategic business plan for the IM&M organization.

Information Movement and Management (IM&M) is the preparation, collection, transport, retrieval, storage, access, presentation, and transformation (processing) of information in all its varied forms (voice, graphics, text, video, data, image, and animation). Movement can take place between humans, humans and machines, and between machines. Management assures the proper selection, deployment, administration, operation, maintenance, and evolution of the IM&M assets consistent with organizational objectives. IM&M is interchangeable with the phrase "Information Technology (I/T)."

Business strategy is the definition of a desired future state for the business, objectives, strategic moves to accomplish the objectives, a change management plan, and a commitment plan. Strategic moves are purposeful and coherent actions to achieve the objectives. They are purposeful in that they directly act to achieve or cause one or more objectives. They are coherent in that they complement and enable each other; they do not block or retard each other.

This book is about IM&M strategy; the discipline of applying strategic business planning to the IM&M arena. It blends the two disciplines together and, in doing so, creates a distinct relevance and accessibility for the IM&M professional. This book assumes the reader is IM&M knowledgeable but not strategic planning knowledgeable. It develops the concepts and techniques of modern strategic planning and then applies them to the IM&M discipline. Consequently, in a single volume, the important issues of what is strategic planning and how it is specifically applied to the IM&M function are addressed. Rather than starting with the technical issues, database, microprocessors, communication protocols, object-oriented languages, etc., we start with the tools of strategic business planning, core competencies, scenarios, strategic intent, value-chain analysis, five-forces analysis, gap analysis, sustainable competitive advantage, etc. Rather than a constrained technology focus, we take a complete business perspective that includes, but is not limited to, technology.

While is it is always difficult to master a new discipline, strategic business planning should prove to be both interesting and challenging to the IM&M professional. Just as IM&M excellence requires skilled application of methodologies, models, and aggressive use of logic, so does strategic planning. The analytical skills that have enabled success in applying technology will equally serve you well in using strategic planning techniques.

Throughout this book, another book, *The Art of War* by Sun Tzu will often be quoted. The *Art of War* was written over two thousand years ago as a book on the strategy of war by a Chinese philosopher-warrior. Though it was directed at the conflict of war, it is written at such a deep level of insight and metaphor about conflict, that its insights transcend war and are applicable to most conflictual situations. Recent editions of the book have been renamed *The Art of Strategy*. The *Art of War* provides persistent value as the primary and enduring reference on strategic thinking. Much of what is presented as new and insightful is little more then the re-packaging, modernization, and tweaking of Sun Tzu's ideas; little more than footnotes to his creative wisdom. Relevant verses from *The Art of War* will be quoted throughout the book to provide philosophical insight into the strategic issue being covered.

This book should be of interest to managers responsible for Strategic Information Systems Planning, Systems Architecture, Product Planning, Application Design, and System Analyst or Chief Information Officer support. It also will be of interest to IM&M technologists who wish to broaden their understanding of how business decisions are made and functional line managers who wish to understand how to use IM&M to build advantage. As the competitive business situation increases in this decade, everyone must become a strategist.

Strategy is the prerequisite for IM&M success. Strategy formulation and execution is a humbling experience. It is a humbling experience because of the enormity of the unstructured problem confronted, the challenge of grasping the entire problem, the struggle for insight, and recognition of the consequences if the wrong choices are selected. Sun Tzu said:

> Act when it is beneficial, desist if it is not. Anger can revert to joy, wrath can revert to delight; but a nation destroyed cannot be restored to existence, and the dead can not be restored to life. Therefore an enlightened government is careful about this. This is the way to secure the nation.

Those who have the responsibility of developing the IM&M strategy must prepare for the challenge.

Among the sages who study such things, it is said, just as it is for individuals and all gradations of societal units, that the nature of many corporations is as follows:

- They focus on the immediate to the exclusion of the distant; they are content to the point of intoxication with what is and resist to the point of violence what will be; they rejoice in the magnitude and wonders of their triumphs without concern to the possibility that their advantages are but temporary and withering; and they hear, see, and applaud that which confirms their views and ignore and disregard that which challenges them.

Now, if all enterprises were of this nature, they would all be the same and these traits would convey neither advantage nor disadvantage; but such is certainly not so. There are at any time, many corporations whose nature is quite contrarian to that which has been described:

- They balance their attention between the current and the distant; they are suspicious that all their advantages and triumphs are but temporary; they celebrate their triumphs and aggressively prepare for even greater accomplishments; and they coldly and honestly assess reality as it is, not as they wish it to be.

It would therefore seem certain that given time, industry, and freedom to compete, the latter will thrive and the former will decline to the point of becoming fossils; but of interest to corporate anthropologists, historians, and sociologists who study the causes of extinction. It was his observation of this profound difference in the natures of people that lead Sun Tzu to assert that "...it is easy to take over from those who do not plan ahead." This book, then, is for those who wish to plan ahead and not become artifacts of interest for business school case studies in failure. While all can be of value, even serving as a bad example, it is preferable to leave that honor to others.

Acknowledgments

The material presented in this book is the culmination of work done to develop a Strategic Business Planning process for the Processing Product Line of the Information Management Services (IMS) Business Division of the American Telephone & Telegraph Company (AT&T). The material builds on a wide range of accepted strategic planning practices, and these sources are footnoted appropriately throughout the text. Much of the value-added provided by the strategy team came through integration and relevance; integration in taking all the individual techniques and creating a comprehensive model that "glued" them together in a coherent manner with well defined interfaces; relevance in crafting the resulting process to meet the particular needs of our Information Technology Product Line Managers.

Many product team managers and team members who have participated in our planning process have made comments and suggestions that have been incorporated into the process. I would like to thank all those who have participated in the planning process. Their comments and suggestions help to continually improve the process.

I would like to acknowledge the leadership of our management team at IMS. It is not easy moving an organization from being technology focused to being customer focused. It is not easy changing from thinking about mips, bytes, and packets to thinking deeply about competencies, capabilities, and strategic intent. It is not easy to realign and restructure a $2 billion business to take it from where it has been and place it on the journey to where it needs to be. Our management team understands change, and only in such an empowered environment could a strategic planning process like ours flourish. The management team does not do what is easy or safe, but does what is necessary to prepare for tomorrow. For the opportunity to be part of this passion for excellence, I thank them.

Lastly, I would like to thank all the authors who graciously permitted me to include materials from their works. This includes IDC, InfoCorp, G2 Research, Dataquest, The Gartner Group, Frost and Sullivan, BCR, IBM, Meta Group, Input, and Northeast Consulting Resources. Their material is appropriately cited where used in the text. I have also included many quotes from classics of strategy, i.e., *The Art of War* by Sun Tzu, *The Prince* by Machiavelli, and *Strategy* by B. H. Liddell Hart. I have supplemented these conventional sources with material from unconventional strategy sources such as "The Divine Comedy" by Dante, "Paradise Lost" by Milton, *The Godfather* by Mario Puzo, and Greek mythology. Let us be candid, strategy can be a dry subject. The use of these nontraditional sources to make points and create allusions hopefully makes the text more interesting, informative, and, most of all, more instructive. It also demonstrates the important point that great strategy requires renaissance people; lateral thinkers. Insight is transferable between disciplines. The wider the scope of interests and knowledge brought to strategy formulation, the wiser the output.

Strategic learning, from whatever source, yields benefits in two dimensions; the obvious and the subtle. The obvious benefit is to achieve the requisite state of competency to intelligently participate in the strategic planning process. The more interesting and substantive benefit is that it prepares one to transmute presented advice into distinct advantage. To maximize the value of any advice, the one who seeks it must be wiser and shrewder than the one who gives it. Machiavelli explained this paradox as follows:

> A prince must always seek advice. He should be a constant questioner, and he must listen patiently to the truth regarding what he has inquired about. Many believe that a prince who gives the impression of being shrewd does so not because he is shrewd by nature but because he has good advice; but this is certainly not so. *A prince who is not himself wise cannot be well advised.*When seeking advice of more than one person, a prince who is not himself wise will never get unanimity in his councils or be able to reconcile their views. Each councilor will consult his own interest; the prince will not know how to correct or understand him. So the conclusion is that good advice, whomever it comes from, depends on the shrewdness of the prince who seeks it (in interpreting it) and not on the shrewdness of the prince on good advice (in seeking it).

The maximum utility of advice is therefore not a function of the raw ideas of the advice giver, but the wisdom of the receiver to interpret, synthesize, build upon, integrate, and customize it to her deeper and unique appreciation of her circumstances. Another can never truly know what you know nor the manner in which you know it. Advantage must therefore always spring from within, not from without. So before seeking advice, we must prepare ourselves so that we can process the advice to achieve the highest return.

1

Introduction

1.1 Purpose

The purpose of this book is to make you "strategy literate." It is intended to teach the methodology, terminology, and "think" of strategic planning, both generally and specifically in terms of how it applies to the Information Movement and Management (IM&M) function. At the completion of this book, you will understand what is meant by strategy, how to formulate it, how to execute it, and how to use it to improve the use of IM&M resources throughout the enterprise. It is assumed that you, the reader, are IM&M literate but not knowledgeable in the ways of strategic business planning. It is this gap we intend to close.

The purpose of strategic planning is to provide direction, concentration of effort, consistency of purpose, and flexibility as a business continually strives to improve its competitive position. Strategic planning focuses on what needs to be done now in order to be properly positioned for the future. What has served us well in the past may or may not serve us well in the future. Past successes, however great, do not assure future successes.

Strategic planning is the process by which corporate objectives for the future are identified in response to perceived opportunities and threats, and, by understanding company strengths and weakness, activities are selected and resources allocated to meet those objectives. It provides the framework that guides those choices that determine the future direction and nature of an organization. It provides the context for all long-range planning and operational planning. It is the highest level of decision making concerning a company's basic directions and purpose in order to assure the long-term health and vitality of the organization. Such decisions are enduring, broad in scope, and concerned with the goals and means of attainment. It is the process of positioning the organization so that it can prosper in the future. It serves to assure continuing competitive advantage for each product and market chosen. By providing direction, focus, constancy of purpose, and flexibility, strategic planning:

1

- Provides a formula to enable the business to compete,
- Provides a clear statement of direction,
- Provides the context for all other business decisions,
- Enables autonomous but coordinated actions throughout the business,
- Creates a shared competitive agenda, and
- Assures the long-term viability of the business.

The act of developing a strategic plan provides the community with intellectual investment in time and resources to shape future actions.

Strategy is the collective output of the strategic planning process, and is the definition of a desired future state for the business, objectives, strategic moves to realize the objectives, a change management plan, and a commitment plan. It is the context for all unifying and integrative decisions a firm makes, determining and revealing the organization's purpose in terms of long-term objectives, action programs, and resource-allocation priorities. It selects the businesses the organization is or will be in. It is also an attempt to achieve a long-term sustainable competitive advantage in each of the firm's businesses by responding properly to both the environmental opportunities and threats and the strengths and weakness of the organization.

Strategy provides purposeful direction. It is purposeful in that it creates a direct path of causation to the objective. Strategy is coherent in that the derivative actions complement and enable each other. Strategic decisions are non-routine, important, complex, holistic, and future oriented. Without strategy, a business stumbles along in a state of masked chaos.

Figure 1.1 illustrates the overall strategic planning process. The process consists of a structured set of steps which cover three major areas:

- *Assessment*—analyzes the current and foreseeable business situation.
- *Strategy*—identifies what is to be done.
- *Execution*—executes and monitors the strategy.

The process is enabled by the use of a robust set of models, frameworks, and analytical techniques which help frame and focus the decision-making steps. While appearing linear in structure, in practice the process is iterative (best described as a forward spiral) and is one of continual discovery.

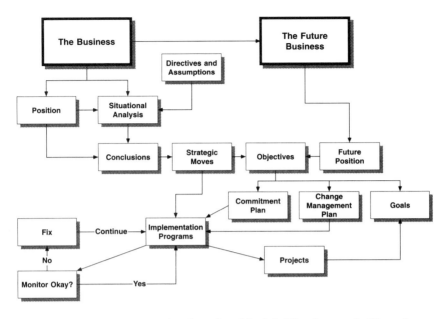

Figure 1.1   **The Strategic Planning Model. The Strategic Planning Model consists of a structured set of steps.**

IM&M or Information Technology (I/T) is the asset/capability base on which the enterprise constructs its business information systems. IM&M may be more rigorously defined as follows:

> Information Movement and Management is the preparation, collection, transport, retrieval, storage, access, presentation, and transformation of information in all its forms (voice, graphics, text, video, and image). Movement can take place between humans, humans and machines, and/or between machines. Management assures the proper selection, deployment, administration, operation, maintenance, and evolution of the IM&M assets consistent with organizational goals and objectives.

Figure 1.2 illustrates this definition. IM&M encompasses the variables of:

- Information collection, preparation, and presentation appliances,
- Geographical distribution and demographics of the senders and receivers of information,
- Availability of the IM&M asset for use,
- Standards used to enable the productive use of the IM&M asset,
- Translation of information between IM&M components,

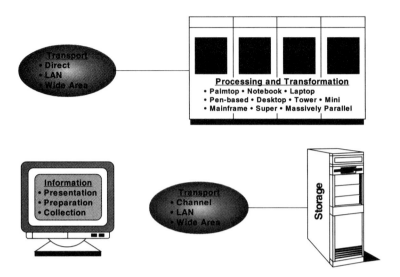

Figure 1.2   Information Movement and Management Model. IM&M encompasses the transport, retrieval, storage, access, presentation, and transformation of information in all its forms.

- Asset scalability (i.e., performance, cost, volume, total users and total concurrent users),
- Transparency of change,
- Accessibility of the IM&M asset, and
- Component to component integration.

IM&M would typically include data processing resources, data communication resources, telecommunication resources, and application development resources. IM&M capital investments account for approximately seven percent of total US capital stock and represents the largest individual item of new capital investments. The IM&M industry is rapidly becoming a one trillion dollar world-wide industry and is increasingly being used by corporations as the foundation or accessory for the development of competitive business advantage.

Historically, IM&M planning has had the following attributes:

- Budget-year oriented as opposed to a strategic three to six year horizon,
- Inwardly focused as opposed to customer or user focused,
- Technology focused as opposed to solution focused, and

- Incremental-change focused as opposed to paradigm-shift focused.

For the most part, the typical IM&M organization has engaged in technology planning but not strategic business planning. As a consequence, many IM&M organizations have tended to be product oriented, repeatedly offering products based on familiar technologies similar to those they have always offered, instead of being user oriented and striving to offer constantly evolving services in synchronization with emerging user requirements without embedded technology prejudice.

This mode of planning is simply inadequate to deal with the challenges of the 1990s. As illustrated in Figure 1.3, the IM&M function is coming under extraordinary pressure from three forces:

1. The business, reacting to intense competitive pressure, is demanding that IM&M resources be deployed in a manner to develop and sustain competitive advantage. The business cannot carry the IM&M function, rather IM&M is needed to accept the role of being a foundation of competitiveness for the business.

2. IM&M technology is changing at an unprecedented pace. When systems were developed 20 years ago, architecture and technology decisions were simple because there were few choices. The situation has completely reversed itself. The IM&M organization is now confronted with a plethora of advantageous technologies which need to be integrated into its platforms and architectures.

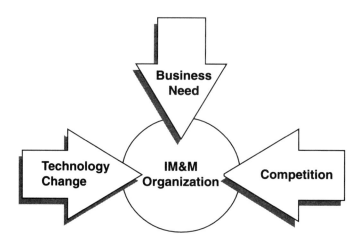

Figure 1.3 IM&M Pincer. The IM&M function is coming under tremendous pressure to change.

3. Competition, for the first time, is a serious threat to the internal IM&M organization. System integrators, facility managers, business consultants, and business re-engineering specialists all provide viable substitute solutions to insourcing (doing IM&M functions internally.) Unless the internal IM&M organization can convince management that it delivers value-added to the business, the outsourcers may win the IM&M business through open and free competition.

It is the thesis of this book that IM&M organizations will benefit tremendously by adopting formal strategic planning methodologies to develop an IM&M business strategy. An IM&M strategy is a set of purposeful and coherent actions which enable IM&M resources to be deployed to build, compound, and sustain competitive advantage for the enterprise. By engaging in proactive strategic business planning, the IM&M organization would accrue the strategic planning benefits of:

- Continuous realignment of the IM&M function with the needs of the user community,
- A formal framework for coordinated action,
- A framework for the priority allocation of resources,
- A process to identify technology shifts,
- A holistic view of the business,
- An opportunity to engage in forward rather than fire-fighting thinking, and
- The ability to realize the true benefits of IM&M technologies.

Though the backgrounds of most IM&M professionals are technical and do not include education or experience with strategic planning methods, this need not be a roadblock. This book will explain how to perform the steps shown in Figure 1.1 and how that process can be directly applied to the IM&M function. By marrying strategic business planning and IM&M in this manner, the techniques and advantages of strategic planning are made relevant and accessible to the IM&M professional.

Figure 1.4 shows a typical IM&M organization chart. To apply strategic planning techniques to the IM&M community, we will treat the IM&M organization as a logical strategic business unit. A strategic business unit has the following attributes:

- A collection of related businesses,
- A distinct mission,

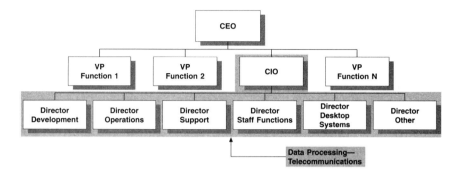

Figure 1.4 The IM&M Organization. To utilize strategic business planning, the IM&M organization should view itself as a strategic business unit.

- A clear set of customers (a market),
- A set of competitors,
- A set of products, commercially defined and managed, which add value for the customer,
- Profit and loss responsibility, and
- A distinct management team.

Viewing the IM&M organization in this way, a business within the business, allows the application of strategic planning methods.

The IM&M management team needs to develop strategic plans which specify direction and purpose for the business. They need to clearly articulate objectives and the associated actions to realize those objectives. They also need to position IM&M services in alignment with the greater needs of the user communities. Through thoughtful adoption of strategic planning methods, the IM&M function can markedly improve its performance, and in doing so, position IM&M as the foundation of competitiveness for the enterprise.

1.2 The Strategic Business Planning Model Overview

The purpose of this section is to provide an overview to the strategic planning process. Figure 1.5 portrays the previously illustrated model, Figure 1.1, but with the three primary steps, assessment, strategy, and execution delineated. The model will be explained in its entirety in Chapters 3–7.

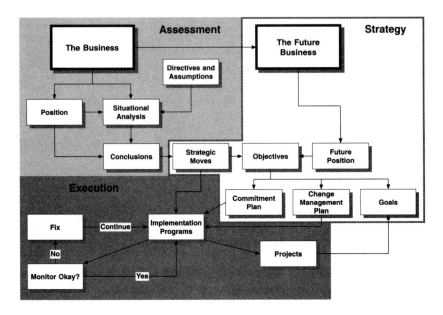

Figure 1.5 **Strategic Planning Model Revisited. The Strategic Planning Model is divided into three primary steps: assessment, strategy, and execution.**

Process Overview

The strategic planning process provides an ordered set of steps designed to culminate in the development and execution of a comprehensive strategic business plan. The process is performed as follows:

- *Assessment* is the activity of developing a clear and thorough understanding of the business situation from both an internal and external perspective. Assessment culminates in the identification of "conclusions" which pinpoint critical issues requiring strategic attention. Two major substeps, positioning and situational analysis, are used to generate conclusions. *Positioning* provides a graphical way to understand the "position" of the business in all relevant strategic areas (i.e., market share, customer satisfaction, core competencies, etc.). *Situational Analysis* is the use of various analytical methods to interpret the data about the company and its environment. Assessment is a data intensive and analytical intensive activity.

- *Strategy* consists of identifying the desired future state of the business (future position), the specific objectives to be achieved, and the strategic moves needed to realize the future state and objectives. *Objectives* are descriptive of what we wish to achieve. *Strategic moves* are prescriptive identifying the actions to be undertaken. To support the realization of the objectives, a commitment plan to focus organizational attention on the objectives and a change management plan to anticipate and reduce resistance to change are also developed. Once a strategy has been defined and communicated, the business can quickly determine which opportunities "fit" and which events pose "threats."

  Unfortunately, there is a great deal of ambiguity in terminology used to describe the various objects of strategic planning. The most confusing is the word *strategy*. Sometimes, strategy is used to mean specific actions to be taken. Other times, strategy is used to means all the objects which compose the strategic plan (i.e., future business scope, future strategic positions, objectives, commitment plan, etc.) Sometimes, in the same sentence or paragraph, the word strategy is used to mean both. To eliminate confusion, we use the word strategy to mean the complete strategic plan and the words *move, initiative,* or *actions* to denote the specific actions taken to achieve an objective.

- *Execution* is the action of putting the plan into motion. It is the translation of intent into reality. Strategies are made operational through implementation programs which are partitioned into multiple projects. *Projects* achieve objectives and interim objectives called *goals*. A process monitoring and control step is used to:

  adjust and tune the projects,

  provide learning feedback from the project experiences, and

  observe the ever changing environment for additional situations requiring strategic response.

  Success of the execution step depends on the commitment and change management plans designed in the strategy step to minimize barriers and obstacles.

Throughout the entire process, quality control actions are interwoven to catch mistakes as close to the point of introduction as possible, and procedural steps are undertaken to maximize organizational input and participation. All steps focus on understanding and achieving the *strategic intent* of the business which represents the long term ambition of the enterprise.

The process is very adaptable to the culture and style of the organization and evolves with the organization. To minimize bureaucracy, the process can be "time-boxed" to force its execution within a specific time period. This prevents "analysis paralysis" and forces the notion that "this is a time for decisions." The process results, specifically strategy, can be leveled consistent with the desired degree of centralization and distribution of decision power within the organization. For very centralized and tightly controlled organizations, the strategy can be extremely specific in detail. For more empowered organizations, emphasis can be put on the definition of the future state of the organization and the specifics of how can be left to the entrepreneurial talents of the management team. The degree of specificity can also be mixed on an item by item basis to reflect varying importance. So by leveling, the process can be used to control or empower.

While this is an extremely abbreviated explanation of the process, it does catch the essence of the process which is to identify exactly where you are (assessment), specify what is to be done (strategy), and do it/ monitor it (execution).

Benefits

This strategic planning approach offers the IM&M strategist a number of distinct benefits in addition to the customary benefits accrued through strategic planning. These supplemental benefits are as follows:

- Completeness

    The model provides a comprehensive process for doing *all* the steps and substeps of assessment, strategy, and execution. Much of the strategy literature and course instruction emphasizes a specific step or technique to the exclusion or minimization of all the others. Focus provides necessary in-depth coverage of the subject area but leaves the aspiring strategist asking, "How did I get here?" or "What do I do next?" This model has synthesized all the individual ideas and packaged them into a composite framework.

- Integration

    Just as the IM&M community is fractured into schools of technology zealots, the strategic planning community is also partitioned into ideological schools. This book integrates the multiple perspectives of the *rationalist school of strategy* (see Figure 1.6). The rationalist school believes that strategy is primarily the product of rational, purposeful, and conscious analysis. Strategy must be developed in this deliberate

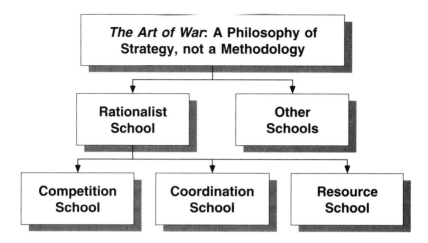

Figure 1.6   Schools of Strategy. The Rationalist School of Strategy is
the basis of this book and is divisible into multiple subschools.

manner because of the irreversibility of commitment, the effort of
forcing organizational alignment, the time to build and nourish
specific sustainable advantages, the effort of accruing the benefits
of leverage, and the difficulties of managing organizational
change.

The three schools of the rationalist approach differ in their assessment of the dominant factor for strategy formulation. The *competition school* emphasizes *strong competitive position* as the essence of
strategy. The *coordination school* asserts the supremacy of winning
through strong directional alignment. The *resource school* emphasizes winning through the development of superior resources (competencies, capabilities, etc.). All the schools agree in their
acknowledgement that meeting the needs of the customer is the
context for their approach.

This book is unbiased and includes methods from each school.
The different approaches result in a variety of perspectives that all
contribute to understanding the essence of the problem. This variety
promotes clarity, stimulates debate, and broadens insight. The techniques presented were therefore chosen for their pragmatic utility,
not their ideological adherence.

The rationalist school is not the only school of strategy. Some propose that strategy is the product of politics. Others propose that
strategy is the by-product of the organizations experience; strategy
emerges from the pragmatic test of what is working in practice. Oth-

ers emphasize speed. The *ready-fire-aim school* or the *trial and error school* holds that success cannot be designed, so strategy consists of blanketing the marketplace with many experiments and then focusing on the identified winners. Some suggest that strategy often equates to no more than hustle.

This methodology generates an *intended and explicit* strategy as opposed to the *emergent and implicit* strategy some of the other schools endorse. It is our intent to maximize the intended strategies that are realized while accepting those that emerge, but we do not count on serendipity as our primary approach. Figure 1.7[1] illustrates this concept as follows:

> *Intended Strategy*—the explicit product of the strategic planning process,
>
> *Unrealized Strategy*—intended strategies that fail,
>
> *Deliberate Strategy*—intended strategies that are realized,
>
> *Emergent Strategy*—realized strategies that were not intended; they emerged from the dynamics of the actual situations, and
>
> *Realized Strategy*—those intended and emergent strategies that work in practice.

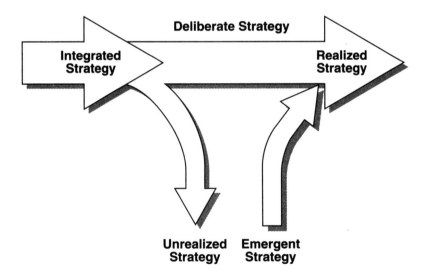

Figure 1.7   Intended vs. Emergent Strategy. The Rationalist School of Strategy views strategy as intended and explicit rather than emergent and implicit. *Source:* Professor Henry Mintzberg.

The rationalist school does reject emergent strategies, and the more opportunities that develop, whether planned for or unforeseen, the better. Nevertheless, the rationalist school's view is that there is more to strategic management than crossing one's fingers and believes that one can bend fortune and not have to be a perpetual victim of it.

A final point about Figure 1.6, *The Art of War* is a philosophy about conflict and strategy, not a methodology. The schools and sub-schools of strategy represent specific insights and codify those insights to permit the multitudes to apply their frameworks. As additional insights are developed, newer frameworks emerge. "The Art of War" remains constant as a reservoir of truth from which to develop novel approaches.

- Analytically Based

  Strategy formulation is extremely difficult. While methods some-times look superficially simple, the value of the outputs are propor-tional to the depth of analytical insight developed by the strategy team. Thinking holistically, abstractly, and with an open mind about a complicated business is a daunting challenge.

  Although the problem is not eliminated by the extensive use of proven analytical methods, it is simplified. The methods help to focus the attention of the debate on proven critical items. By elevat-ing the discussion to an abstract level without the clutter of the details, the essence of the problem can be studied. The use of mod-els insures that all relevant bases are touched and that multiple views of a problem are studied in order to generate a variety of insights. In Chapters 3–7, numerous analytical models will be intro-duced and explained. These models are invaluable for effectively and efficiently performing the analytical tasks. The use of models provides a robust toolbox from which the IM&M strategist can attack the dual problems of understanding *what is* and deciding *what to do*. A few points about analytical models:

    The utility of the models is preeminent during the assessment step. As one would expect, developing frameworks to model *what is* is simpler than developing formal frameworks to model *what should be*. As one moves from assessment to strategy, there is decreasing utility of analytical models and increasing utility of vision, intu-ition, feel, business savvy, etc. as means of decision making.

    The analytical models "clip-onto" the strategic planning model at the appropriate step (Figure 1.5). The strategic planning model serves as an overall infrastructure on which analytical models are appended to perform specific steps. This makes the methodology easily extensible and flexible. As analytical models are developed or discarded, they can simply be clipped-on or removed from the framework as required.

It will become obvious that it is impossible to use all the techniques in a given planning period. The techniques should be viewed as tools which are selected based on problem appropriateness. Additionally, it will become clear that the time and effort in using some techniques could not be done within one planning period. Consequently, in a given period, the results of previously sponsored studies are included in the process and new studies are sponsored for inclusion in future planning cycles.

The tools which will be presented were, in general, developed independently. They do not automatically integrate and interface with each other. They were developed as focused solutions to specific problems. In Chapters 3 and 4, an effort will be made to synthesize the tools to work in harmony with each other.

To be used effectively, many of the tools would require an entire book of explanation or extensive classroom training. Consequently, the tools will be introduced and explained, but it is not intended that all the nuances and procedural details of usage will be developed to a point where from this book alone the reader can use the technique. Readers should refer to the references to obtain more detailed knowledge for the specific tools they wish to use.

Except for three models, the IM&M Architecture (see Section 3.3), the Reach/Range/Maneuverability Architecture (see Section 2.1), and the IM&M Matrices (see Section 2.2), all the models used in this book are generic strategic planning models. This provides added credibility to the assertion that IM&M is not "special and different" and can be managed strategically just the same as any other business function.

- Participatory

    The planning model encourages broad organizational participation. As will be explained in Chapter 7, there are numerous process points to encourage strategic planning participation from all levels of the organization. The model does not encourage the few to go off into an isolated corner and develop a plan for the many.

- Quality Focus

    The process is interwoven with quality control steps. Chapter 6 suggests numerous techniques to infuse quality throughout the entire planning process.

While there is value in strategic planning and its benefits, there are also limitations. The critical limitation is always having to remember the difference between a method, however good, and an execution of that method. In the end, the results of the process are only as good as the intellectual investment of the participants in thinking deeply about the issues. What makes the difference is insight, not rote execution of analytical steps. The strategic planning process works best only for those who are prepared and committed to work extremely hard at thinking through the issues. Sun Tzu calls this "winning by intelligence."[2] Recall that what the Greek army of Achilles, Ajax, and Ulysses couldn't achieve in ten years of brutal combat in the Trojan War, they achieved in one evening through the ruse of the Trojan Horse.

An Example

A good example is both informative and entertaining. In doing the research for Strategic Planning, I came across an example which met both requirements in a most unlikely place; a scene from *The Godfather*.[3] The scene is as follows: Tom Hagen is *consigliori* (advisor) to the Coreleone Family, a New York City mobster family in the late 1940s. The family has been approached to enter the drug business. Don Coreleone, the head of the family, requests counsel from his *consigliori*. Tom Hagen gives the following advice:

> Now we have the gambling and we have the unions and right now they are the best things to have, but I think that narcotics is the coming thing. I think we need to have a piece of the action or we risk everything we have. Not now, but maybe in ten years. There is more money potential in narcotics then any other business. If we don't get into it, somebody else will. With the revenue they earn, they can amass more political and police power. There family will be stronger then ours. Eventually, they will come after us to take away what we have. It's just like countries, if they arm, we have to arm. If they become stronger economically, they become a threat to us.

Figure 1.8 shows how Hagen's counsel closely mimics the strategic planning model. Mr. Hagen:

- Clearly understands his current position,
- Engages in a cold and calculated situational analysis,
- Derives a pointed conclusion,
- Defines a future position, and
- Defines strategic moves to assure "a piece of the action."

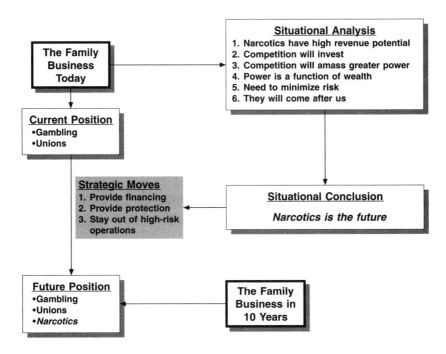

Figure 1.8   Analysis of Hagen's Strategic Advice. *Consigliori* Hagen's counsel closely mimics the Strategic Planning Model.

While Mr. Hagen's choice of application is deplorable, his strategic planning skills are laudable. Don Coreleone refused the deal; Tom's reaction was, "He wasn't looking far enough ahead." Hopefully, we will apply equal or better strategic planning skills to much more positive undertakings and "look far enough ahead."

Summary

It is obviously important that one must begin reasoning based on valid notions of the objects of inquiry. If we construct a system of arguments based on invalid notions, we build a tower of fallacy. Philosophers have asserted that people often have an incorrect notion of "time." Time is correctly understood as an "accident" of motion. Accident in this usage meaning a "by-product of" or "consequence of;" it does not mean an unplanned for and negative event. To command time, one would have to alter the motion of the cosmos; time being a derivative

object is not subject to direct manipulation. Rather, because it is a derivative, an accident, to command it requires commanding the primary
object from which it derives its character and existence. It is only meaningful to take actions against primary objects; one cannot take actions
against accidents.

We begin our reasoning about strategy with the notion that sustainable
business success is an accident of strategy. Strategy is to business success
what motion is to time. To command business success, a derivative,
means to common strategy, a primary object. Fortunately, strategy, unlike
the motion of the cosmos, is within the limits of mortals to shape and execute. It is based on this rationalist notion of strategy and its relationship to
business success that we build our arguments on the art of strategic business planning for information technology.

1.3   Book Overview

The remainder of this book will build on the initial ideas introduced in
this chapter and fully explain the strategic business planning model and
the application of that process to the IM&M discipline. This will be
accomplished in the following manner (see Figure 1.9).

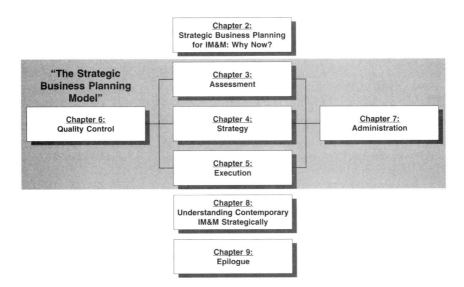

Figure 1.9   Book Structure. The core of the book explains the Strategic
Planning Model in its entirety.

- Chapter 2: *Strategic Business Planning for IM&M: Why Now?*

  This chapter will explain the necessity of adopting strategic planning practices. Given the triple pincer which is closing in on the IM&M organization (business need for competitive advantage, technology shift, and competition), adopting strategic planning methods is not an optional extra for the IM&M management team. This chapter will explain fully the etiology of each pincer point.

  Chapters 3–7 explain the strategic planning model. Chapters 3–5 explain the major steps of assessment, strategy, and execution, and Chapters 6–7 explain quality control and administration and apply equally to Chapters 3–5.

- Chapter 3: *Assessment*

  This chapter will explain in detail how to perform the assessment step. It will explain the notion of a business scope, organizational alignment, positioning, situational analysis, and conclusions. Assessment is the first step of strategic business planning, and its output, *conclusions*, feeds the next step, *strategy*.

- Chapter 4: *Strategy*

  This chapter will explain the attributes of the strategy step. Strategy defines what is to be done. The plan consists of a desired future state (future positions), objectives and goals, strategic moves, a commitment plan, and a change-management plan. The strategy provides clear direction and purpose for the organization.

- Chapter 5: *Execution*

  This chapter will explain the mechanics of executing the plan. Major activities include formulating implementation programs, dividing these programs into manageable projects, and monitoring the environment. Execution makes strategy happen. Its success is tightly tied to the preparation work done in previous steps to plan for the elimination of obstacles.

- Chapter 6: *Quality Control*

  This chapter will explain quality control methods to be applied throughout the process. Quality control methods will be partitioned into three types:

  Completeness checks assure that the plan is comprehensive and complete,

  Logical Checks assure that the plan logically flows and is logically whole, and

Correctness Checks test the plan to assure that it is the best possible plan for the organization.

Quality control is interleaved throughout the entire planning process.

- Chapter 7: *Administration*

    This chapter will explain how to administer the entire process. Topics covered include roles and responsibilities, calendar scheduling, interfacing with other organizational processes (budgeting, objective setting, etc.), maximizing organizational participation, and data collection.

- Chapter 8: *Understanding Contemporary IM&M*

    This chapter will leverage the newly developed strategic planning skills to analyze contemporary IM&M issues and news items. Most major IM&M issues are poorly analyzed in the industry press due to a paucity of strategic-planning skills. Given that this shortcoming has been eliminated, major IM&M issues can be analyzed using the skills learned from this book, and a decision can be made concerning exactly why or why not these issues are of strategic importance. Better strategic understanding of issues leads to the formulation of implementation programs and wins necessary support for investment. It also prevents the waste of time and money on buzzword and short-term fads that are without enduring, strategic benefit.

- Chapter 9: *Epilogue*

    Some final thoughts on strategy.

The book provides knowledge at three levels. First, it provides a philosophy of strategy. This is built on the works of Sun Tzu and Machiavelli. Second, it teaches a generic set of strategic planning methods and techniques. These techniques are extracted from the most current thinking of academic and industry practitioners. Lastly, it teaches applied IM&M strategy. By this we mean applying both the philosophy and generic techniques directly to the IM&M discipline and its current and emerging situation. This makes the book focused to the specific needs of the I/T strategist. The book, consequently, can aid the IM&M strategist in both seeing the trees and the forest and moving dynamically between the two perspectives.

Strategic planning is a difficult subject to teach because in order to understand the whole you must first understand the parts; but to understand the parts, you must first understand the whole. So while the book is presented in a linear order by necessity, you may find it advantageous to read the book more than once. In this way, terms which are used to describe certain subjects before they themselves are fully developed, will take on richer meaning in the second reading.

1.4   Summary

Machiavelli, the acclaimed political strategist, understood only too well the true nature of success:

> ...Some princes flourish one day and come to grief the next without appearing to have changed in character or in any way. This I believe arises because those princes who are utterly dependent on fortune come to grief when their fortune changes. I also believe that those who adapt their policy to the times prosper and, that those whose policies clash with the times do not. This explains why prosperity is ephemeral.... If time and circumstances change, he will be ruined if he does not change his policy. If he changed his character to the times and circumstances, then his fortune would not change.[4]

Figure 1.10 diagrams Machiavelli's simple but deeply insightful summary of the eternal challenge facing all management teams in all times. It is the endless treadmill of time and changing circumstances and the need to adapt policy to the times that creates the *reason d'être* for strategic planning. Figure 1.11 illustrates the change in stock market valuation (stock price times number of shares) of IBM, AT&T, and the Regional Bell Operating Companies. At the time of the AT&T divestiture in 1984, IBM, having won the government antitrust case, was considered the winner, and AT&T, by consenting to divestiture, was considered the loser. But, as it is with individuals, adversity builds character and strength, and success often breeds complacency and arrogance. So AT&T and the Regional Bells have prospered and IBM sits at the brink of divesting itself; doing to itself what the justice department failed to do. IBM, which was the most admired Fortune 500 company for the second year in a row in 1983 and had the highest stock market valuation of all US companies at $74,508 billion, was worth 121% of AT&T on 18 November 1983, 430% of AT&T on 21 November 1983 (when-issued divestiture shares), but only 42% of AT&T on 31 December 1992. Its stock market valuation had decreased to $28,741.1 billion, an almost unbelievable 61% devaluation. Fortune and misfortune change the rules of the game, and some adapt their character to the times and circumstances better than others. The boatman Charon will have many passengers from IBM to ferry across the river Acheron.

Many IM&M organizations have enjoyed "good fortune" over the past decades. The host-centered computing model (large mainframes housed

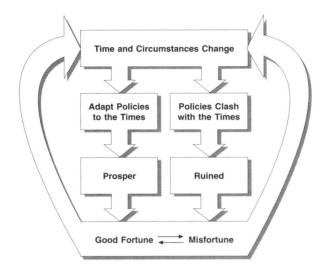

Figure 1.10   Eternal Challenge. The Eternal Challenge dates your business idea and provides the *reason d'être* for strategic planning.

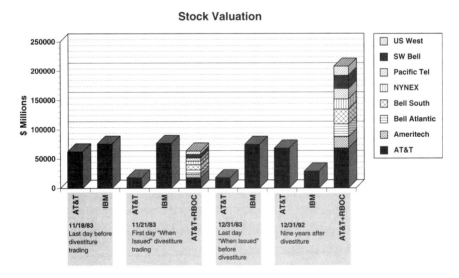

Figure 1.11   Fortune. Time and circumstances have resulted in misfortune for IBM and good fortune for AT&T and its progeny, the Regional Bell Operating Companies.

in data centers and tended to by an elite group), dominated architecturally, technologically, and economically by a single vendor, supported, enabled, and promoted an IM&M organization hegemony over the information-processing resources of the firm. IM&M planning, characterized as technology-focused, incremental, short-term, and self-promoting, was compatible with the times. IM&M organizations engaged in a *moat strategy,* defending and perpetuating with extreme prejudice the host-centered computing model. They relished in their "good fortune" and dismissed the waves of change about them as "not real computing." A noted industry observer captured the essence of the IM&M organization perspective when noting, "Not only do they not understand the business, they proceed arrogantly oblivious to it."

As will be documented in the next chapter, "good fortune" has turned her back to us and we now find ourselves confronted by a demanding business, exponential technology change, and ambitious and capable competitors. Machiavelli said:

> Time sweeps everything along and can bring good as well as evil, evil as well as good.[5]

We must either react to this challenge with a fresh agenda or become irrelevant. Some barbarians are at the gate of the data center fortress, and others are simply bypassing us. The moat has been bridged. We must change.

The emerging IM&M paradigm of network computing coupled with a smorgasbord of feature and functionality-rich technologies requires new vision and commitment. It requires comprehension of fundamental shifts and perseverance to remake and reshape the IM&M organization to master the possibilities. This will not be the product of planning approaches which embrace small steps, tunnel vision, and self-serving assessments.The adoption of strategic-planning methods offers the IM&M organization an extraordinary turnaround opportunity and the chance to create its own fortune. Armed with vision, clear objectives, and insight, the IM&M organization needs only to rely upon itself to leverage the changing technology landscape. Fortune is a fickle friend who whimsically comes and goes. Fortune is a deceiver; her greatest deceit being to plunge one into great misfortune after having raised one to great fortune. Her only constancy is everlasting change. We are much better off entrusting our destiny to thoughtful and carefully crafted strategies of our own making. We are much better off designing our future than wishing for it or hiding from it. We are much better off anticipating and solving our customer's needs than having them go elsewhere for solutions.

Footnotes

1. The notions of intended and emergent strategy and this illustration are based on the work of Professor Henry Mintzberg.
2. Sun Tzu, *The Art of War.*
3. Paraphrased from *The Godfather,* Mario Puzo.
4. Machiavelli, *The Prince.*
5. Machiavelli, *The Prince.*

2

Strategic Business Planning for IM&M: Why Now?

In the strategy lexicon, the phrase, *strategic imperative,* is of particular importance. A strategic imperative is an action which must be undertaken; it is an action of unquestionable critical import. A meaningful response to the IM&M pincer is such a strategic imperative (Figure 1.3). The suggested appropriate response is the partnership of IM&M and strategic business planning to provide a context for a renewed and successful IM&M organization.

The purpose of this chapter is to explain the etiology of this imperative. Why now? What chain of events have occurred which point to this conclusion? Why not simply continue our past successful practices? Why do the hardest thing of all, change?

We will provide evidence to answer these questions as follows:

- *Section 2.1: Business Need*—This section will explain the changing business situation which demands increased competitiveness from the IM&M organization.

- *Section 2.2: Technology Change*—This section will explain the emergence of new IM&M technologies that are obsoleting the technologies which have been the basis of IM&M for the past few decades.

- *Section 2.3: Competition*—This section will examine the threat posed to the internal IM&M organization by a variety of outsourcing alternatives.

- *Section 2.4: Summary*—This section will summarize the key ideas presented in this chapter.

The marriage of strategic business planning and IM&M can be used to meet the challenges presented in this chapter. While change is very difficult, it is most preferable to extinction.

2.1 Business Need

The business environment in the 1990s is best described as intensely competitive. Business is under extreme pressure to react to multiple socioeconomic forces. These forces include (but are not limited to):

- *Changing demographics*—changes in the distribution of ethnic groups, age groups, and gender in the work force,
- *Micromarketing*—the need to service ever finer market segments with discreet products and services,
- *Corporate volatility*—the need to deal with mergers, acquisitions, divestitures and alliances,
- *Cost control*—relentless pressure to contain and reduce expenses,
- *Consumerism*—the need to react to demanding and selective consumers,
- *Education crisis*—the need to deal with employees who are graduates of a disintegrating educational system,
- *Environmentalism*—the need to react to the growing concern for the environment,
- *Quality*—the "ante" to play the game,
- *Health costs*—the need to simultaneously cap expenses and meet employee needs for protection,
- *Globalization*—the need to source, compete, and sell globally, and
- *Regulation*—government constraints on actions.

Most pressing of all, however, is an absorbing competitive rivalry. The competitive situation is best described as intense, diverse, complex, and global. Assets which have served corporations for years as competitive advantages are now merely strengths. Markets are characterized as having reduced barriers to entry, more sophisticated, discriminating, and demanding buyers, short product life cycles, constantly emerging substitute products, and global rivalry. While meeting customer needs remains the goal, dealing with competition is the dominant business driver.

Against such pressures, a business must set high objectives in order to be successful. Typical objectives should include:

- To be best in class in selected markets,
- To maintain a low cost structure and/or adopt a differentiated approach to meeting market needs,
- To achieve 100% customer satisfaction,

- To defend and grow market share, and
- To be ever more customer responsive through faster and more effective processes.

Against this picture, we believe that corporate America will undertake a massive re-engineering of their business systems. Business re-engineering is the fundamental rethinking and basic redesign of an entire business system including processes, jobs, organizational structures, management systems, and use of IM&M technologies to achieve dramatic (order of magnitude) improvements. The heart of business re-engineering is to redesign business processes on a clean slate, unencumbered by the existing business processes, and employ the novel use of advantageous IM&M technologies to radically improve process performance.

The logic of business re-engineering is as follows:

1. Business entities *have to* become competitive and will *have to* redesign business systems to infuse them with advantage.

2. They will benchmark best-of-breed competitors to find out what is necessary to achieve minimum competitive parity. This is the advantage step-off point.

3. Business entities will discover that world-class competitors have linked critical business practices to specific and new enabling technologies. Business solutions drive the selection of IM&M technologies.

4. Desirable and enabling technologies have the following attributes:

   price/performance advantage,

   feature/functionality advantage, and

   enable dramatic maneuverability.

5. A new generation of IM&M systems will be constructed which will increasingly emphasize the newer technologies to the denuding of the traditional technologies. Why?—price/performance advantage, feature/functionality advantage, and/or dramatic maneuverability.

6. The new IM&M technologies, the technologies of business re-engineering, will permit the business not just to automate but to engineer applications; to "imagineer" them.

While this scenario may seem ambitious, it is actually conservative. Figure 2.1 depicts a market estimated to grow at 46% annually.

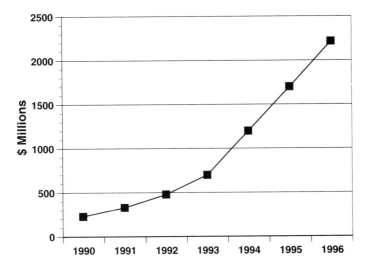

Figure 2.1   Business Re-engineering Forecast. The Business Re-engineering services market is expected to grow at 46% annually.

The goal of this massive re-engineering investment is to exploit IM&M
to enable and support the building of sustainable competitive advantage
(SCA) for the business. *SCA* is the distinct asset, capability, skill, resource,
process, etc., which creates a capability gap between the company and its
competitors. Without sustainable competitive advantage, a business has
no edge in the marketplace. The goal is to use IM&M for any and all of
the following purposes:

1. Build new SCA into business processes, and create new advantage
   gaps.
2. Extend existing SCAs in business processes, and elongate advantage gaps.
3. Reduce the advantage of others by narrowing the SCA gap
   between their business processes and your own.

In most corporations, at least 25–50% of all software investment is targeted toward this end. We will discuss SCA extensively in Chapter 3.

This positioning of IM&M brings us to ask the crucial question: What
is the real purpose of IM&M technology? A typical answer is that the purpose of IM&M is to improve productivity, save money, and improve decision making. While true and beneficial, this is a tactical and shortsighted
response. The strategic purpose of IM&M is to enable management to act

and react to the dynamics of the marketplace and to enable management to build, sustain, and compound competitive advantage. The purpose of IM&M is *competitiveness!*—creating a business edge through the superior use of information. Figure 2.2[1] helps to illustrate this point. The business needs IM&M to build systems on an architecture which has the following three attributes:

1. *Maximum Reach*—Anyone (or any processor), anywhere, anytime can access the IM&M assets.

2. *Maximum Range*—Any information object (data or process) can be shared.

3. *Application Maneuverability*—On top of the reach and range platform applications are built with the maneuverability attributes itemized in Table 2.1. Maneuverability will require migration to a network-computing architecture which will impose dramatic change on the IM&M organization (see Table 2.2).

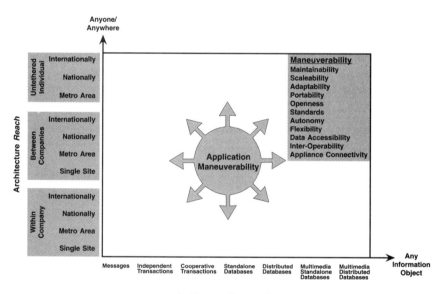

Figure 2.2   Reach, Range, and Maneuverability Architecture. The business requires that the IM&M architecture permit the development of maneuverable applications. *Source*: **"Implementing Client/Server Computing: A Strategic Perspective," Bernard H. Boar, McGraw-Hill, 1993 with permission of publisher.**

Table 2.1
Maneuverability. Maneuverability is the primary business requirement imposed on the IM&M function. *Source*: **"Implementing Client/Server Computing: A Strategic Perspective," Bernard H. Boar, McGraw-Hill, 1993 with permission of publisher.**

Architecture Attribute	Definition
Maintainability	The ease of maintaining the architecture
Modularity	The ability to add, modify, and remove pieces of the architecture
Scalability	The ability to scale the architecture by the dimensions of transaction volume, data storage volume, concurrent users, and/or total users
Adaptability	The ease of change
Portability	The ability to move applications across the architecture
Openess/Standards	The compliance of the architecture with open standards which enables many of the other attributes
Autonomy	The ability of each part of the architecture to function both independently and as part of the whole
Flexibility	The ability to grow and contract the architecture as required
Data Accessibility	The ability to access decoupled data both locally and remotely
Inter-Operability	The ability to work cooperatively between multiple heterogeneous processors
Appliance Connectivity	The ability for a wide variety of information appliances with a versatile set of human-interface metaphors (character, full-screen, graphical, voice, real-time 3D, motion, virtual reality, etc.) to attach to the architecture
Maneuverability	The summation of all the attributes which positions the enterprise to both act and react expeditiously to the dynamics of the competitive marketplace with alacrity

A reach/range/maneuverability architecture would consist of, at minimum:

- A corporate-wide local, metropolitan, and wide-area network based on a standard set of communication protocols,
- Gateway capability to interface with the networks of suppliers, the extended trading community, and customers,

- Support for both traditional and wireless communication technologies,
- Support for synchronous, asynchronous, store and forward, file transfer, messaging, bursty, and non-bursty traffic,
- Industrial grade operations, administration, and maintenance capabilities to life cycle operate and administer the network computing environment, and
- Standard application program interfaces (API's) that enable communication between heterogeneous clients and servers. Service-based API's would encompass messaging (e-mail), data access (SQL), remote procedure calls (RPC's), file transfer, distributed transaction management, output services (print, CD-ROM, etc.), and systems management. This set of APIs is increasingly referred to as bonding products or middleware.

Table 2.2
Comparison of host-centered computing vs. network computing. The characteristics of the two environments are radically different. *Source*: **"Implementing Client/Server Computing: A Strategic Perspective," Bernard H. Boar, McGraw-Hill, 1993 with permission of publisher.**

Host-Centered Computing	Network Computing
Uni-processor orientation	Multiple processor orientation
Self-contained environments	Interoperability
Hardware-centered architecture	Software-centered architecture
Proprietary products	Open systems and standards
Homogeneous environment	Heterogeneous environment
"A" primary vendor	Mix and match suppliers
Little portability	Portability key advantage
Dumb clients	Intelligent clients
Development and production environments equate	Build here—run there
Vertical configuration management (often provided by vendor)	Horizontal configuration management (provided by you)
Product engineering (systems support) function in "parts" business	Product engineering function in systems integration business

Maneuverability promotes the IM&M architecture to the status of a *pivot position*. A pivot position permits a business to create and react to surprises. Pivot positions will be discussed in more detail in the next chapter.

Maneuverability is the prime requirement of competitiveness. Maneuverability permits a business to change and control the terms of competitive engagement. Maneuverability permits the IM&M organization to deal with the needs fragmentation of the user communities. Rather than being homogeneous, users' needs are often quite different. Maneuverability permits us to react to specific application demands for distinct IM&M technologies, but, at the same time maintain application bonding with the overall business. Maneuverability means that each business capability can be customized to optimize its competitive advantage.

Maneuverability means speed. Sun Tzu said:

> Some win through speed.... Use swiftness to wear them out.... Get the upper hand though extraordinary swiftness...be as fast as the lightning that flickers before you can blink your eyes.[2]

Speed is the value-added of maneuverability.

Competition is all about moves and counter-moves. With maneuverability, the business can attack and put competitors off balance or it can quickly parry competitor moves. What the business wants from IM&M more than anything else in the 1990s, is systems maneuverability; the ability to dictate the competitive agenda.

A final item of evidence on this point. Figure 2.3[3] is a list of issues which top corporate information technology leaders have identified as the most critical IM&M issues for corporate America. More then half directly support the exploitation of IM&M for business competitiveness. Indirectly, they all do.

Sun Tzu said:

> Struggle means struggle for advantage; those who get the advantage are victorious. [4]

The 1990s are an era of total competition. What the business requires of IM&M is a foundation for competitiveness; the capability to maneuver its systems. That is the business imperative imposed on the IM&M organization. An imperative which can only be realized through a reach, range, and maneuverability IM&M architecture. An imperative which indicates a shift from the primacy of IM&M efficiency to the primacy of business impact of IM&M.

Top 20 Senior I/T Issues	'92	'91	'90	'89	'88
Aligning I/S and Corporate Goals	1	2	4	2	1
Re-engineering Business Processes Through I/T	2	1	1	11	N/R
Creating an Information Architecture	3	8	9	5	5
Utilizing Data	4	5	7	6	7
Improving the H/R Resource	5	13	11	8	8
Instituting Cross-Functional Information Systems	6	3	3	7	N/R
Improving Software Development Quality	7	7	14	N/R	N/R
Improving Leadership Skills in I/S	7	10	N/R	N/R	N/R
Boosting Software Development Productivity	9	4	6	13	12
Developing an I/S Strategic Plan	10	6	5	4	2
Cutting I/S Costs	11	11	10	14	17
Instituting Total Quality Management in I/S	12	N/R	N/R	N/R	N/R
Integrating Information Systems	13	9	16	12	6
Using I/T for Competitive Breakthroughs	14	12	8	1	4
Managing Dispersed Systems	15	19	N/R	16	13
Educating Management on I/S	16	14	2	3	3
Promoting the I/S Function	17	17	15	N/R	N/R
Updating Obsolete Systems	18	N/R	13	N/R	18
Capitalizing on Advances in I/T	19	20	N/R	17	N/R
Connecting to Customers and Suppliers	20	15	19	N/R	N/R

**Figure 2.3   1992: Top 20 I/T Issues. A survey of top I/T executives indi-
cates that more than half of the critical IM&M issues directly support
business competetiveness.** *Source*: CSC Index.

2.2   Technology Change

The purpose of this section is to explain the extreme changes which are
taking placing in IM&M technologies. These changes are obsoleting existing IM&M organizational competencies. If the IM&M organization is to
remain relevant, it will need to respond to these changes. Unfortunately
for those who prefer technological stasis, the mean time to technological
obsolescence is accelerating.

In Chapter 1, we defined IM&M.

Information Movement and Management is the preparation, collection, transport, retrieval, storage, access, presentation, and transformation of information in all its forms (voice, graphics, text, video,
and image). Movement can take place between humans, machines,
or humans and machines. Management assures the proper selection,
deployment, administration, operation, maintenance, and evolution
of the IM&M assets stays consistent with organizational goals and
objectives. [5]

For succinctness, the essence of this definition can be reduced to an
equation of the form:

IM&M	=	Information Form (sound, data, image, text)
	x	Information Function (presentation, processing, storage, transport, OAM)
	x	Information Movement (people/people, people/machines, machines/machines)

Understanding IM&M in this manner leads us to a set of matrices, represented by Figure 2.4, Figure 2.5, and Figure 2.6. These models let us position and visualize IM&M change in a structured manner. Respectively, IM&M change can be modeled as a change in the relationship of information forms to applied information functions, as a change in the movement of information between people and machines, and as a change in the relationship of OAM to information functions.

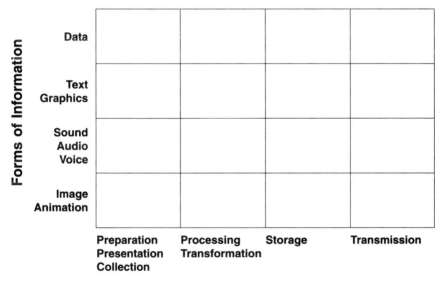

Figure 2.4   IM&M Change: Form vs. Function. IM&M change can be understood as any change in the relationships between information forms and applied information funtions.

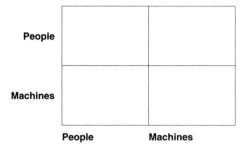

Figure 2.5   IM&M Change: People vs. Machines. IM&M change can be understood as any change in the relationships between people and machines.

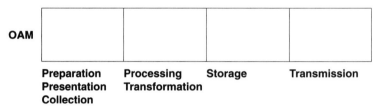

Functions of Information

Figure 2.6   IM&M Change: Function vs. OAM. IM&M change can be understood as any change in the relationships between information functions and OAM.

Historically, as shown in Figure 2.7, voice communications and data processing represented the application of IM&M functions to sound and data, respectively. This simple IM&M model is antiquated. In this section, evidence will be presented to show that IM&M is undergoing radical transformation that will need to be matched by a parallel transformation of the IM&M organization.

To structure this section's argument, an analytical method called *Theory/Hypothesis* will be applied (see Figure 2.8). A *theory* is a systematically related set of statements, including some law-like generalizations, that is empirically testable. The purpose of a theory is to increase understanding through a structure capable of both explaining and predicting phenomena. It provides a framework for understanding. Theories serve as the basis for developing hypotheses which can be tested for validity. An *hypothesis* is a predictive assumption made to test logical consequence. Hypotheses are alternately referred to as assertions, postulates, or propositions. From a theory, multiple hypotheses are postulated. If they can be proven correct, it tends to prove the theory. If they are proven false, it denies the theory. By using this method, seemingly disparate and unconnected information can be linked into a coherent whole. The use of this method will be augmented by using the IM&M change models to summarize the change evidence presented in proving the hypothesis.

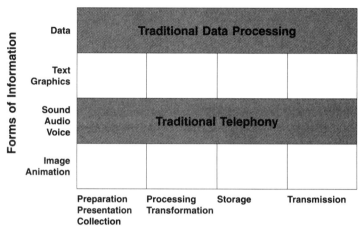

Figure 2.7   Traditional IM&M. Traditional IM&M was the limited application of information function to sound and data.

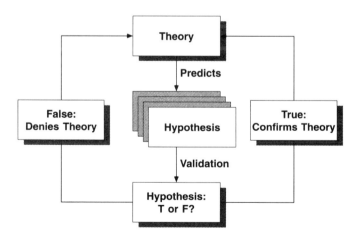

Figure 2.8   Theory/Hypothesis Analytical Model. The Theory/Hypothesis Analytical Model provides a structured approach to analyze and relate a large amount of seemingly disparate data.

Theory

We assert the following theory to explain the technology revolution occurring in the IM&M industry:

> Businesses will re-engineer their business systems to compete successfully, and the most opportunistic technologies of re-engineering are not the traditional IM&M technologies. This business re-engineering is fueled by changing computing economics and rich feature/functionality/maneuverability technologies which favor network computing over traditional host-centered computing.

Hypothesis

We will present a series of hypotheses to demonstrate the validity of this theory. Each hypothesis will be presented in the following format:

- *Hypothesis:* succinct statement of the assertion,
- *Rationale:* a brief explanation of why one would expect this to be true given the theory, and
- *Evidence:* data to prove the validity of the hypothesis.

The evidence will make extensive use of market research forecasts. Many, with good reason, are skeptical of market forecasts and automatically discount their validity. In Section 3.2, market forecasts will be discussed. For now, the important point in judging forecasts is to focus on direction, general magnitude, and inter-forecast synergy (i.e., do the forecasts complement each other). Precision accuracy of dates or volumes is not important.

1. *Hypothesis*: Competitive pressures will drive IM&M users to re-engineer their information systems to infuse them with advantage.

    Rationale: Core premise of theory.

    Evidence: The evidence to support this assertion was presented in Section 2.1.

2. *Hypothesis*: There exists a growing and compelling set of re-engineering IM&M technologies.

    Rationale: Core premise of theory.

    Evidence: Eleven exemplary IM&M technologies which can be used to re-engineer business processes will be reviewed. These technologies provide robust alternatives and complements to traditional host-centered computing.

A. Multimedia and Imaging

Multimedia and imaging provide new approaches to the design of the user interface and the management of any paper-based application. Multimedia includes information in all its forms (text, voice, image, graphics, video, and animation) with primary applications including marketing, sales, education, and decision support. The multimedia market is anticipated to grow from approximately $600 million in 1991 to over $12 billion in 1996, stimulated by high-speed communications, standards, and packaged multimedia applications.

Imaging provides the basis for re-engineering any form-intensive application. Since over 90 billion business documents are created each year, adding to the over 1 trillion business documents already stored, and over 300 billion photocopies made annually, imaging is the premier multimedia application. Benefits of imaging include concurrent document processing, document accessibility, space saving, avoidance of misfiling, and archival access. The imaging market is anticipated to grow from approximately $3 billion in 1991 to $9 billion in 1996.

Imaging and multimedia are IM&M resource-intensive applications:

- One second of sound consumes 15 kb to 150 kb of digitized information.
- Ten seconds of sound consumes about 1 mb of digitized information.
- Seventy-five minutes of fidelity music consumes approximately 600 mb of storage.
- One pixel of video/animation requires up to 24 bits of information.
- One frame of video consumes approximately 1.5 mb of storage.
- An 8" by 11" image @ black and white requires 50 kb to 100 kb of storage, @16 bit color requires 200 kb to 400 kb storage, and @ 24 bit color requires 1.2 mb to 2.4 mb storage.

These requirements stimulate the need for high communications bandwidth (also needed to assure audio/visual synchronization and continuity—for video/animation, a frames per second rate of 30-90 must be maintained), MIPS to handle data compression and decompression, and media to support the exponential storage growth requirements. Optical storage (CD-ROM, WORM, and Rewritable) is anticipated to grow from an $800 million business to a $1.2 billion business from 1991 to 1994 in response to these huge storage demands.

B. E-Mail and Groupware

E-mail and groupware are technologies of collaboration. They allow collocated and remote employees working on a common project to share information. E-mail, while of independent value to allow direct messaging, is increasing in importance as the back-end transport mechanism for groupware. The advent of mail enabled APIs such as VIM, OCE, MAPI, SMF, and APIA is promoting e-mail to the primary conduit for inter-employee electronic communication.

The Electronic Mail Association expects e-mail messages to soar from under 3 billion per year in 1991 to 15 billion by 1995, while the number of e-mail users triples from 8.9 million to 27 million. The total market for e-mail services from 1991 to 1996 will grow from $3 billion to $11 billion.

The groupware market is also anticipated to grow tremendously, driven by the quality emphasis on teams, the need to improve the productivity of office workers, and the need for global collaboration by global companies. The overall groupware market is anticipated to grow from $10 million in 1991 to $600 million in 1995. Workflow-management software that automates the movement of documents and forms between users within a workgroup (collocated and distributed) is expected to grow in number of users by 1000%.

C. Video-Conferencing

Video-conferencing is also a technology of collaboration. In March 1992, AT&T announced a new $400 CODEC chip that replaces circuit boards to perform video signal compression, code the signal, transmit it, and decode the signal. Combined with the stimulant of the CCITT Px64 standard, the market for video-conferecing equipment is expected to grow from $50 million in 1991 to $600 million in 2000. While the other forms of video-conferencing (room-based, desktops, and roll-abouts) will also grow, disproportionate growth will occur for PC-based capabilities.

D. Pen-Based Computing

Pen-based computing is the use of electronic character recognition through a stylus as the means of user input to a computer. Pen-based computing is the evolution of the pen and paper metaphor to computing with the electronic stylus serving as the pen and the terminal serving as intelligent electronic paper. Since pen and paper are the primary means of communication, there is ample reason to believe that pen-based computing will become the dominant form of computing interface as the most comfortable and natural form of input evolution.

Figure 2.9 illustrates the evolution of computerized character recognition which is the enabling technology. Typical applications would include field work force automation, any clipboard user, inventory, doctors, insurance adjusters, and quality control. The pen-based computing market is expected to grow from .5 million units in 1991 to 16 million units in 1998.

E. Mobile Computing

Mobile computing encompasses all forms of portable personal computers. Typical examples of this are:

- the HP 11 ounce palmtop computer,
- the IBM 9075 PC radio,
- the Sony Palm Pentop PTC-300, and
- the NCR 3170 notebook which includes cellular and wireless messaging communications.

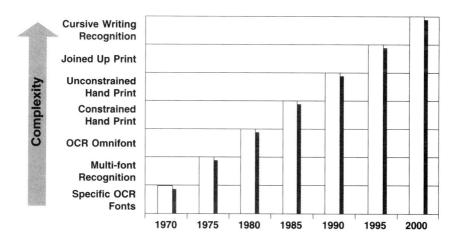

Figure 2.9   Electronic Character Recognition. The evolution of character recognition technology enables pen-based computing.

Mobile computers usually include notebooks, pentops, subnotebooks, and palmtops. By 1996, it is predicted that 85% of all portable computers will include data and fax modem capabilities.

Portable computing increases the reach of the IM&M architecture. The overall market for portable PCs will increase to 75 million units in 1988 from 8 million units in 1991, while notebooks will increase by a factor of five. Improved wireless communications, extension of battery lifespan between recharging, color, and an increasingly mobile work force all conspire to stimulate the market (see Table 2.3).

F. Wireless Communication

Wireless communication technologies increase the reach of the IM&M architecture. Wireless technologies include both wide-area and local-area technologies. Examples of wide-area technologies include:

- Easylink "Wireless Mailbox" mail service from AT&T/Skytel,
- EMBARC (Electronic Mail Broadcast to a Roaming Computer) wireless e-mail service from IBM, Motorola, and Ardis,
- RAM Mobile Data wireless mail service from Bell South and RAM Broadcasting, and
- Cellular Data Broadcasting System from Oracle and McCaw.

Table 2.3
Extending Portable Lifespan. A number of changes in portable technologies are extending the time period required between recharging.

Current Technology	Anticipated Change
Nickel Cadmium batteries last 2–4 hours	Nickel Hydride batteries last 2.5–5 hours
	Lithium-Ion batteries last 8–16 hours
	Lithium Polymer batteries last 16–20 hours
	Zinc Air batteries last 16–20 hours
Limited power management	Power management chips suspend keyboard, processor, disk, and screen power consumption when not in use
5 volt microprocessor chips	3.3 volt microprocessor chips

In the spring of 1992, a consortium of companies lead by IBM announced Celluplan II which enables voice and data to share the same analog cellular network @ 19.2 kbps. Industry analysts forecast the wide-area wireless market to grow to 5 million users by 1997 and $8 billion by 2000 while growing at a 30–40% rate per annum.

In the Fall of 1992, AT&T bought a 33% stake in McCaw Cellular Communications. The move completed a series of moves:

1. An investment in EO Corporation, a maker of personal communication devices,

2. A marketing agreement with GO corporation which makes a pen-based operating system for portable computers,

3. An announcement of the Hobbit microprocessor which is designed to support wireless communication for hand-held computers (NEC, Matsushita, and Toshiba have agreed to use the Hobbit in designing their own personal communicator products),

4. Wireless mail services from AT&T Easylink Services, and

5. An announcement of the V32MX Complete Modem Chip Set which enables the building of low-power modems that work both over land-lines and RAM Mobile Data's Mobitex wireless network.

These moves position AT&T to participate in wireless growth and focus on the mobile communications user. At the end of November, 1992, AT&T announced its first hand-held communiator, the Personal Communiator 440. Demand for wireless and mobile data services will be driven by the needs of sales, field-engineering, and field-service positions.

Table 2.4 illustrates the essential attributes of the three prominent wireless LAN technologies. The wireless LAN marketplace is anticipated to grow in revenue from $20 million in 1991 to $700 million in 1996.

G. Voice Processing and Speech Recognition

Voice-processing and speech-recognition systems refer to a wide range of voice technologies which include:

- *Voice messaging*—systems that digitize voice messages and store them for later recall,

- *Voice response*—computer-generated voice output,

Table 2.4
Wireless LAN Technologies. There are three emerging wireless LAN
technologies to select from.

	Spread Spectrum	Narrowband Microwave	Infrared
Exemplary Vendor	NCR Wavelan	Motorola Altair	BICC Infralan
Data Rate (Raw)	2 Mbits per second	15 Mbits per second	4/16 Mbits per second
Maximum Radius	800 feet	80 feet	80 feet
Security	Data scrambling and encryption	Data scrambling	None
Antenna	Desk/Wall	Ceiling/Wall	Wall/Floor stand
Alignment Aids	Software	Leds	Leds
Line of Sight	No	No	Yes
Max Users/Subnet	No limit	32	No limit
Minimum Cost/User	$1,390	$830	$500
Inter-Building Use	Yes	No	Yes

- *Interactive voice response*—systems that allow a requestor to receive specific information from a database using a touch tone phone,
- *Transactional voice processing*—systems that enable both data retrieval and input,
- *Text to speech*—systems that convert text to speech using speech synthesis technologies, and
- *Speech translation*—systems that translate continuous speech from one language to another.

These technologies are appropriate for a wide range of applications including order processing, customer service, marketing, employee support, financial services, university student support, taxpayer support, scheduling and dispatch, and general information entry and retrieval. Typical benefits include staff reduction, improved service, and reduced telecommunications costs.

The market for all voice technologies was approximately $2.2 billion in 1990 with voice mail growing at 16% and interactive voice response growing at 25%. The voice mail equipment and services market is expected to grow to $7 billion in 1996 from $1.5 billion in 1991.

In the spring of 1992, AT&T announced an emerging language-translation technology called VEST (Voice English/Spanish Translator) with the following features:

- translates spoken speech between English and Spanish,
- recognizes 450 words in any combination and translates them into a synthetic voice, and
- the translation is performed in less than one second.

VEST, however, does have limitations. It is individual user-trained and has an application-specific vocabulary.

In November 1992, IBM announced a series of speech-recognition capabilities for a number of its platforms. These products which convert spoken input to text included the following:

- *DragonDictate-7K*—a text dictation system for DOS based PCs,
- *Dragon Talk-To-Plus*—a speech recognition system for Microsoft Windows,
- *Speech Server Series*—a network-based speech recognition system for RS/6000 servers and OS/2 clients, and
- *Continuous Speech Series Developer's Program*—speech recognition application development tools.

The market for speech recognition hardware and software is expected to quadruple to $600 million in 1995 from $150 million in 1991.

H. Electronic Commerce (Figure 2.10)

Electronic commerce is the networked-based coordination of materials, processes, and people to facilitate commercial exchange. Electronic commerce includes electronic data interchange (EDI), electronic funds transfer (EFT), interactive voice response (IVR), electronic bulletin boards, database buying services, electronic trading, and reservation systems. Electronic commerce binds a business with a supplier and/or customer and offers benefits in speed, quality, and process improvement, and creates competitive barriers to entry. The US EDI market (including software, network services, and professional services) is anticipated to grow from $100 million in 1989 to $750 million in 1995. Coupled with other messaging tech-

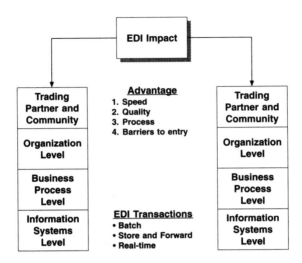

Figure 2.10   Electronic Commerce. Electronic commerce replaces paper-based transactions with more effective and efficient electronic ones. *Source*: "Implementing Client/Server Computing: A Strategic Perspective," Bernard H. Boar, McGraw-Hill, 1993 with permission of publisher.

nologies, electronic commerce is fundamentally changing the way people communicate with each other. As shown in Figure 2.11, business processes will require message-handling filters for managers to handle the surge in electronic communication.

I. Artificial Intelligence

Artificial intelligence is the automation of business knowledge. Major applications include scheduling, monitoring, configuration, diagnosis, design, and compliance. The expert systems tools market is expected to grow to $850 million in 1996 from $200 million in 1989.

J. Object-Oriented Technologies

Object-oriented technologies include object-oriented programing, object-oriented analysis and design, object-oriented database management systems, and object-oriented application interoperability frameworks. By virtue of the key object-oriented concepts of encapsulation, messaging, inheritance, and the unit of work being an object, object-oriented technologies offer the promise of tremendous productivity improvement through reusability. Object-oriented market forecasts are summarized in Table 2.5.

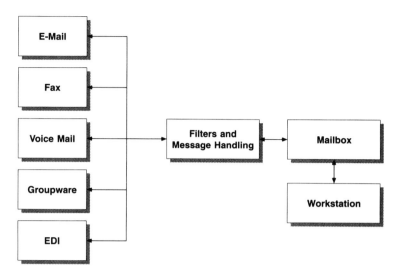

Figure 2.11 Message Integration. Future employee communications will be message-based.

Table 2.5
Object-Oriented Market Forecast. The productivity advantages of object-oriented technologies will stimulate tremendous market growth.

Object-Oriented Market Segment	From		To	
	Year	Revenue	Year	Revenue
Object-Oriented Software Products (Languages, Tools, Case, and DBMS)	1990	$200 million	1996	$3.5 billion
Object-Oriented DBMS	1991	$13.5 million	1996	$445 million
Object-Oriented Analysis and Design Tools	1991	$20 million	1996	$250 million

K. Massive Parallelism

Massive parallelism is the building of high-performance processors based on the combination of microprocessor technology and parallel processor architectures. In a conventional serial computer, one instruction works on one data item at a time. In a massively parallel SIMD machine, many data items are manipulated simultaneously by one instruction. In massively parallel MIMD machines, multiple processors act independently and concurrently on different data items. Typical applications for massively parallel processors are financial analysis, marketing analysis, process-intensive decision support, and database. Exemplary vendors include:

- *Intel*—the Paragon XP/S systems consisting of 120–4,000 I860 RISC processors yielding 5 billion–300 billion flops,
- *Thinking Machine*—the CM-5 system consisting of 16,000 processors yielding 1 trillion flops, and
- *NCUBE*—a 512 processor system yielding 5000 MIPS.

The market for massively parallel machines expected to grow to $600 million in 1994 from $150 million in 1990.

Table 2.6 assesses each of the re-engineering technologies by its primary benefit. Table 2.7 illustrates the impressive growth rates for the technologies discussed. The primary conclusion which can be reached is not only that there is a growing and compelling set of re-engineering technologies, but that the locus of computing is moving with these technologies to the desktop (see Figure 2.12).

3. *Hypothesis*: There is a shift to network computing from host-centered computing.

    Rationale: Core premise of theory.

    Evidence: Figure 2.13 and Figure 2.14 illustrate the major transition that is occurring, from host-centered computing to network or client/server computing. Host-centered computing was characterized by the following processing model:

    - A user at a dumb terminal (an input device which did not have a processor) would enter a transaction,
    - The transaction would be sent to a host processor where all services (presentation, processing, and data manipulation) would be performed, and finally,
    - The resulting output would be sent back to the dumb terminal for display.

Table 2.6
Re-engineering Technology Advantages. The re-engineering technologies encompass all the different motivators explained in Section 2.1 for re-engineering.

Re-engineering Technology	Primary Competitive Business Advantage		
	Maneuverability	Price/Performance	Feature/ Functionality
Multimedia			x
Imaging			x
Optical Disk		x	
E-Mail	x		
Groupware		x	
Workflow Software		x	
Video Conferencing		x	
Pen-Based Computing			x
Wireless Communications	x		
Voice Technologies		x	
Electronic Commerce		x	
AI			x
Object-Oriented Technologies	x		
Massive Parallelism		x	

Table 2.7
Re-engineering Technology Growth Summary. The re-engineering
technologies all share impressive growth potential.

Re-engineering Technology	From	To	Growth Factor
Multimedia	1991	1996	20 times
Animation Software	1991	1996	4.5 times
Color Scanners	1992	1996	3 times
Audio Boards	1992	1994	2.66 times
Imaging	1991	1996	3 times
Optical Storage	1991	1994	1.5 times
E-Mail Messaging	1991	1995	5 times
E-Mail Services	1991	1996	3.66 times
Groupware	1991	1995	60 times
Workflow Software Users	1991	1996	1000 times
Video Conferencing	1991	2000	12 times
Pen-Based Computing	1991	1998	32 times
Mobile Computers	1991	1998	9.5 times
Wireless LANS	1991	1996	14 times
Voice Mail Equipment and Services	1991	1996	4.33 times
Speech Recognition Hardware and Software	1991	1995	4 times
US EDI	1989	1995	7.5 times
AI	1989	1996	4.25 times
OODBMS	1991	1996	16 times
OO Analysis and Design Tools	1991	1996	12 times
Massively Parallel Computers	1990	1994	4 times

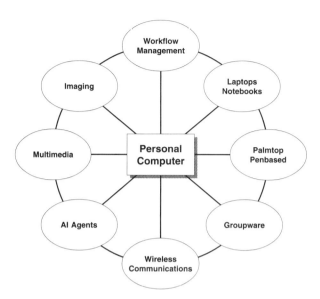

Figure 2.12 Workgroup Becomes Locus of Computing. The re-engineering technologies support moving the locus of computing to the desktop from the mainframe.

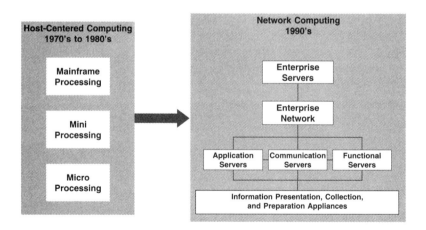

Figure 2.13 Fundamental Paradigm Shift. Host-centric, mainframe, mini, and personal computing is shifting to a network computing architecture.

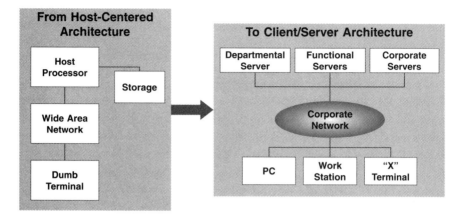

Figure 2.14   A Second View of the Shift. Presentation, processing, and data manipulation services will be distributed across the network in accord with the needs of each application.

This is in contrast to client/server computing where the presentation, processing, and data services are partitioned across multiple processors which cooperate transparent to the user to complete the transaction.

There is ample evidence of this shift through vendor announcements, seminars, user success stories, and the changing patterns of IM&M expenditures. The following provides market research evidence which confirms the shift:

- Figure 2.15 illustrates the number of new monolithic applications (host-centered) declining in half by 1995,
- Figure 2.16 illustrates the rapidly increasing percent of users planning to build distributed applications,
- Figure 2.17 illustrates the movement to a predominantly decentralized networked computing architecture, and
- Figure 2.18 illustrates the ever increasing percent of I/T spending consumed by microsystems.

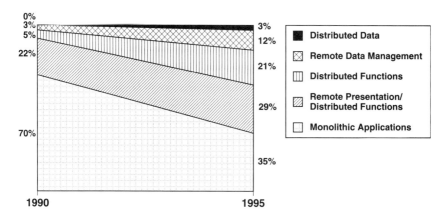

Figure 2.15   New Application Architectures. By 1995 two thirds of new applications will have distributed architectures. *Source*: Gartner Group.

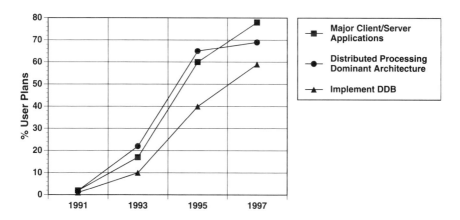

Figure 2.16   Move To Distributed Architectures. By 1997, the clear majority of users will have implemented a variety of distributed architectures. *Source*: Input.

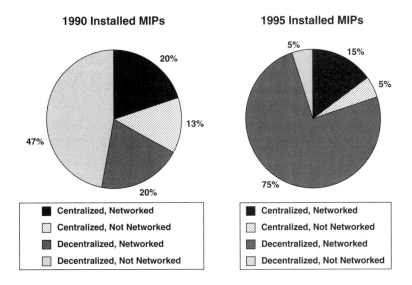

Figure 2.17   MIPS Directions. By 1995, 90% of all MIPS will be networked. *Source*: Dataquest.

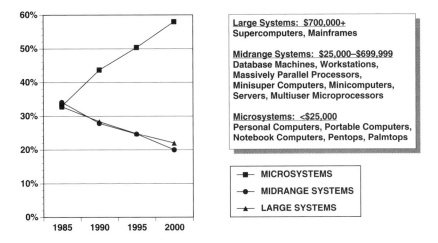

Figure 2.18   Spending Trends. Microsystems will continue their upward surge as a percent of expended IM&M dollars through the turn of the century. *Source*: Infocorp.

The following quotes from 1991 and 1992 Gartner Group seminars best summarize the shift to the new network-processing architecture illustrated in Figure 2.19:

1. "Business requirements will drive I/T to highly flexible network systems."
2. "Users will take the time to standback and re-examine their fundamental architecture premises."
3. "IBM has gotten serious about allowing and enabling non-IBM products to interoperate with SAA products."
4. "The importance of MVS has diminished from the mainframe dominated world of the 70s and 80s"
5. "The role of the mainframe will change to that of manger of enterprise level data, technologies, and computational server."
6. "Computing is undergoing a major change from monolithic processing to distributed processing in all its varieties."
7. "MVS will be rejuvenated to become a major participant in client/server computing."

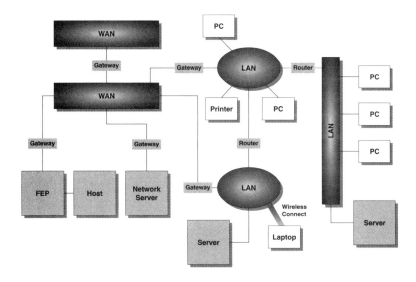

Figure 2.19 **I/T Architecture of the 90s. The IM&M architecture of the 90s will be a network of networks.** *Source*: **"Implementing Client/Server Computing: A Strategic Perspective," Bernard H. Boar, McGraw-Hill, 1993 with permission of publisher.**

8. "Mid-range performance will match requirements of 80% of commercial processing by 1993 and 95% by 1995."

9. "The coincidence of multiple industry shifts will establish mid-range systems as preferred enterprise information technology platforms."[6]

From 1991 to 1996, the world-wide software market will more than double from $45 billion to $100 billion. The client/server's share will increase sevenfold from 3% to 21%. The fascination with network computing is not a temporary aberration; the computing paradigm is undergoing a fundamental change.

It is important to understand that the motivation for the shift to a network architecture is not because the business world has suddenly realized the need for distribution of computing intelligence. In fact, the business world has always had a distribution need, but computing-technology limits and constraints have imposed the host-centered solution. The move to network computing is therefore not the adoption of a new technological dogma, but the more natural mapping of presentation, processing, and data services to where they most naturally and advantageously belong throughout the business.

4. *Hypothesis*: Microprocessor-based technologies are further increasing their price/performance advantage.

   Rationale: More powerful and cost-effective microprocessors are required to enable the process-intensive re-engineering technologies and to provide favorable price and performance advantages over mainframe computing to justify the migration to network computing.

   Evidence: Few technologies have offered both the power improvement and the price and performance productivity which are exhibited by microprocessor technology. Figure 2.20 illustrates this tremendous price and performance trend. Figure 2.21 shows the consequences of this trend with PCs realizing a 700:1 price and performance advantage over mainframes by the turn of the century. Figure 2.22 shows the continuing decline in unit costs of microprocessors. The new Intel "P5—Pentium" chip rated at 100 MIPS, a clock speed of 66MHz, and 3 million transistors, is expected to start selling at about $700 per 1,000 chips. This is all the more surprising given the dominance Intel has in CISC microprocessors. Intel is forecasting a product called "Micro 2000" with the following attributes:

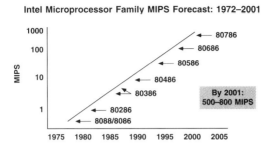

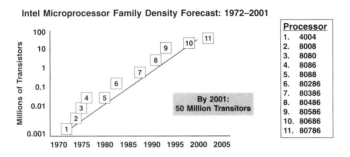

Figure 2.20   Intel Microprocessor MIPS and Density Forecast. By the turn of the century, an Intel chip will perform at 500–800 MIPS. *Source*: **Gartner Group.**

- 50 million–100 million transistors with each transistor 1/25th the size of an I386 transistor,
- 250 MHz clock speed (a 8086 processor was rated at 10 MHz),
- A multiprocessing chip with 4 CPUs @ 700 MIPs/processor yielding 2 BIPS per chip,
- 2 MB of cache memory,
- Graphics unit with HDTV quality for full-motion video,
- 386 compatibility, and
- Suitability for a full range of process-intensive applications including telepresence, continuous speech recognition and translation, cursive handwriting recognition, vision, artificial intelligence, and virtual reality.

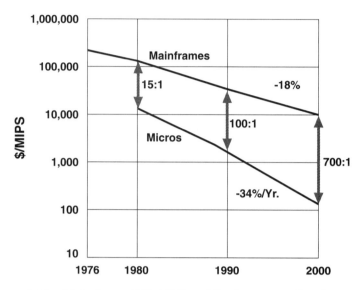

Figure 2.21   Mainframe/Mini/PC and Performance. By the turn of the century, microprocessor-powered PCs will enjoy a 700:1 price/performance advantage over mainframes. *Source*: Gartner Group.

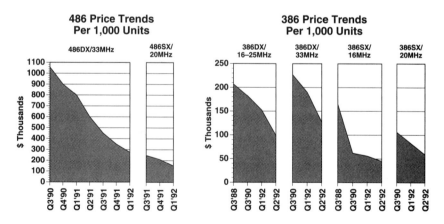

Figure 2.22   Intel Price and Performance Trends. In spite of dominating the CISC microprocessor market, Intel has provided striking price/performance improvements.

Comparative RISC/CISC Performance

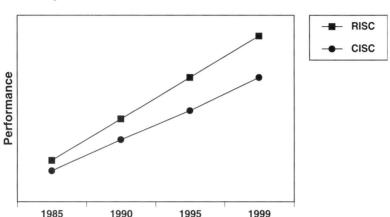

**Figure 2.23   Comparative RISC/CISC Price/Performance. RISC proces-
sors offer a price/performance substitute to Intel-based CISC processors.** *Source*: **Gartner Group.**

As impressive as Intel's chips have been, the emergence of RISC chips
offers the promise of even better price/performance. Figure 2.23 shows
RISC processors maintaining superior price/performance. As the RISC
market is much more competitive with five vendors (SUN/SPARC, HP/
PA-RISC, IBM/POWER, MIPS/RX000, and Intergraph/Clipper) all having double digit market shares, competition should continue to drive
down prices, improve performance, and provide a strong substitute to
Intel. All the major players in the fault-tolerant marketplace (1991 revenues of about $1.2 billion): Tandem (MIPS chip), Stratus (PA-RISC chip),
and DEC (ALPHA chip) have committed their processors to RISC technology.

The DEC ALPHA RISC chip represents a major shift in the DEC product line. DEC's adoption of RISC includes the following:

- The entire product line will shift to the RISC chip,
- The 64 bit ALPHA will power all DEC processors from palmtops to
  supercomputers,
- VMS, Ultrix, OSF/2, and Windows NT will all run on ALPHA,
- Multiple OS will be able to run concurrently, and
- The ALPHA will be scaled to run up to 200 MHz and 400 MIPS.

Competitors have already hinted at their responses which include the SUN Supersparc at 150 MIPS and the HP/ PA chip at 150 MIPS.

5.   *Hypothesis*: Center of competition and innovation is shifting to microprocessor-based operating systems and graphical user interfaces.

Rationale: As the locus of computing shifts to the desktop, one would expect intense vendor competition for control and influence.

Evidence: The 32 bit power operating system marketplace is increasingly competitive with a wide number of viable players as illustrated in Table 2.8. Figures 2.24 and 2.25 illustrate the anticipated PC OS growth. Three major OS trends of particular importance are as follows:

- The new PC operating systems are designed to support multiple environments. Figure 2.26 exhibits this trend,

Table 2.8
32 Bit OS Players. The 32-bit PC operating system market is intensely competitive.

Vendor	OS	Availability	GUI	Platforms
Apple	System 7	Now	Finder	Motorola 68000
IBM/Apple	Pink	Mid 1990s	PM, Motif	Motorola 68000 Ix86 Rs6000
IBM/Apple	Power/Open	1994	AIX Windows and Mac	Power/RISC Power/PC Motorola 68000
IBM	OS2/2.0	Now	PM	Ix86
Microsoft	Windows NT	Now	Windows	Ix86, Alpha, Mips Rx000
Next	Nextstep	Now	Nextstep	Motorola 68000 Ix86
Sunsoft	Solaris 2.0	Now	Open Look Windows	Ix86 Sparc
SCO	SCO Open Desktop	Now	Motif	Ix86
USL	Destiny UNIX System V R4.1	Now	Open Look Motif	Ix86

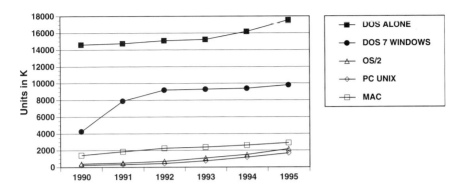

Figure 2.24   PC OS Explosion. Annual OS shipments will grow to 18 million by 1995.

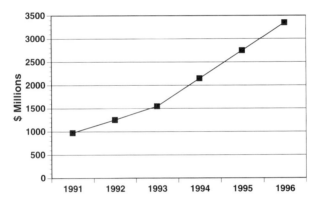

Figure 2.25   PC OS Explosion: Revenue View. PC OS revenue will grow to $3.5 billion by 1996.

- The PC operating systems are dividing into specialized client and server versions:

  Windows is dividing into Windows NT for servers and Windows 4.0 for clients,

  OS/2 is dividing into a client version with multimedia support, pen support, voice support, and a server which supports DCE, multiprocessing, and built in networking, and

  UNIX System V R4 is dividing into a client version which does DOS emulation, Windows emulation, X-windows, and a server version that supports multiple clients and is multi-platform portable, and

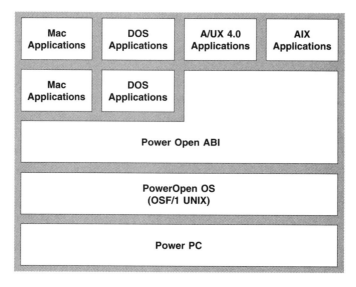

Figure 2.26   Poweropen PC Architecture. The new PC operating environments can typically host multiple operating systems.

- The pen-based OS situation is wide open as illustrated in Table 2.9

Figure 2.27 illustrates the market penetration of various graphical user interfaces. Control of the user interface is critical to convincing developers and users to build applications.

Table 2.9
Pen-Based OS Alternatives. The Pen-based OS market is wide open.

Vendor	Pen Only OS	Pen and Keyboard OS
Go	Penpoint OS	
Microsoft		Windows for Pen Computing
Grid Systems	Penright	
Communication Intelligence		Pendos
Nestor		Penshell

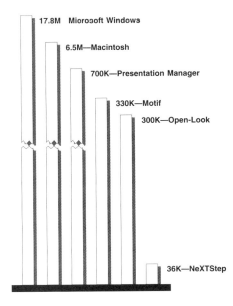

Figure 2.27   GUI Installed Base. Microsoft Windows dominates the GUI market.

6. *Hypothesis*: Tremendous market growth in LAN-based PCs and workstations.

    Rationale: Consistent with transition to network computing and the need of the re-engineering technologies for compute intensive resources at the point of human interface, one would expect LAN-based PCs and workstations to evolve to the preferred work environment.

    Evidence: Table 2.10 summarizes major trends which support this hypothesis. These trends are being stimulated by declining prices as illustrated in Table 2.11, Figure 2.28, and Figure 2.29. The movement to LAN-based architectures is stimulating the market for backup capabilities as illustrated in Figure 2.30. Key LAN-based backup media are digital audio tape (DAT), .25 inch cartridge (QIC), and 8 mm tape. DAT and 8 mm tape combined revenues are expected to increase 400% from 1991 to 1997. Figure 2.31 shows the planned evolution of DAT technology to be able to store 16 Gbytes by 1995.

    The point of all this evidence is convergence. While the evidence crosses a wide range of disparate technologies, they all contribute to making LAN platforms viable. This is an excellent example of the value of taking holistic views.

Table 2.10
PC/LAN Trends. Multiple perspectives demonstrate the tremendous
growth trends for LAN-based solutions.

Technology	From	To	Trend
"X" Terminal Market	1992	1996	500% growth
Workstation Market	1990	1995	600% growth
LAN-based Uninterruptible Power Supplies (UPS)	1991	1995	240% growth
LAN-based E-Mail boxes	1990	1995	900% growth
LAN Server Shipments	1991	1995	200% growth
Overall LAN Support and Product Revenues	1990	1995	250% growth
PCs On LANS	1991	1995	150% growth
LAN Remote Access Products	1991	1996	600% growth
LAN/Mainframe Controllers	1990	1996	1100% growth
LAN Superservers	1991	1995	500% growth
LAN OS Licenses	1989	1995	200% growth
LAN DBMS Licenses	1991	1995	400% growth

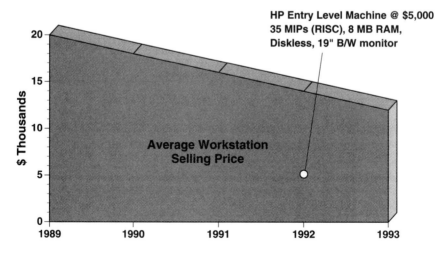

Figure 2.28   Workstation Price Trends. Workstation prices are declining to the point where they will overlap with high-end PCs.

Table 2.11
Declining PC Prices. PC prices are anticipated to continue to decline
due to severe competition.

386sx PC with Monitor and Hard Disk (Various Configurations) Change in Prices from 2nd/3rd Quarter 1991 to 2nd Quarter 1992		
PC Supplier	From	To
AIR	$3491	$1999
AST	$3390	$2950
Compaq	$4997	$2567
Dell	$2599	$1799
HP	$3597	$2297
IBM	$4495	$3630
NEC	$4847	$2457
Zenith	$4367	$3467
Zeos	$2295	$1995

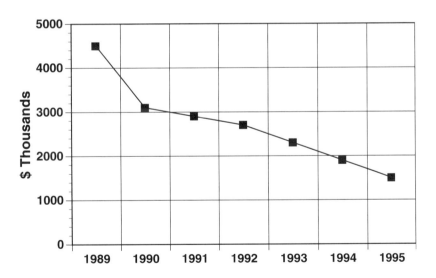

Figure 2.29   "X" Terminal Price Trends. "X" terminals are demonstrating a steady decline in cost.

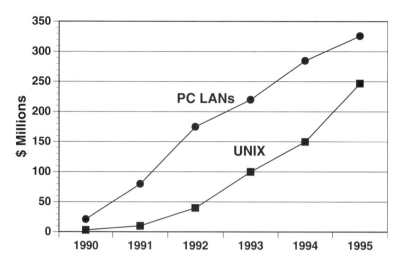

Figure 2.30   Spending on Backup Trends. As more data and applications migrate to LANs, there will be an ever growing need for backup capability. *Source*: Gartner Group.

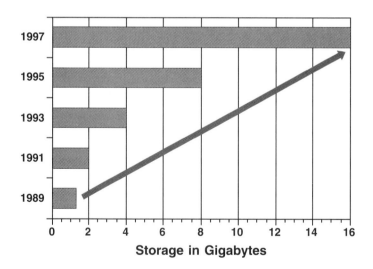

Figure 2.31   DAT Storage Growth. While the storage capability of DAT is expected to grow by a factor of 12, the form factor is expected to decrease to 3.5" from 5.25" and the transfer rate to accelerate to 2+ Mbps from 183 Kbps.

7.   *Hypothesis*: Memory price/performance continues to improve.

Rationale: Resource-intensive re-engineering technologies require large and cost-effective memory.

Evidence: Figures 2.32 and 2.33 show continued price/performance improvements for memory. 1992 DRAM purchases exceeded 1991 purchases by approximately 15%. Three additional events which confirm this hypothesis are as follows:

1.   In December 1991, IBM and Siemens AG announced they had developed 64 Mbye DRAM chips. They will be commercially available in 1995. The market for 64 MB DRAMS is expected to grow from $7 million in 1995 to $7.5 billion in 1998.

2.   In June 1992, IBM announced they had fabricated the world's smallest transistor at 1/75,000th the size of a human hair. From it, they will be able to make 4 Gbit DRAM chips. Such chips should be available about 2008.

3.   In July 1992, IBM, Toshiba, and Siemens announced a joint venture to develop 256 Mbit DRAM chips. The targeted availability date is 1998.

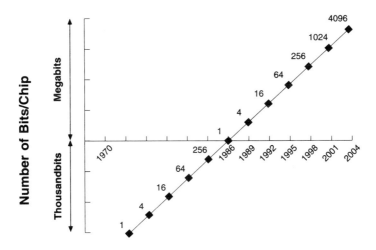

Figure 2.32   Memory Chip Density Time Line. Memory densities are anticipated to continue to quadruple past the turn of the century.
Source: **Gartner Group.**

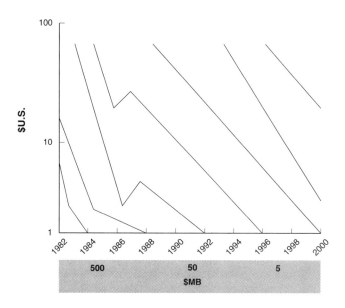

Figure 2.33   DRAM Pricing History and Forecast. Price/performance of memory is expected to improve by a factor of 100 from 1984 to 2000. *Source*: **Gartner Group.**

There is ample evidence to conclude that through the first decade of the next century, memory chips will continue to demonstrate improving price/performance, thereby enabling the new re-engineering technologies.

8. *Hypothesis*: Storage price/performance trends favor microprocessor-based solutions.

    Rationale: Both cost-effective and high-volume storage is required to support the resource-intensive re-engineering technologies and the migration of business data to LAN platforms.

    Evidence: The following data provides evidence in support of this hypothesis:

    • Figure 2.34 shows that in 1989 the aerial density for PC/workstation disks started to exceed that for mainframe storage,
    • Figure 2.35 illustrates the price/performance trends for PC-based storage. In the spring of 1992, Intel made a flash memory product announcement introducing 20 MB, 10 MB, and 4 MB flash memory cards at prices of $611, $331, and $163, respectively. A flash

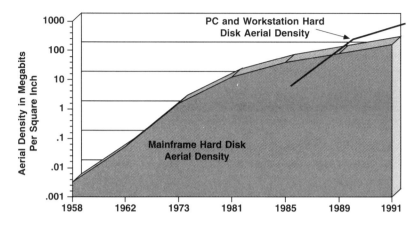

**Figure 2.34   Aerial Disk Density. In 1989 the aerial density of PC/
Workstation storage began to exceed that of mainframes.** *Source*: **IBM.**

memory card is the size of a credit card and is made in compliance with Personal Computer Memory Card International Association (PCMCIA) standards. Microsoft announced support for
the Microsoft "Flash Memory File System" to support flash memory cards. The flash memory card market is expected to grow by
a factor of 12 from 1991 to 1995. During the same time, the market
for PC hard disks (2.5" and smaller) is anticipated to grow by a
factor of 5,

- Figure 2.36 shows the anticipated shrinking of the form factor for
  PC disks and the concurrent increase in storage capabilities. In
  the summer of 1992, HP announced a 20 MB 1.3" disk, and, by
  December 1992, 80 MB 1.8" disks are expected,

- Figure 2.37 shows the forecasted price trends for mainframe storage with Storage Tek's RAID Iceberg technology superimposed.
  Comparing it with Figure 2.35 shows the clear PC disk cost
  advantage per megabyte. Iceberg is RAID technology which uses
  arrays of 5.25" disks. Redundant Arrays of Inexpensive Disks
  (RAID) technology brings the advantage of not only cheaper cost
  but also high volume to the LAN. The RAID marketplace is
  expected to grow by a factor of 16 from 1991 to 1994,

- Table 2.12 summarizes some embryonic storage technologies
  which will possibly offer further improvements in storage quantity, speed, and price/performance in the next century.

Table 2.12
Future Exotic Storage Technologies. These are all possible storage technologies for the twenty-first century.

Future Storage Technology	Attributes
Optical Cubes	1. Store 6.5 terabits/square centimeter 2. No moving parts 3. Tenfold improvement in access speed
Holographic Storage	1. No moving parts 2. Tenfold increase in storage capacity 3. One-thousandfold increase in access speeds
Bacterium	1. Fivefold increase in access speeds 2. Store 500 gigabytes in 5 cubic centimeters 3. No moving parts
Mangeto-Optic Storage	1. Store 45 billion bits per square inch 2. Under development by Bell Labs
Atomic Force Microscope	1. Stores 30 billion bits per square inch 2. One hundred times the capacity per equal size optical disk 3. Bit storage is one micron or one fiftieth the width of a human hair. 4. Under development by IBM

The price/performance and storage capabilities (typically 60–108 Gbytes) of RAID complexes will enable the migration of large files to the LAN.

9. *Hypothesis*: On-Line Transaction Processing (OLTP) applications are migrating to network computing.

   Rationale: OLTP applications which "run" a business are driven by cost and performance. It is therefore reasonable to expect that OLTP applications would want to take advantage of the economies, features, and functionality of network computing.

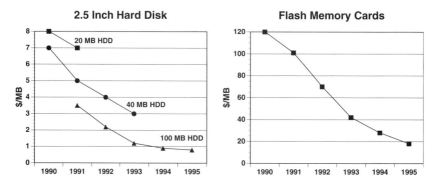

Figure 2.35   Declining Cost of PC Disk and Flash Memory. PC storage demonstrates excellent price / performance curves. *Source*: Input.

Year	Megabytes Per Platter	Platter Size (in.)
1991	80	3.5
1993	325	2.5
1997	325	1.8
2000	1,000	2.5

Declining Platter Size Forecast			
1991	1992	1995	1998
2.5"	1.8"	1.2"	0.5"

Figure 2.36   Declining Platter Size. PC disk platters continue to shrink and increase in storage density.

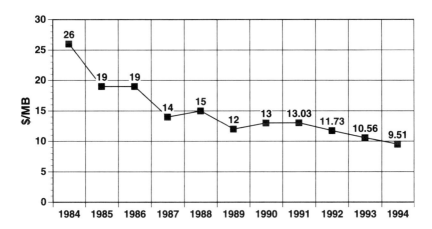

Figure 2.37   IBM Mainframe Storage Cost Per Megabyte. While mainframe storage costs continue to decline, they are still more expensive than PC-based storage. *Source*: **Gartner Group.**

Evidence: Figure 2.38 illustrates the anticipated changing components of OLTP with the contribution of PCs more than doubling. Figure 2.39 shows tremendous growth in the use of UNIX for OLTP. UNIX OLTP is characterized by distributed transaction processing using transaction monitors such as Tuxedo, Cooperation, and Transarc. The UNIX OLTP market is anticipated to grow from $4 billion to $11.5 billion between 1990 to 1995.

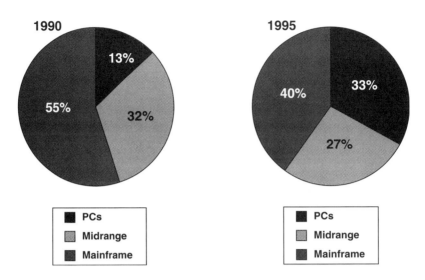

Figure 2.38   OLTP Reconfiguration. The PC component of OLTP will grow by almost 250% by 1995. *Source*: Gartner Group.

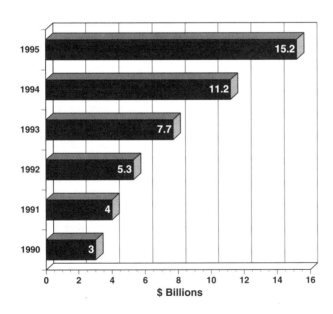

Figure 2.39   Unix OLTP. The Unix OLTP market is expected to grow by a factor of five. *Source*: Gartner Group.

10.   *Hypothesis*: Communication trends are enabling network computing.

Rationale: Network computing requires both cost-effective and high-bandwidth communications (local and wide area).

Evidence: Table 2.13 summarizes major communication trends which support the migration to network computing. Key requirements for the migration are support for bursty traffic, high bandwidth, network management, and interoperability. Figure 2.40 and Figure 2.41 show the trends to which the technologies in Table 2.13 are responding. Figure 2.42 shows the evolution of AT&T high-speed services. These services are designed to support a variety of speed requirements, bursty and non-bursty traffic, and information in all its forms (voice, data, image, and video). The entire communications field is in a major transitional state in order to enable the "network" in network computing.

Table 2.13
Communication Trends. Communication trends support the migration to network computing. Inter-LAN networking vendors such as Cisco and Wellfleet have experienced greater than 190% annual growth over the last few years.

Technology	From	To	Trend
Frame Relay	1991	1995	1100% growth
Bridges	1991	1995	280% growth
Intelligent Hubs	1991	1995	150% growth
Routers	1990	1995	300% growth
FDDI	1990	1995	3000% growth
Cellular and Mobile Communications	1990	1995	18% CAGR
LAN Connectivity	1990	1995	48% CAGR
Fiber Optics	1991	1996	1200% growth
ATM	1993	1997	1100% growth
LAN Superservers	1991	1995	1500% growth
TCP-IP/OSI	1991	1996	2400% growth
Network Management	1991	1996	300% growth
DSP Chips	1991	1996	400% growth

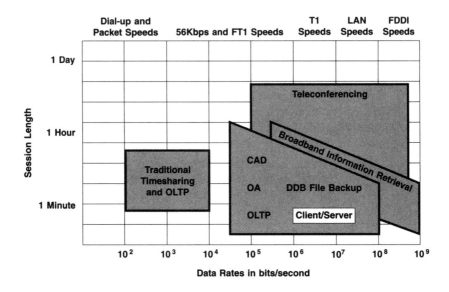

Figure 2.40   Applications Drive Communications Bandwith I. Communication Bandwith is responding to the application challenge. *Source*: BCR.

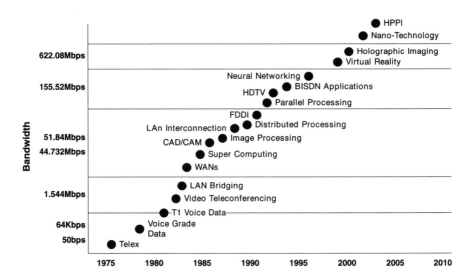

Figure 2.41   Applications Drive Communications Bandwith II. Communication bandwith has to evolve to match emerging application requirements. *Source*: MCI.

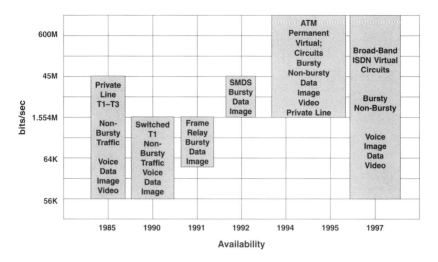

Figure 2.42   AT&T Broadband Services. AT&T is evolving its Broadband Services to support bursty and non-bursty traffic at a wide range of speeds.

Conclusion

Table 2.14 summarizes some of the incredible changes taking place in IM&M technologies. Figures 2.43, 2.44, and 2.45 overlay the technologies examined in this section onto a set of IM&M change matrices. If you compare these with Figure 2.7, the magnitude of IM&M change is vivid. You are confronted by a revolution in technology, seeding a revolution in opportunity.

If you still have any doubts about the extent of the occurring revolution, consider the counter theory:

> Reacting to competitive pressures, users will fund major new investments in traditional host-centered computing. The interest in network computing and re-engineering technologies is only a short-lived fad.

Now do two things:

1. Generate a set of hypothesis and supporting evidence, and
2. Explain away all the evidence just presented.

It is obvious to all except those living in a total state of denial that the evidence in support of our theory is overwhelming and compelling. Such is the power of the theory/hypothesis approach which links seemingly disparate information into a coherent and comprehensive argument.

Table 2.14
Price/Performance Trends. IM&M technologies demonstrate absolutely
incredible price/performance trends through the 1990s.

Technology	From	To	Trend
Microprocessor Transistor Density/Chip	1978	1996	From 29,000 to 3 million
Microprocessor Transistor Density/Chip	1978	2001	From 29,000 to 100 million
Microprocessor Mips	1978	2001	From .5 Mips to 800 Mips
Microprocessor Clock Speeds	1978	2001	From 10 MHz to 250 MHz
PC/Mainframe Price Performance	1978	2001	700:1
DAT Storage	1989	1997	Twelve times increase per unit
DRAM Density	1970	2000	From 1 thousand bits/Dram to 4096 Mbits/Dram
$/MB Dram	1970	2000	From $500 Mb to 5 Mb
PC disk form factor	1991	1998	From 2.5" to .5"
MB/PC disk Platter	1991	1995	Twelve times increase
Video Compression	1978	1993	Bandwidth requirement to carry video conference signal reduced from 6 Mbps to 80 Kbps

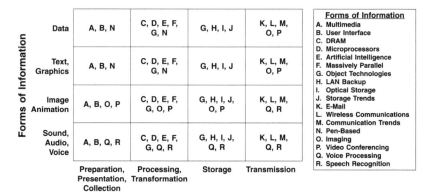

Figure 2.43   IM&M Form vs. Function. The evidence indicates tremendous change in the relationships of IM&M form to IM&M function.

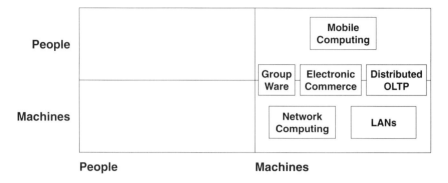

Figure 2.44   IM&M People vs. Machines. The evidence indicates tremendous change in the relationships between people and machines.

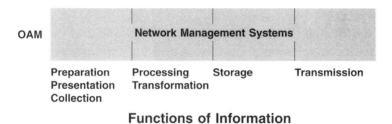

Functions of Information

Figure 2.45   Function vs. OAM. The evidence indicates change in the relationship of OAM to IM&M functions.

2.3 Summary

The purpose of IM&M is competitiveness. The future actions of decision makers can then be forecasted as follows:

- Host-Centered or User-Centered Computing (Figure 2.46)

    Given additional money for investment in IM&M resources, will the decision makers choose to construct another generation of systems on the host-centered architecture, or will they choose to build the next generation of advantage applications on user-centered technologies?

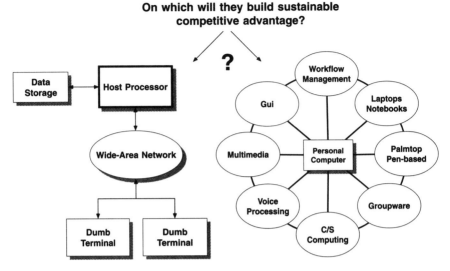

Figure 2.46   Host-Centered vs. User-Centered Computing. Which architecture will the decision maker choose for the next generation of applications?

- The Reach/Range/Maneuverability Game (Figure 2.47)

    The decision makers must pick a game piece to play the game of reach, range, and maneuverability. They may pick a host-centered game piece or a network computing game piece. They need to be able to integrate all the emerging technologies discussed in this section as well as position the organization for unparalleled IM&M maneuverability. Which will they pick?

The answer to these choices is obvious. Our technology heritage is under attack by vibrant substitutes.

Sun Tzu said:

    It is easy to take over from those who do not plan ahead. [7]

Strategists must analyze information with objective detachment and be ready to accept and react to unpleasant facts and trends. The endless stream of IM&M technologies that can be anticipated needs to be appreciated within a greater context: we, as a technology community, are in the barbarism stage of evolutionary development. I/T historians will look back at today as the primordial period. While most people in our field are intoxicated with their skills and accomplishments, the unpleasant reality is that IM&M as a commercial engineering discipline is only roughly 35 years old. When we imagine what will be possible and needed and com-

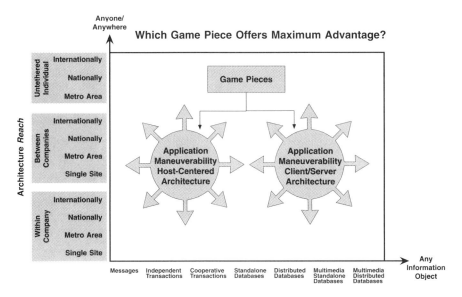

Figure 2.47   Host-Centered vs. Network Computing. Which architecture will the decision maker choose for the next generation of applications? *Source*: "Implementing Client/Server Computing: A Strategic Perspective," Bernard H. Boar, McGraw-Hill, 1993 with permission of publisher.

pare that with the crude state of IM&M and systems development methodologies today (the structured techniques of the 70s were no no more than medieval bloodletting), we must soberly anticipate that similar to most engineering disciplines, the technologies of the early stages are but an amateurish preview of what is to come. We must plan for incredible change now not only because we are immediately confronted with a major transitional period, but because as IM&M matures, its rate of change will ever accelerate.

2.3.   Competition

The purpose of this section is to understand the threat of substitution to in-house IM&M by a variety of competent and ambitious outsourcers. Historically, the internal IM&M function enjoyed an elitist status, immune to competition. This era is rapidly coming to an end. Reacting to the need for competitiveness, companies are migrating their IM&M services to a free-market economy. Users are being given discretionary control of their budgets and are now "free to choose." The internal IM&M organization must compete for business.

Sun Tzu said:

> What causes opponents to come of their own accord is the prospect of gain. What dissuades opponents from coming is the prospect of harm. [8]

There is ample prospect for gain to attract them. How will we parry their advance? Machiavelli said:

> ...One must never allow disorder to continue so as to escape a war. Anyhow, one does not escape; the war is merely postponed to one's disadvantage. [9]

We must not be slothful.

Definitions

Outsourcing is a contractual relationship between an external vendor and a user in which the vendor assumes responsibility for one or more functions. It is usually characterized by a transfer of assets or personnel. Two major types of outsourcing raising the "ante" of competition for the internal IM&M organization are:

- *Facilities Management (FM)*—A form of outsourcing in which the vendor assumes responsibility for establishing and operating a client's telecommunications operations, data centers, and voice networks.

- *Systems Integration (SI)*—A large (typically $1 million plus) customized project that requires multiple components (such as hardware, professional services, software, and communications) and addresses a significant problem. An external contractor manages most or all phases of systems development and assumes a high degree of the project's risk. [10]

Facility managers and system integrators are strategic competitors to the typical in-house IM&M organization. A *strategic competitor* is an existing or potential provider of services to your market who has the assets (commitment, competencies, resources, reputation, financial resources, geographic coverage, etc.) to win a meaningful market share.

Companies turn to outsourcers to reduce costs, gain expertise, supplement internal labor shortages, meet deadlines, improve IM&M performance and responsiveness, and to permit management to focus on the core business and leave IM&M to the experts. Companies go to outsourcers because they believe they will be more competitive by using an external provider than they would using the internal provider of IM&M services.

Sun Tzu said:

So the rule is not to count on opponents not coming; but to rely on having ways of dealing with them; not to count on opponents not attacking; but to rely on having what cannot be attacked. [11]

Sun Tzu was, of course, correct. They are coming. Armies of system integrators, facility managers, consultants, and every form and shape of outsourcer. They are coming to take the internal IM&M organization's job.

The Market

Systems integrators and facility managers offer a wide range of attractive services for clients. Typical SI services include business consulting, I/T auditing, feasibility studies, systems architecture, systems design, systems development, systems installation, training, and project management. Typical facility management services include operations management, vendor management, contracting, and planning.

Both SI and FM are attractive growth industries and have attracted major players. The size and growth of these markets are illustrated in Figure 2.48, Figure 2.49, and Figure 2.50. Major players in these market include IBM, through its Integrated Systems Solution Corporation (ISSC) subsidiary, Electronic Data Systems (EDS), Computer Science Corporation (CSC), and Arthur Andersen Consulting (AAC).

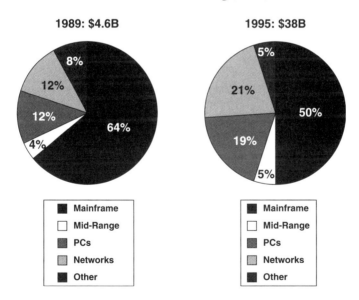

Figure 2.48 **Outsourcing Market. While outsourcing will grow significantly, the focus of outsourcing will start to shift to the network and PCs.** *Source*: **Frost & Sullivan, Inc.**

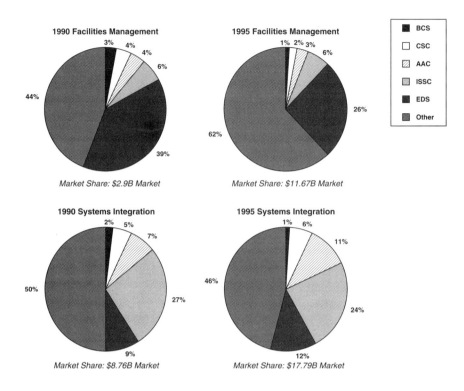

Figure 2.49   SI and FM Markets. Major players in both markets are ISSC, EDS, CSC, and AAC. *Source*: **Gartner Group.**

The markets have distinct success factors. The FM market is a cost-savings driven market; the basis of competitive advantage is offering a cost advantage to the client. The SI market is a value-added driven market; the basis of advantage is offering the client a differentiated service. Table 2.15 identifies what the vendors must do well to succeed in each of the marketplaces.

The Players

There are more than 50 major players in the outsourcing business. Four key players are listed below:

- *Arthur Anderson Consulting (AAC)*—AAC is a strategic business unit of Arthur Andersen & Co. AAC has over 150 offices worldwide with over 800 partners. AAC focuses on systems integration with an increasing focus on network computing.

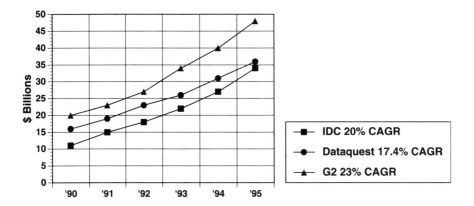

Figure 2.50   SI Market Forecast. The composite forecast of the three
market forecast firms is a CAGR of about 20% for the SI Marketplace.
Souce: IDC, Dataquest, and G2.

Table 2.15
SI and FM Critical Success Factors. SI and FM have distinct critical
success factors.

Critical Success Factors	
Systems Integration	**Facilities Management**
Business consulting	Asset to large pools of capital
Methodology-based development	Cost control and operations efficiency
World-wide geographic coverage	Legal and contract skills
Project management	Vendor management
Wide range of technology skills	Technology and operations management
Reputation—technology and business expertise	Reputation—operations expertise
End-to-end services	Economies of scale

- *Electronic Data Systems (EDS)*—EDS is an independent subsidiary of
General Motors. It was established in 1962, and reorganized itself in
the Fall of 1992 to grow both globally and support becoming a $35 bil-
lion company. EDS has traditionally made its revenue on facilities

management but is now branching more into business consulting and systems integration. In December 1992, EDS renewed its master contract with GM for a period of five years worth $3 billion. The contract included incentives wherein EDS would share savings produced through business re-engineering efforts. This growing shift to shared savings and incentive-based contracts will put added competitive pressure on internal IM&M organizations as they are required to link revenue to specific results.

- *Computer Science Corporation (CSC)*—CSC was established in 1959 and has three major business units:

  1. CSC Consulting which does commercial systems integration,
  2. Industry Services Group which offers services to vertical markets, and
  3. Systems Group which does government systems integration.

  CSC has historically gotten most of its revenue from government SI contracts, but due to defense cutbacks, it's targeting commercial SI.

- *Integrated Systems Solution Corporation (ISSC)*—ISSC is a subsidiary of IBM and was formed in April 1991. ISSC does not have an independent sales force but sells through the national sales force and targets both commercial and government opportunities. ISSC is anticipated to grow at a compound rate of 75% through the mid 1990s. Like EDS, ISSC provides IM&M services to its parent and is expected to have total 1993 revenue greater than $4 billion.

Table 2.16 provides descriptive information about these SI/FM players. Table 2.17 summarizes the sizes of some of the major deals. We are witnessing extremely large SI/FM deals being made in multiple industries.

The intent of all these companies, as well as the other SI/FM players, is to replace the internal IM&M service provider by offering superior economies for facilities management and superior development capabilities for systems integration. The composite business objectives of these vendors are:

- To offer a seamless suite of services,
- To offer total, end-to-end, solutions,
- Worldwide presence (global capabilities for global clients),
- Double digit annual growth, and
- To be a vision leader by providing IM&M blueprints.

Table 2.16

Competitor Profiles. EDS, ISSC, AAC, and CSC, collectively, offer competition to internal IM&M organization in almost any industry.

Vendor 91; Revenue; Staff Size	AAC; $2.3B; 21K
Marketing	1. Uses demonstration centers; 2. Sells high by positioning with CEO, CFO, CIO, and MIS director; 3. Presents selves as leader in all segments; 4. Heavy advertising and promotion; 5. Consulting pulls through other business
Strengths	1. Business consulting; 2.Client relationships; 3. Proprietary tools; 4. Complete array of services; 5. Reputation; 6. Global; 7. Professionalism; 8. Commitment to employee development
Sample Contracts	1. 1992 Winter Olympics; 2. 1994 Winter Olympics; 3. Hungarian railroad; 4. Thames Water; 5. Budget Rent A Car; 6. Schuller International
Alliances/ Purchases	1. Microsoft strategic integrator; 2. NCR integrator; 3. HP Case Tool for client/server; 4. Client/server airlines system
HR Policies	1. Comprehensive and standardized training in methodology, professionalism,service orientation, and AAC culture; 2. 6.3% of budget spent on training; 3. Four training centers; 4. Hires top graduates at premium; 5. At least eleven years to become a partner
Vendor 91; Revenue; Staff Size	EDS $7.1B 64K
Marketing	1. Uses enterprise technology centers to demonstrate prowess; 2. Promotional advertising in *Wall Street Week, Business Week,* etc.
Strengths	1. Long-term presence and experience; 2. Financial strength; 3.Large infrastructure; 4. Broad range of services; 5. Proprietary products; 6. Economies of scale; 7. GM as base customer
Sample Contracts	1. Anchor Glass; 2. Blue Cross of Massachusetts; 3. FAA Corn project ; 4. Enron; 5. Smith Food and Drug; 5. Summer 92 Olympics; 6. Continental Airlines; 7. PPG; 8. GE PC services; 9. GM; 10. MSRC; 11. California Department of Health—Medicaid; 12. Washington Water Power; 13. Del Monte Foods; 14. Memorex Telex; 15. Brunos; 16. Bethlehem Steel
Alliances/ Purchases	1. NCR integrator; 2. Compaq Integrator; 3. Avcom; 4. IBM VAR; 5. Microsoft Integrator; 6. Consilium; 7. Versant Object Technology; 8. Lante; 9. Everett Systems; 10. Apple VAR; 11. Hospitality Franchise Systems; 12. Lotus Notes VAR; 13 Purchased Energy Management Associates; 14. Purchased Cummins Cash and Information Services; 15.Purchased 2% of 4th Dimesnion Software
HR Policies	1. Fiercely competitive culture; 2. Strong company loyalty; 3. Tenacious management style; 4. "Get It Done" culture

Table 2.16 *continued*

Vendor 91; Revenue; Staff Size	EDS; $7.1B; 64K
Marketing	
Strengths	1. Federal government experience and references; 2. Project-management skills; 3. End-to-ends services; 4. Client retention; 5. Worldwide presence
Sample Contracts	1.WCI Steel; 2. General Dynamics; 3. State Department Communications Network; 4. Treasury Network; 5. IRS Financial Systems; 6. NYS Medicaid; 7. Burpee; 8. Australian Mutual Provident Society; 9. JCALS Department of Defense; 10. British Home Stores
Alliances/ Purchases	Bought 1. Compu-Source; 2. Butler-Cox; 3. Intelcom Solutions Corp. Alliances 1. Sun Microsystems
HR Policies	
Vendor 91; Revenue; Staff Size	ISSC; $1.9B; 5K
Marketing	1. Industry-specific marketing; 2. Sells through regular sales force; 3. Offers a short-term outsourcing program called Term Capacity Plan
Strengths	1. IBM product expertise; 2. Established customer relationships; 3. Vertical market expertise; 4.Size; 5. Financial resources; 6. Worldwide presence; 7. Reputation
Sample Contracts	1. Foremost Insurance; 2. Health Dimensions Inc.; 3. Zale Corp.; 4. Supermarkets General; 5. First Tennessee Bank; 6. Continental Bank; 7. Eastman Kodak; 8. United Technologies; 9. Yankee Gas Services Co.; 10. Hertz; 11. Norrell; 12. Hook-SuperRx; 13. McDonnel Douglas; 14. Kaiser Permanante; 15. Chase Manhattan Bank; 16. Qualex
Alliances/ Purchases	1. Coopers Lybrand; 2. Policy Management Systems Corp.; 3. Advantis with Sears
HR Policies	

An IBM advertisement summed up their thrust:

We now have management consultants to help our customers decide what to do, systems consultants to show them how, technical experts to help them get their systems up and running, and even an organization that will actually run their systems for them.

Table 2.17
Contract Sizes. Half billion dollar contracts or greater have not been unusual.

Client	Value	SI/FM Vendor
General Dynamics	$3B	CSC
McDonnel Douglas	$3B	ISSC
Continental Airlines	$2.1B	EDS
Australian Mutual Provident Society	$1.5B	CSC
Massachusetts BC/BS	$800M	EDS
Enron Corp.	$750M	EDS
Continental Bank	$700M	EDS
First City Bancorp	$600M	ISSC
Eastman Kodak	$500M	ISSC
National Car Rental	$500M	EDS
Bethlehem Steel Corp.	$500M	EDS

This advertisement is a lighthouse. Isn't this what the in-house IM&M organization was chartered to do? You are forewarned. They are aggressive, purposeful, and ambitious competitors.

Summary

It is not surprising that the Arthur Andersen's *et al.* are coming. There is much to gain. Able, ambitious, motivated, and full of momentum, they offer a viable substitute to the internal IM&M organization. They seem to recognize much better than complacent IM&M organizations that "what is" is getting old, and they do not show hesitancy to adopt the newer technologies.

I sometimes wonder if I am overly pessimistic in my assessment of the ability of many internal IM&M organizations to respond to this threat. A recent article in an industry trade magazine, however, convinced me that I am probably too optimistic. The article entitled "Ten Reasons to Stand by Your Mainframe" summarized the view of "mainframe diehards." The author asserts that "a mainframe is the only platform we would trust to run nearly all our mission-critical applications." He presents the following ten reasons for his mainframe-centric perspective:

1. We need to handle massive transaction volumes.
2. We want to shield users from system issues.
3. The mainframe keeps our IS costs down.
4. We need to ensure that data is timely, secure, and accessible.
5. We feel we can attract a more highly professional IS staff.
6. The mainframe helps us keep pace with user applications needs.
7. Custom application development is easier on the mainframe.
8. We want to preserve and leverage our systems investment.
9. We are assured of vendor support in upward migrations.
10. We hold a lot of clout with our systems vendor.

The article ends with a call to arms: "Our mainframe will never die." Given what you have learned in this chapter, particularly the importance of reach, range, and maneuverability, and what you will learn in the ensuing chapters, I leave it to you to judge whether the "high walls and deep moat" the author of this article has built to protect himself will suffice.

I would like to offer an informative analogy to place this defense in a timeless perspective. A traumatic transition for the American Navy was the evolution from sail-powered man-of-wars to steam-powered man-of-wars.[12] A compact chronology of related events follows:

*   1690—American naval shipbuilding begins in Portsmouth, New Hampshire, with the construction of *The Falkand*.
*   1807—The *Clermont*, constructed by Robert Fulton and the first commercially successful steamboat, is launched.
*   1820's—The Navy Board's position is "a steamer would never do as a sea-going man-of-war."
*   1822—The largest sail-powered man-of-war ever built in the United States, the 120 gun Pennsylvania, is under construction at the Philadelphia Naval Yard.
*   1841—The *Congress* is built. It is to be the last new design for sail-powered man-of-war frigates.
*   1842—The *Mississippi* and the *Missouri*, steam-powered man-of-wars, are launched. "These ships marked the beginning of the decline in importance of sailing man-of-wars, though it was 20 years more before the last die-hards would recognize the supremacy of the steamship."

- 1842 1845—A boon occurs in the construction of sail-powered man-of-wars. "The Navy Board and senior officers were anxious to utilize any available funds in the construction of sailing vessels at the expense of steamers. Satisfied with the existing state of events and living on past glories, they came to resent and fear any innovation."

- 1861—"Slowly but surely steamers replace sailing man-of-wars. The innovation of the screw propeller hastened the end of the sailing ship. A fire in the Norfolk Naval Yard provided a funeral pyre for ten great sail man-of-wars. There was no longer a valid reason for their existence other than sentimental preservation of an era."

I would suggest that when the history of computing is written in the 21st century, "Ten Reasons to Stand by Your Mainframe" and its conclusion "Our mainframe will never die" will prove equal in insight and foresight to the Navy Board's statement in the 1820s that "steamers would never do as sea-going man-of wars." The Ptolemaic earth-centric view of the cosmos lasted as established science for 1500 years. Galelio was tried and convicted of heresy for promoting the Copernican view that the earth revolved around the sun. It is not difficult to surmise how the Navy Board or our mainframe enthusiast would have voted at Galileo's trial.

What is particularly interesting about both the mainframe zealot and the Navy Board is the degree of "self-satisfaction" each achieved. Each was completely self-assured and confident in their position. They were powerful and important people, heirs of successful technology, believed themselves to be all knowing, intellectually and technically excellent, and the final arbiter of what was correct. They had reached a state where they no longer could learn from or evaluate new information; they could only pass judgment on it. So like all self-satisfied people, they become complacent, arrogant, and self-serving. Their view of the world became "right by entitlement." They lost the common perspective of all those who lead. The perspective that life is a struggle which has to be won each and every day by having the capacity to act in new and creative ways. Why would anyone involved with technology believe that any technology is anything other than passing; transient until another comes which offers superior price/performance, feature/functionality, or flexibility? Only those who would rather live off the labors of the past and forget, to their own demise, that the need to create new advantage is eternally recurrent. Will we be able to react to the competition, or are we like the Navy Board, consumed with what was rather than what will be? The Navy was well positioned to fight the last war. Are we likewise well positioned to build yesterday's systems?

Sun Tzu said:

Compare the strength of the enemy with your own, and you will know whether there is sufficiency or lacking. After that, you can assess the advisory of attack or defense.[13]

The era of the IM&M organization hegemony is in collapse and it's becoming a war of all against all. The best attack and the best defense for us is the same thing, excellence in the use of IM&M for competitive advantage for the business. We need a plan.

2.4   Summary

Dr. Nilolai Kondratiev was a Russian economist during the Stalinist era. His studies of Western economies culminated in a concept called "Kondratiev Waves" (Figure 2.51). Dr. Kondratiev argued that Western productivity grew in distinct waves with each wave being fueled by a few dominant technologies. Extrapolating Dr. Kondratiev's ideas, Figure 2.51 asserts that we are now in the electronics and information technology wave. The periods of transition when one wave ebbs and another rises are difficult and dislocating periods as balances of power are broken and new orders are developed.

Dr. Kondratiev's wave theory is an excellent context to understand the change which has been presented in this chapter. As illustrated in Figure 2.51, the electronics and computing wave is divisible into subwaves which share the same characteristics of change as the megawaves. The early computing subwaves, batch, big iron, OLTP, and demassification of microcomputers were not disruptive of the IM&M order; they represented change but were evolutionary. The current subwave, network computing, is dislocating. It requires a major shift in roles and responsibilities, power bases, and control and utilization of IM&M resources. The era of host-centered computing and "one size IM&M fits all" is in decline, and the era of network computing and pick and match IM&M technologies is on the ascent.

Information systems in the 1990s will be very different than their predecessors. Key characteristics will be:

- Exploitation of workgroup-centered technologies to re-engineer the business for competitive advantage,
- Exploitation of mobile technologies to increase speed, productivity, and information sharing with mobile workers,
- Exploitation of standards to bond the organization with its suppliers and customers,

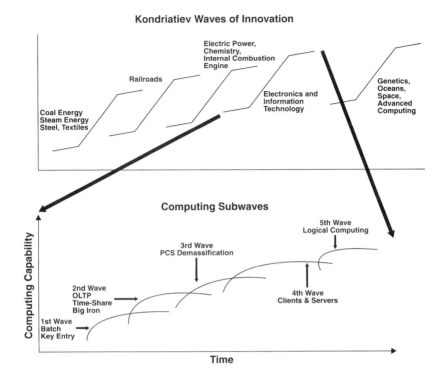

Figure 2.51 Waves of Change. Productivity is stimulated in any era by a few dominant technologies. *Source*: "Implementing Client/Server Computing: A Strategic Perspective," Bernard H. Boar, McGraw-Hill, 1993 with permission of publisher.

- Movement to microprocessor-based solutions to take advantage of changing computing economics,
- Leveraging of ease-of-use features of new user-interface technologies to broaden the usage and utilization of information technologies,
- Integration of information in all its forms into the IM&M application base, and
- Adoption of network computing to maximize reach, range, and maneuverability of the IM&M asset.

While critical IM&M success factors during the host-centered era were utilization efficiency, centralized control, and slow adaptation, critical success factors in the 1990s will be:

- Open architecture-based IM&M,
- Business re-engineering philosophy,
- Continuous learning,
- IM&M positioned as foundation of business competitiveness by permitting unparalleled maneuverability,
- Re-education of staff, and
- First extension and then replacement of the embedded IM&M base.

The ability to respond to this challenge is compromised by an interesting but unfortunate paradox of organizational behavior. Figure 2.52 illustrates this paradox. Sun Tzu says:

> What the aware individual knows has not yet taken shape. If you see the subtle and notice the hidden when there is no form, this is really good. What everyone knows is not called wisdom. A leader of wisdom and ability lays deep plans for what others do not figure on.[14]

The pinnacle of strategic insight is to sense, understand, or foresee the ripples of change and opportunity when they are but scarcely visible; when they are "formless." An organization blessed with such foresight has maximum degrees of strategic freedom of action and time to accommodate the shift.

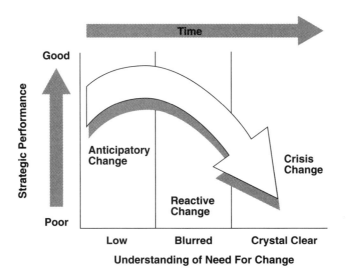

Figure 2.52   Degrees of Freedom of Action vs. Understanding of Need for Change. Paradoxically, the organization refuses to adopt change when it is most advantageous.

Unfortunately, when the evidence is slight and the need "formless," the multitudes do not see the need for change. They resist, argue, fight, and defend "what is" as though "what is" is immutable. They take on the character of an ethnocentric group whose "folkways" have been elevated to the status of dogma. All is rated and evaluated in reference and subordination to their "clearly superior" beliefs. Dr. Andrew Grove, CEO of Intel, referring to Intel's transformation from a DRAM vendor to a microprocessor supplier, summed up the problem laconically as follows:

Emotionally, it is easier to change when you're hemorrhaging.

By the time the need to change becomes visible to all, the options available to deal with the change are extremely limited. Such is the paradox of organizational reaction to change. If the multitudes embrace change early, multiple alternatives exist for a gradual and successful adaptation. Waiting until the evidence is sufficiently glaring to convince even the most determined cynic leaves the organization with few strategic change options. Paradoxically, the multitudes act against their own interests in embracing what was rather than what will be. Machiavelli summarized the situation:

All wise rulers must cope not only with present troubles but also with ones likely to arise in the future and assiduously forestall them. When trouble is sensed well in advance it can easily be remedied; if you wait for it to show itself any medicine will be too late because the disease will have become incurable.... Disorders can be quickly healed if they are seen well in advance (and only a prudent ruler has such foresight); when, for lack of a diagnosis, they are allowed to grow in such away that everyone can recognize them, remedies are too late. [15]

We are well along the strategy and change line of Figure 2.52. The degrees of freedom of action decline with each day of inaction. One no longer needs to be an extraordinary strategist to recognize the need for change. Only the most closed-minded can deny the evidence presented in this chapter. The need for change has already happened, it has become obvious. We must not tarry.

To succeed in the 1990s, the IM&M organization must plan, act, and think strategically. As Sun Tzu says:

They do not wander when they move. They act in accord with events. Their action and inactions are matters of strategy. [16]

In the following chapters, we will learn how to manage IM&M strategically.

Footnotes

1. Adapted from P. Keen's *Shaping the Future.*
2. Sun Tzu, *The Art of War.*
3. CSC/Index.
4. Sun Tzu, *The Art of War.*
5. We use the term "Operations, Administration, and Maintenance (OAM)" to refer to the management functions.
6. Gartner Group Seminars: 1991/1992.
7. Sun Tzu, *The Art of War.*
8. Sun Tzu, *The Art of War.*
9. Machiavelli, *The Prince.*
10. These definitions are from The Gartner Group, "Outsourcing: Threat or Salvation."
11. Sun Tzu, *The Art of War.*
12. H. I. Chapelle, *The History of the American Sailing Navy.*
13. Sun Tzu, *The Art of War.*
14. Sun Tzu, *The Art of War.*
15. Machiavelli, *The Prince.*
16. Sun Tzu, *The Art of War.*

3

Assessment

The purpose of this chapter is to explain the "assessment" step of the strategic planning process. *Assessment* is the thorough analysis of the business environment to decide what to focus on. There is an endless amount of detail and petitioners competing for management attention. Assessment filters the candidates to a preferred set which demands strategic attention and response.

Figure 3.1 is an enlargement of the assessment step. We will explain this step in the following manner:

- Section 3.1: *The Business Scope and Alignment*

    This section will define the notion of a business scope. A *business scope* defines the key describers of a business. A corollary concept to a business scope is alignment. *Alignment* is the process of assuring that all business functions operate in harmony with each other to support the business scope.

- Section 3.2: *Directives and Assumptions*

    This section explains how the IM&M function aligns itself with the greater business through the notion of directives and assumptions. The strategic planning for the IM&M organization takes place within the context of an overall business which the IM&M function must support. The business strategic planning function provides directives and assumptions which bound (guide) the IM&M effort.

- Section 3.3: *Position*

    This section explains the concept and development of positioning the business. *Position* illustrates the state of one or more business areas. Position answer the question "Where are we?"

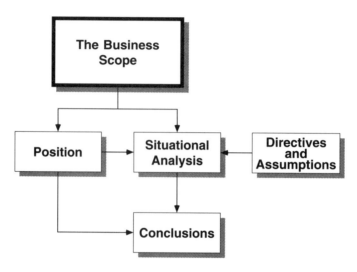

Figure 3.1   **Assessment. Assessment is the first step of the strategic planning process.**

- Section 3.4: *Situational Analysis*

    This section explains how to perform a situational analysis. *Situational analysis* is the collection and analysis of information about the business for developing conclusions about the state of the business. Situational Analysis is performed by using various analytical methodologies.

- Section 3.5: *Conclusions*

    This section explains the notion of conclusions which are the culmination of the assessment step. *Conclusions* are explicit statements describing the overall situation of the business. They represent a set of imperatives requiring remedial or exploitative strategic action.

- Section 3.6: Summary

    This section summarizes the key points of the chapter.
Sun Tzu says:

    If you know others and know yourself, you will not be imperiled in a hundred battles; if you do not know others but know yourself, you will win one and lose one; if you do not know others and do not know yourself, you will be imperiled in every single battle.[1]

He teaches that assessment was the necessary preamble to a winning strategy. He says:

> The one with many strategic factors in his favor wins, the one with few strategic factors in his favor loses.… Observing the matter in this way, *I can foresee who will win and who will lose.*

Sun Tzu's seven strategic factors in order of importance and their modern equivalents are as follows:

Sun Tzu Strategic Factor	Definition	Modern Day Equivalent
1. The Way	Inducing the people to share the same aims as the leadership through justice and benevolence	Culture, ethos, ethics
2. The Leadership	Intelligence, sterness, trustworthiness, humanity, and courage	Same
3. The Weather	The seasons	Industry Dynamics
4. The Terrain	The lay of the land	Competition
5. The Discipline	Organization, chain of command, and logistics	Managment systems, capabilities, and processes
6. Troop Strength and Training	Number and competence of troops	Same
7. Reward and Punishment System	Procedures for rewarding valor and punishing disobedience	Human Resource Architecture

Adaptation to events takes place within the context of the assessment of these factors. It is remarkable that these strategic factors remain as relevant today as they were 2500 years ago.

The first step of strategic planning, therefore, is assessment, the act of knowing oneself and all other aspects of the business environment. Without assessment, we would proceed without forethought: a sure formula for failure.

3.1 Business Scope and Alignment

We understand a business as consisting of a business scope and a set of organization units to realize that business scope. The business organizes into units to accomplish the business scope. Relative to each other and the

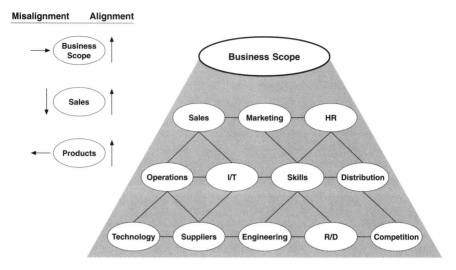

Figure 3.2   The Business Scope Model. A business may be understood in terms of a business scope which defines the essential parameters of the business and organizational units which act to realize the business scope.

business scope, functional units may be in a state of alignment or misalignment. Figure 3.2 illustrates these ideas.

Business Scope

Table 3.1 itemizes the attributes of a business scope. After reviewing a business scope, one should clearly understand the nature of a business. Each attribute of a business scope will now be explained:

- *Vision*—A vision provides a guiding theme that articulates the nature of the business and its intent for the future. A vision should be informative, shared, competitive, empowering, and worthy of an extended personal commitment.
- *Mission*—A mission clearly defines the purpose of the business. It should remove any doubt as to what is intended to be accomplished.
- *Values*—Values describe what the business believes in. Values are important for success from at least two perspectives:

1. Values are the root system for staff behavior. Management cannot expect winning behaviors to develop throughout the organization without building a foundation of values which stimulate and support desirable behaviors.

2. Values provide the basis for autonomous action by empowered employees. Executive management cannot be everywhere all the time making every decision. If teams are to make rapid decisions without endless top management review, they require a framework of values to guide their decision making. Values provide such a guide.

- *Customers/Markets*—Customers/Markets define the recipients of products and services.
- *Products/Services*—Products/Services define what is sold.
- *Geography*—Geography defines the "space" of the marketplace. As companies compete globally, space takes on increased strategic significance because financial systems, standards, products, human resource practices, and capabilities all have to adapt to the new geography of the marketplace.
- *Strategic Intent*[2]—Strategic Intent describes the long term ambition of our efforts. It may be viewed a grand selfish vision. A strategic intent has the following attributes:

  It is the long term stable ambition of a winner. It defines winning and is worthy of an extended corporate attention plan.

  It represents ambition out of all proportion to the resources and capabilities of the organization. It promotes leveraging the resources of the organization to reach the intent rather than settling for limited objectives.

  It provides a compelling target for organizational commitment and effort.

  It provides a future to fold back against. One must constantly ask "What must I do now to get closer to my strategic intent?"

Strategic planning cycles, therefore, are not disconnected. Each planning cycle should be understood as a stepping stone to the strategic intent. Challenges and hurdles are addressed in each planning cycle to move us closer to the stable long term intent. As illustrated in Figure 3.3, the business does not wander from planning cycle to planning cycle but moves forward toward a defined end; the end of a winner.

Table 3.1
Business Scope Definition. The business scope defines the essential character of a business.

Business Attribute	Definition
Vision	Business guiding theme
Mission	Purpose of the business
Values	Distinguishing beliefs—Ethos
Customer/Markets	To whom we sell
Products/Services	What we sell
Strategic Intent	Long-term ambition of our efforts
Driving Force	Primary determiner of products/services and markets
Geography	Where we sell
Sustainable Competitive Advantage	Asset, capability, process, etc., which attracts us to our customers and deters our competitors

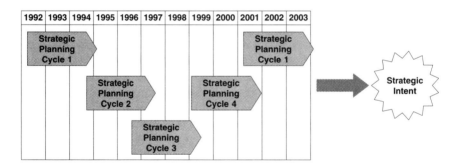

Figure 3.3   Strategic Intent. Strategic planning cycles are not indepen-dent but link together to reach the strategic intent of the business.

Given that the purpose of IM&M is competitiveness (Section 2.1), the strategic intent of an IM&M organization must include the realization of a reach/range/maneuverability architecture (Figure 2.2). By moving ever closer to a reach, range, and maneuverability architecture, an infrastructure is put in place that permits rapid IM&M system development, deployment, and evolution.

An ancillary concept to strategic intent is that of "market leader." One may assert that there are three types of companies:

1. Those that ask customers what they want and are perpetual followers,
2. Those that temporarily succeed in leading customers in directions they don't need to go, and
3. Those that lead customers where they need to go.

A strategic intent driven company is always the later type of company; it anticipates what the customer will need rather than selling the customer what they wanted six months or a year ago.

Two interesting examples of "market leader" companies in the IM&M field are as follows:

1. *Intelligent Vehicle Highway System (IVHS)*

    The IVHS is a joint initiative of AT&T and Lockheed to market IVHS services such as delivering traffic information to vehicles, automated toll collection, and delivering navigational information to vehicles. While the market is embryonic today, it is projected to grow to $200 billion by 2012. A spokesperson for IVHS is quoted as saying "The biggest challenge is convincing customers that they need such services."

2. *IBM/Time-Warner Interactive Home Services*

    This is a joint venture of IBM and Time Warner to bring interactive entertainment and services to the computer-television of the near future. Examples of such services are catalog shopping, home video, information services, financial services, view control, e-mail, and video-conferencing. A spokesperson for the venture has stated "Does anyone really want this stuff?"

Both of these cases exemplify companies that are trying to lead customers to desirable services in full recognition of the risks involved in creating a market.

Market leaders are often vision driven. Sun Tzu says:

What everyone knows is what has already happened. What everyone knows is not called wisdom. What the aware individual knows is what has not yet taken shape; what has not yet occurred. If you see the subtle and notice the hidden so as to seize victory when there is no form, this is really good.[3]

Visionaries provide insights that allow for discontinuous improvements in the strategic situation of a business. Much can be gained if you can take action while to most "there is no form."

- *Driving Force*[4]—Driving Force is an explicit statement of what will be the primary determiner of the scope of future markets and products. Table 3.2 illustrates a variety of driving forces from which a firm may choose. The selection of a driving force is a pivotal decision, since it will have a great influence on day-to-day decision making throughout the organization.
- *Sustainable Competitive Advantage*—Sustainable Competitive Advantage (SCA) are the resources, capabilities, assets, processes, etc., that provide the enterprise with a distinct attraction to its customers and unique advantage over its competitors. Table 3.3 lists the seven attributes that describe an SCA. An SCA may result in an advantage in cost/productivity, value-added/differentiation, or customer focus. The assessment, development, nurturing, and compounding of SCA is a major thrust of strategy development. SCA defines how the business will win. Table 3.4 may be used to analyze existing and candidate SCA for potency.

A business scope defines the essential characteristics of a business. It encapsulates the idea, concept, and formula of the business.

Alignment

A business accomplishes its objectives by mobilizing all the units toward realizing its business scope. To be successful, a business must realize a tri-state of alignment:

1. The business scope internally aligned between its elements.
2. All internal business units aligned with each other.
3. The aligned internal business functions, as a whole through the aligned business scope, aligned with the needs of the external marketplace.

The essence of alignment is coordination, perseverance, and concentration of effort toward a shared set of objectives. A business which is aligned is said to be in a state of "strategic fit."

Strategic fit or alignment should be understood as a continuum of states which include the following key data points in increasing achievment of alignment:

Table 3.2

Driving Force. A driving force is the primary determiner of future products and markets for the business.

Driving Force	Definition	Example
Products offered	Continue to produce and deliver products similar to those it has	Automobile manufacturer
Market needs	Provide a range of products to meet current and emerging needs in the markets it serves	Hospital supply
Technology	Only offers products derived from its technological capability	Pharmaceutical
Production capability	Only offers products driven by its production know-how/capability	Lodging
Method of sale	Selects products and serves markets based on its primary method of sale	TV home shopping
Method of distribution	Selects products and markets based on its distribution channels	Catalog house
Natural resources	Offers products and services based on its natural resource asset	Oil company
Size/Growth	Provide a range of products to meet size/growth objectives	Mergers and acquisitions
Return/Profit	Provide a range of products to meet return/profit objectives	Conglomerate

- *Entropy (chaos)*—Gross misalignment. Collaboration within and between functions, processes, and the external marketplace is a rare accident.
- *Misfit*—Collaboration between functions and processes is minimal.
- *Mixed*—There exists a mixture of alignment and misalignment. A reasonable number of functions and processes are "kind of" going in the same direction.
- *Threshold (minimal)*—A minimal level of alignment exists so that products and services can move through the value chain and to the customer. Businesses at less than a threshold level will eventually implode if the state is not improved.
- *Harmony*—General and continuing collaboration

Table 3.3

Sustainable Competitive Advantage. Sustainable competitive advantage defines the logic for attracting new customers, retaining existing customers, and growing existing customers.

Attribute	Definition
Customer perception	The customer perceives a consistent difference in one or more critical buying factors.
SCA linkage	The difference in customer perception is directly attributable to the SCA.
Durability	Both the customers perception and the SCA linkage are durable over an extended time period.
Transparency	The mechanics/details of the SCA are difficult to understand by competitors.
Accessibility	The competitor has unequal access to the required resources to mimic the SCA.
Replication	The competitor would have extreme difficulty reproducing the SCA.
Coordination	The SCA requires difficult and subtle coordination of multiple resources.

Table 3.4

SCA Evaluation Matrix. Existing and candidate SCA's can be evaluated by analyzing each SCA against the list of SCA attributes.

SCA	Customer Perception	SCA Linkage	Durability	Transparency	Accessibility	Replication	Coordination
SCA "1"							
SCA "2"							
SCA "3"							
SCA "4"							
SCA "5"							
SCA "N"							

- *Perfect alignment*—Not only does a state of harmony exist but the state has been achieved in a manner which provides sustainable competitive advantage to the firm.

As will be presented in the next section, achieving a level of stratetgic fit at and preferably superior to threshold is a foundation requirement of strategy.

Alignment does not mean automatons marching mindlessly in straight lines. Alignment is a wide highway, not a thin line. Alignment includes skunk works, "crazy money," and encourages creative independence. Alignment may include parallel projects as well as contradictory projects. The issue is that it is purposeful from the perspective of the whole rather than the individual optimizations of individual parts at the expense of the whole.

As shown in Figure 3.4, strategy crosses all functional areas. It is therefore not possible to develop or execute strategy without an objective of forcing a strategic fit. Without alignment, a business proceeds in a state of chaos with each unit optimizing its own provincial view of the world at the expense of the whole business (see Figure 3.5).

Figure 3.4   Strategy Is Comprehensive. Strategy development and execution crosses all business functional areas.

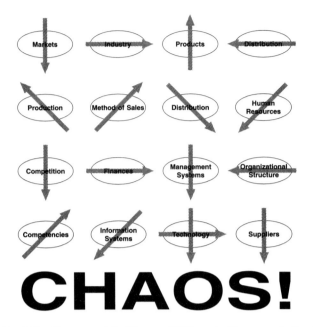

Figure 3.5   Misalignment Is Chaos. Without alignment, the business
proceeds in a state of chaos.

Sun Tzu says:

> Those whose upper and lower ranks have the same desire are victorious.... Those skilled in strategy achieve cooperation in a group so that directing the group is like directing a single individual with no other choice.... Employ the entire force like employing a single individual.[5]

Alignment is best conceptualized as the civilizing (throttling) of intra-organizational conflict to a point where a shared agenda and common purpose can be established. Alignment beyond that point is probably detrimental. Just as external competition provides the overall impetus to improve products and services, healthy and spirited debate during both the assessment and strategy steps leads to maximizing creative and innovative responses. This is the consequence of the clash of competing ideas. When fortune inevitably changes, new necessities will demand fresh responses. The novelty of these responses springs from the breadth of organizational diversity rather than from the depths of uniformity. For the execution step to succeed, however, a state of civilized alignment must be obtained or we will expend and exhaust our energies battling each other rather than our competitors. Alignment must therefore walk a delicate balance, maximizing current uniformity while not squashing the diversity required to seed tomorrow's adaptability.

As shown in Figure 3.6, a fundamental activity of strategic planning is moving the organization from its current state of alignment into a strategic fit state with the new business scope. A continual effort to reach alignment is imperative. While immediate business needs and opportunities will often cause misalignments as functions and processes move forward on varied schedules, if an effort is not maintained to reassert alignment then the seeds of future strategic problems will be sown. It is hard enough for the business to reacting to external change beyond its control without having to take strategic actions to rectify problems created by its own negligence to maintain synergy. So the nature of alignment is best understood as an endless race to achieve rather than an effort to maintain. Alignment is a continual journey, not a one time event.

Figure 3.6   Strategic Alignment. A basic objective of strategic planning is moving the organization to a new strategic fit.

It should be obvious from this discussion of business scope and alignment that a potentially traumatic event for any organization is a change, however small, in any element of the business scope. If any business scope element is redefined, all the functional units have to realign themselves. It would then logically follow that the worse thing that could happen to an organization is concurrent and major shifts in all (or almost all) of the business scope elements. Massive business scope redefinition would cause a transition state of chaos as the business functions struggle to achieve a new state of alignment.

This is exactly what is happening to many IM&M organizations today. As illustrated in Table 3.5, many of the business scope elements are being redefined in response to the IM&M pincer we discussed in Chapter 2. It is therefore not surprising that IM&M organizations find defining an identify for the 90s difficult when they are in a state of such mass transition.

Summary

Sun Tzu said:

Strategy is a problem of coordination, not of masses.[6]

Table 3.5
Changed IM&M Business Scope. IM&M organizations are undergoing massive realignment due to the massive change in their business scope.

Business Scope Element	Old IM&M Business Scope	New IM&M Business Scope
Mission	Build functional organizational systems	Build enterprise systems
Values	Optimize IM&M	Serve the business
Customers/markets	Data center user	Workgroup, departmental, and corporate user
Strategic intent	???	IM&M as basis for competitive advantage for the business
Driving force	Production capability/products	Market needs
Geography	Domestic	Global
Sustainable competitive advantage	Internal monopoly	World-class efficiency and effectiveness of the IM&M resource
Products/services	One size fits all	Cut and paste network computing

The basis of success is not the quantity of resources employed but the manner of employment. The businesss scope provides an unambiguous shared agenda for the organization. Alignment provides the vehicle to bring all functions into accord with the shared agenda. The objectives of the business as a whole are primary; the agenda of each unit is secondary. All strategic actions take place in the context of optimizing the business as a whole. Strategies of the individual units only have purpose toward that end.

3.2 Directives and Assumptions

The IM&M organization exists to provide competitiveness to the rest of the business. Its direction, as a whole, needs to be in alignment with the needs and requirements of the greater business. All strategic thinking and actions takes place in the overriding context of meeting the information movement and management needs of the customers. Though not constantly restated, whether one is doing business scope development, positioning, objective definitions, commitment plan, etc., all of strategic planning is done in constant (even when silent) reference to serving customers needs.

It should therefore be anticipated that the strategic planning effort of the business, as a whole, will provide directives and assumptions to guide, prioritize, lead, and shape the IM&M strategic planning effort (see Figure 3.7). These directives and assumptions bound the strategies which are permissible for the IM&M organization to undertake, and, in so doing, help assure a strategic fit between the business and the IM&M function (see Figure 3.8). The more valued a business partner the IM&M organization is viewed by the functional business units, the greater participation and influence the IM&M organization will have in shaping both overall business strategy and in bounding IM&M directives and assumptions.

The optimum strategic planning situation would therefore have a high degree of concurrency and interlock between the business strategic planning activities and those of the IM&M organization. In this situation, the IM&M planning would occur slightly staggered but in parallel to the business planning with the chief IM&M strategist (the CIO) actively participating in the business planning. In this and only this situation is the degree of collaboration, coordination, communication, and alignment maximized.

3.3 Position

A *position* is an illustration of the state of a strategic area along one or more strategic dimensions. Position is best expressed graphically, quantitatively, and lastly, qualitatively. A *strategic dimension* is a variable which

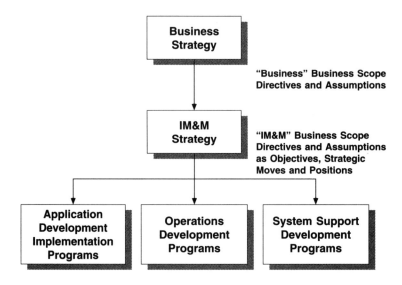

Figure 3.7   Direction and Assumption Planning Chain. Each level of planning provides guidelines and boundaries for the next.

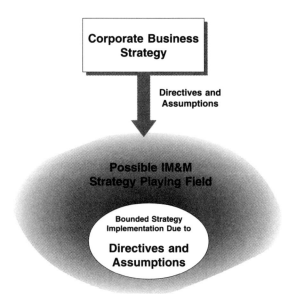

Figure 3.8   Bounding Strategy. The assumptions and directives provided to the IM&M function defines the permissible strategy playing field.

is critical to business success. Positions are descriptive of the state of the business and their correctness should not be argumentative. Position analysis yields a series of position charts which cross all strategically important business areas and collectively answer the question "Where are we?"

The underlying notion of this technique is that the strategic position (Position) of a business, $P_{BUSINESS}$, can be expressed as a set of positions, i.e.,

$P_{BUSINESS} = (P_{MARKET}, P_{FINANCIAL}, P_{TECHNOLOGY}, P_{SALES}, P_{OPERATIONS}, P_{DISTRIBUTION}, P_{ENGINEERING}, etc.).$

A position may also reflect the state of a resource such as a competency or process capability. Positioning is a recursive concept and any position, P_{XYZ}, may itself be a set of positions. This point will be fully demonstrated later in this section when we discuss positioning of a product.

It is asserted that any business area can be positioned. Table 3.6 provides a typical list of business areas which are included in strategic planning analysis and are candidates for positioning. The strategic planning team has the responsibility to:

- Define which areas are to be included in the analysis and require positioning,
- Define what are the strategic dimensions which illustrate the status of the area,
- Collect the required data to do the positioning, and
- Define the presentation format, preferably graphically, of the position.

Positioning, like situational analysis, needs to be done in multiple dimensions:

- Current (period ending) position—What is the collective strategic position of the business as of the ending of the current period?
- Strategic intent position—What would be the position of the business if the strategic intent was reached?
- Competitor position—What is the present situation and what is projected to be the position of the collective competition?
- Desired future state position—What positions does the business wish to attain by the end of this planning cycle?

The resulting gaps between the current position and the other positions is used to develop conclusions, objectives, and strategic moves.

Positioning forces "fantasy convergence." The graphical format of a position and the explicit statement of the position forces clarity and eliminates confusion. A shared agenda cannot be developed if agreement isn't reached on the present state of the organization or if there is gross misunderstanding among those who are trying to reach agreement. Positioning addresses this problem and forces resolution of differences we possess on the state of the business.

A business area must be positioned in a manner that provides understanding and insight into its strategic dimensions. The remainder of this section will demonstrate the positioning of multiple business areas or resources of particular importance to the IM&M function. These are common but exemplary positionings. Each positioning will be developed using the following structure:

Table 3.6
Functional Business Areas. These 17 areas are primary candidates for strategic positioning.

Functional Business area	Internal Analysis	External Analysis	Relative Importance to IM&M Strategist
Products/Services	X		Very high
Markets	X	X	Very high
Customers	X	X	Very high
Technology	X	X	Very high
Production methods	X		High
Method of sale	X		Medium
Method of distribution	X		Medium
Natural resources	X	X	None
Suppliers		X	Very high
Human resources	X		Very high
Organization structure	X		High
Management systems	X		High
External environment (socioeconomic factors)		X	Medium
IM&M (internal use)	X		High
Finances	X		High
Competition		X	Very high
Industry		X	High

- *Definition* of the business area or resource being positioned,
- *Description* of the business area or resource being positioned, and
- *IM&M strategic planning impact* analysis of the implications of the positioning to the IM&M strategic planning activity.

A strategic area which is selected and positioned is said to be under "position management."

1. Financial Position

Definition: Financial position is used to display the financial state of the business. It is the most common and readily understood type of positioning.

Description: There are numerous ways to illustrate financial position, i.e., balance sheet, revenue and expense, forecasts and history, per unit revenue and expense, and net margin as well as multiple financial ratios such as:

- *liquidity ratios*—measure the firm's ability to meet short-term financial obligations,
- *profitability ratios*—measure performance,
- *leverage ratios*—measure the extent of debt and equity funding, and
- *activity ratios*—measure resource utilization.

All these candidate financial measures may be point of time and time-line oriented.

IM&M Strategic Planning Impact: The critical issue is to define and reach consensus on which are to be the measures of performance for the IM&M function. Is the IM&M organization to be measured on return on investment (ROI), cash-flow, expense/employee, IM&M as a percent of revenue, cost savings, or other? Financial performance has been and remains the measure of success (or failure). Financial positioning, therefore, demands the explicit definition of which measures are the ones against which IM&M success is to be judged.

2. Market Position

Definition: Market position defines the market segmentation and associated position for each IM&M product and service.

Description: For each product and service, a market position defines:

- the size of the market,

- the market compound annual growth rate (CAGR),
- the market share, and
- market shares of major competitors products.

This information is often illustrated in the form of a pie chart as shown in Figure 3.9. Market segmentation is important because it clearly identifies:

- what we are selling,
- to whom we are selling, and
- what need(s) we are attempting to meet.

Market segmentation is also important because many of the positioning techniques and situational analysis techniques are best executed at the market segment level.

Market segmentation is done in the following manner:

1. Identify key variables which segment the market, i.e., product feature, buyer type, cost, geography, distribution channel, etc.
2. Assign discrete values for each segmentation variable.
3. Construct a segmentation table (2/3 dimensions).
4. Test the segmentation table for validity by positioning the industry competitors in the table.

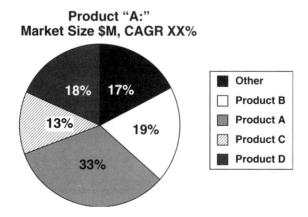

Figure 3.9   Market Position. It is important to understand the market size, its CAGR, market share, and competitor market share.

Figure 3.10 illustrates how database management system (DBMS) products have traditionally been segmented by the key variables of operating platform and the data model supported.

With the emergence of reach/range/maneuverability architectures, market segments are fragmenting. *Segmentation* presents the idea of a group of users with the same need. *Fragmentation* represents the idea of users with very distinct needs. Since network computing permits "cut and paste" solutions, users will start demanding information appliances and technologies that specifically optimize their business practices. There will be a shift from the question of what technologies to offer which make it easiest for the IM&M organization, to the question of what technologies to offer which maximize the end users' competitive advantage. This has a number of important implications for IM&M providers:

1. Systems integration skills grow in importance.
2. Architecture will be critical to define the "bonding" mechanisms among the specialized solutions.
3. The number and types of IM&M technologies that will have to be supported will proliferate.
4. A versatile staff will be more valuable than a specialized staff.
5. The services provided will be more valuable to the customer, lack traditional economies of scale, and thus be premium priced.

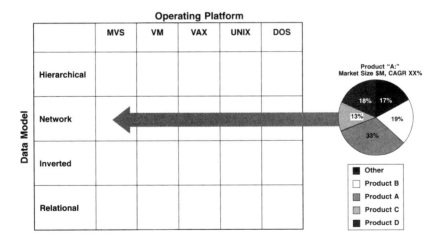

Figure 3.10 Traditional DBMS Market Segmentation. The DBMS market has been traditionally segmented by operating platform and data model supported.

6. Fragmentation is both an advantage and a disadvantage from the perspective of competition. Competitors will lose economy of scale advantages and expertise in competing for the in-house account, but conversely, smaller, boutique vendors will become rivals.

Fragmentation represents a major paradigm shift to the IM&M organization that historically operated on "one size processing fits all," and it will require a number of organization realignments to deal with the change from one big user segment to multiple user fragments.

IM&M Strategic Planning Impact: A market perspective creates a proper customer/supplier relationship between the IM&M organization and the users. The internal IM&M user community is now viewed as a marketplace with needs that the IM&M organizations has to meet through competitive products and services.

Market research is critical to successful market positioning. Sun Tzu says:

> What enables an intelligent leader to overcome others and achieve extraordinary accomplishments is foreknowledge. All matters require foreknowledge.[7]

The better one understands customer needs, the better one can position her products and services to satisfy them.

The ideal way of understanding one's customers is to understand them strategically. Recursively, do a strategic analysis of each customer. What are their critical success factors? What are their cost drivers in their value chains? What are their threats and opportunities? What is their basis of sustainable competitive advantage? If you understand your customer strategically, then you can begin to design IM&M solutions and introduce emerging technologies that directly contribute to building their sustainable competitive advantage. You will then be regarded as a cherished partner rather than an expense.

3. Core Competency Position

Definition: Core competency represents the collective learning of the organization; especially hard to coordinate diverse skills which integrate multiple streams of technologies.[8]

Description: Core competencies provide "roots" for competitive advantage because they can be leveraged to support multiple products and services in multiple market segments. A core competency has four primary attributes:

1. It provides access to a wide variety of markets.
2. It makes a significant contribution to the customer's perceived benefits of the product.

Table 3.7
Core Competency Evaluation Matrix. A core competency must have
four attributes.

Core Competency (CC)	Market Access	Direct Relationship to Customer's Perceived Value	Difficult to Imitate	Complex Coordination of Skills/Technologies
CC 1				
CC 2				
CC 3				
CC 4				
CC "N"				

3.   It is difficult to imitate.
4.   It is often the complex coordination of multiple technologies and applied skills.

Existing and candidate core competencies can be evaluated using Table 3.7. Care must be taken to prevent core competencies from becoming dated core rigidities which prevent adaptation to changing customer needs.

Figure 3.11 illustrates the power of the core competency concept. The foundation competencies are leveraged into multiple core products which in turn are multiplied into numerous end products. Core products are highly reusable building blocks. End products are families of differentiated products to meet diverse customer needs (see Figure 3.12). An end product consists of three layers:

1.   *Core layer*—satisfies the overt user need,
2.   *Tangible layer*—attributes of the product such as functionally, quality, price/performance, branding, size, etc., and
3.   *Augmented layer*—attributes of distinction such as reputation, warranty, service, investment protection, etc.

By designing success around competencies, a company uses skill investment as opposed to capital investment as the basis of advantage. A company can therefore position itself so that a portfolio of competencies supports a portfolio of products for a portfolio of markets (customers).

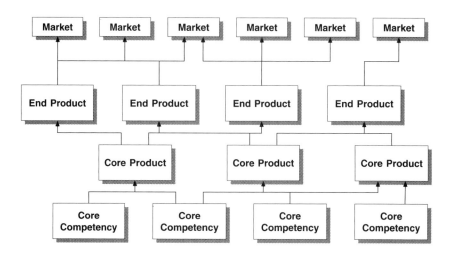

Figure 3.11   Core Competency Architecture. Core competencies provide leverage by being assembled into multiple core products which in turn become the basis for multiple end products.

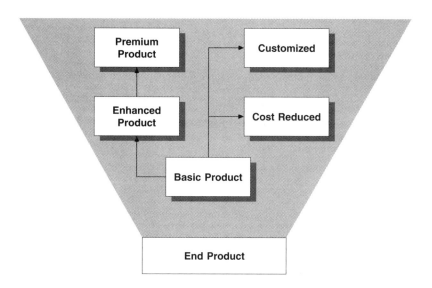

Figure 3.12   End Product Exploded. Core competencies feed the development of families of end products, each with layers of value for the customer.

IM&M Strategic Planning Impact: The pressing question is what is the set of core competencies that the IM&M organization requires to be successful in the 90s given the challenges we outlined in Chapter 2? Figure 3.13 illustrates a candidate core competency architecture. Core competency and Capabilities (which follows) are two major frameworks from which an organization can be managed and positioned strategically.

4. Capabilities Position

Definition: Capabilities is a strategic framework which asserts that the focus of strategy is the nurturing of the primary business processes and practices which deliver value and satisfaction to the customer. Strategic positioning should concentrate on enabling the infrastructure to support robust capabilities and selecting which capabilities to compete on.[9]

Description: A capabilities perspective asserts that the logic of competition is not *with whom* to compete nor *with what* to compete nor *for whom* to compete but is *how* to compete. Success therefore depends on transforming key processes into strategic capabilities that consistently provide superior value to the customer. A capability has six attributes:

1. *Speed*—The process can quickly respond to customer demands and the incorporation of a stream of new ideas and technologies (the capability must be maneuverable).

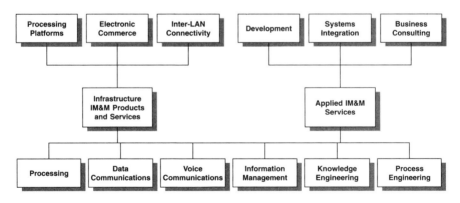

Figure 3.13   IM&M Core Competencies. A successful IM&M organization will be built upon foundation of six core competencies.

2. *Process consistency*—The process can unfailingly produce a product which meets or exceeds customer expectations.

3. *Agility*—The process is highly malleable to accommodate unique customer requirements. (The capability must deal with market fragmentation.)

4. *Cross functional*—The process crosses multiple business areas in its execution.

5. *Begins and ends with the customer*—The process is a closed loop starting with acquisition of a customer need and ending with satisfying that need.

6. *Complements core competencies*—The process puts core competencies into motion, and in doing so translates the competency into value for the customer.

Table 3.8 may be used as an aid to evaluate existing and candidate capabilities.

Capabilities puts two other contemporary business practices into a broader perspective. As illustrated in Figure 3.14, capabilities links quality initiatives and business reengineering to strategy. Capabilities provides a specific strategic framework that emphasizes process as the winning strategic dimension. Quality programs provides a tactic to continuously improve capabilities while business re-engineering provides an approach to radically overhaul processes.

Capabilities along with core competencies, strategic alignment, and sustainable competitive advantage represent the major contemporary paradigms of what should sit at the foundation of strategy. Table 3.9 itemizes the primary attributes of each competing perspective. My view is that the frame

Table 3.8
Capabilities Evaluation Matrix. A capability must meet six criteria.

Capability	Process Speed	Process Consistency	Agility	Cross-Functional	Begin and End with Customer	Related to Core Competency
Capability 1						
Capability 2						
Capability 3						
Capability 4						
Capability "N"						

Table 3.9
Major Frameworks Compared. Core Competencies, Capabilities, Sustainable Competitive Advantage, and Strategic Alignment compete for the role of foundation of business strategy.

Core Competencies	Capabilities	Strategic Alignment	Sustainable Competitive Advantage
1. Market access 2. Customer perception 3. Difficult to imitate 4. Coordination	1. Process speed 2. Process consistency 3. Agility 4. Cross functional 5. Begins and ends with customer 6. Relationship to core competency	1. Coordination 2. Perserverance 3. Concentration of effort 4. Commitment	1. Customer perception 2. Linkage 3. Durability 4. Accessibility 5. Transparency 6. Replication 7. Coordination

works complement each other, as shown in Figure 3.15, strategic alignment provides a necessary foundation layer for success while core competencies and capabilities are often the basis of sustainable competitive advantage.

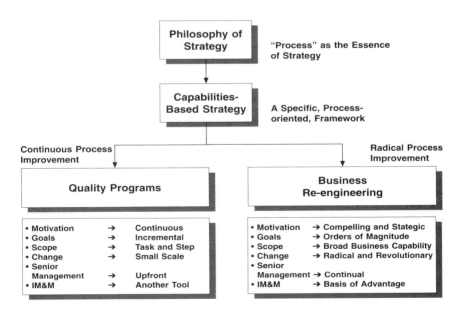

Figure 3.14 Capabilities, Quality, and Business Re-engineering. The concept of capabilities links the contemporary practices of quality programs and business re-engineering to strategic planning.

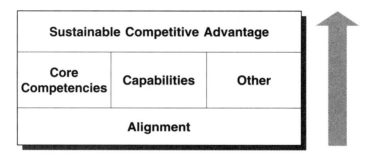

Figure 3.15   Integrating Frameworks. The major strategy frameworks complement each other in a hierarchical relationship.

IM&M Strategic Planning Impact: What are the critical capabilities for the IM&M organization for the 90s? The following starter list is suggested:

- *Systems integration*—the ability to build complex operational systems through the integration of heterogeneous technologies,
- *Project management*—the ability to manage large and complex projects,
- *Network computing operations management*—the ability to operate complex network computing systems in an effective and efficient manner,
- *Configuration management*—the ability to manage the bill-of-material of complex network computing architectures composed of components from a heterogeneous set of vendors,
- *Infrastructure development*—the ability to rapidly amend and append the IM&M infrastructure with ever changing opportunistic technologies, and
- *Supplier management*—the ability to work closely with selected suppliers to create working IM&M environments.

5. Human Resource Position

Definition: Human resource position defines the alignment of human resource systems and practices with the strategic direction of the business.

Description: Values define what a company believes in. Behaviors are the daily way that employees individually and collectively express the values and operationilize them. Human resource systems provide the linkage between the two. As show in Figure 3.16, the human resource systems serve a dual purpose:

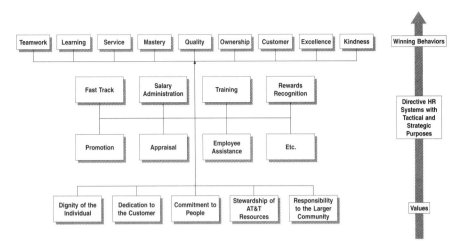

Figure 3.16   HR Architecture. The HR architecture illustrates the translation of the business scope values into desired behaviors through directed HR systems. *Source*: **"Implementing Client/Server Computing: A Strategic Perspective," Bernard H. Boar, McGraw-Hill, 1993 with permission of publisher.**

1. The traditional tactical mission of administrating a functional responsibility, and

2. The strategic mission of incenting and stimulating desired behaviors in the populace.

As shown in Figure 3.17, each HR system should be positioned so that:

• Its tactical and functional purpose is clearly understood, and

• The inclusion of behavior incentives to stimulate desired behaviors is present.

As a consequence of the above, a high-powered human resource environment is created where each desired behavior is stimulated through multiple HR systems, and each HR system supports the development of multiple desired behaviors.

IM&M Strategic Planning Impact: IM&M strategic planning in conjunction with the human resource organization needs to:

• Identify the value set,

• Develop and reach consensus on the desired behaviors set,

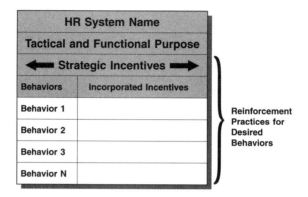

Figure 3.17   HR System Exploded. HR systems serve the dual purpose of executing a tactical function and incenting strategic cooperative behaviors.

- Take inventory of human resource systems,
- Identify the current tactical purpose of each HR system, and
- Design into the HR systems incentives to stimulate winning behaviors.

The HR Architecture provides the strategy team with "knobs" to turn to influence staff behaviors. This becomes extremely important as part of the Change Management Plan to encourage cooperation during the execution step of the strategy process.

6. IM&M Position

Definition: IM&M position defines the state of the IM&M resource. This state is presented in the context of an encompassing IM&M architecture.

Description: IM&M is often a resource in a state of chaos. Table 3.10 provides a framework to position the "greater" IM&M resource. Along the strategic dimensions of infrastructure, information, applications, and organization, it is important to understand the state of:

- *Inventory*—What exists?
- *Principles*—What are the established high-level rules which guide decision making?
- *Models*—structural models (data models, organization structures, business models, etc), which illustrate our IM&M, and
- *Standards*—the agreed to products, methods, vendors, interfaces, etc., which bond our IM&M environment together.

Table 3.10
IM&M Architecture. This approach provides a complete, information architecture. *Source*: **CSC/Index.**

Strategic Dimension	Inventory	Principles	Models	Standards
Infrastructure				
Information				
Applications				
Organization				

The "infrastructure" row is commonly referred to as the IM&M technology architecture, and it is this architecture that we suggest is best realized by the reach/range/maneuverability model. It is obvious that the matrix only serves as a conceptual placeholder and that positioning an IM&M architecture requires exploding each cell in a manner consistent with the contents of that cell.

IM&M Strategic Planning Impact: The positioning of an IM&M is of vital importance to IM&M strategic planning. For IM&M to achieve its strategic objective of competitiveness, it is necessary for IM&M management to have control and knowledge of what they are managing. The IM&M Architecture provides the required framework. Changes in IM&M equate to reconfiguring the architecture. IM&M management can therefore understand the before and after pictures of proposed changes.

The information contained in Table 3.10 has been what most IM&M organizations have historically equated to IM&M strategy. While it is obviously important, alone it is insufficient. It is part, but only part, of the overall strategic thinking and plan required. It is inadequate to strategically manage the buisness.

7. Strategic Progress Position

Definition: Strategic progress is a point of time report of the status of existing strategy implementation programs from previous strategic planning cycles.

Description: Strategy implementation programs are often multi-year projects. The state of existing projects is of prime importance from a number of perspectives:

1. Are present strategy implementation programs working?

2. Do programs in progress or programs in the planning stage need to be modified?

3. What has been learned from these experiences?

4. Does current data collection indicate that the present portfolio of actions is still a preferred set of actions?

For each outstanding project, it is important to know its due date, current implementation status, planned implementation status, and lessons learned.

While we are very interested in current status, we are not bounded by it. Each planning period should be "zero based." Just like the budgeting method of zero-based budgeting in which all financial expenditures must be cyclically re-evaluated and compete for new funding and resources, the same is true for strategy. What is in progress has no halo effect; all problems start with equal rights to our attention and resources.

IM&M Strategic Planning Impact: As will be discussed in Chapter 5, strategic moves are implemented through projects. The selected project management system must meet the standard requirement of status reporting.

8. Five Forces Position

Definition: The Five Force model is an analytical method used to determine the state of competition at an industry or business level.[10]

Description: The Five Force model asserts that competition in an industry is a function of the dynamic interplay of five forces:

1. *Supplier power*—the power of industry suppliers to control prices, quality, and the overall conditions of purchase,

2. *Buyer power*—the power of the customers of an industry to exploit their position to influence pricing, quality, and the overall conditions of purchase,

3. *Threat of entry*—the ease of entry of new competitors,

4. *Substitute products*—the availability and attractiveness of substitute products, and

5. *Rivalry of existing competitors*—the intensity of competition among the incumbent players.

Figure 3.18 illustrates the Five Force model. When "the industry" is in the center, the Five Force model analyzes the overall competitive situation of the industry. When "your business" is put in the center, it can be

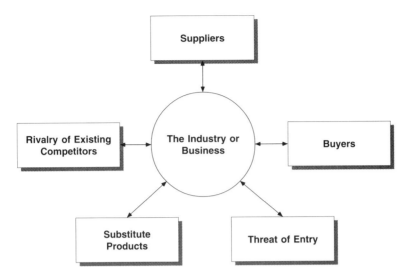

Figure 3.18   Five Forces. The Five Force Model is used to understand the competetive state of an industry or business.

used to understand the competitive situation of your business alone, relative to its external environment. The business is in a constant battle to improve or at least maintain its overall competitive position. To do this, it must undertake initiatives to improve its position relative to some Five Force. Likewise, it must be on vigilance to react to the initiatives of others who are trying to reposition themselves at the enterprise's expense. Tables 3.11 through 3.15 summarize the factors which compose each Five Force. Figure 3.19 illustrates a way to graphically depict a Five Force and its associated factors.

At any given time, the Five Forces may be impacting the business in any of the following ways:

- *No impact*—a Five Force factor is dormant,
- *An act by another*—a supplier, customer, rival, etc., takes an action to improve its position at your expense,
- *An act by you*—you initiate an action to improve a Five Force position, or
- *An external act*—an event outside the immediate Five Force domain (war, economic swing, etc.) occurs which can alter the balance of the Five Forces.

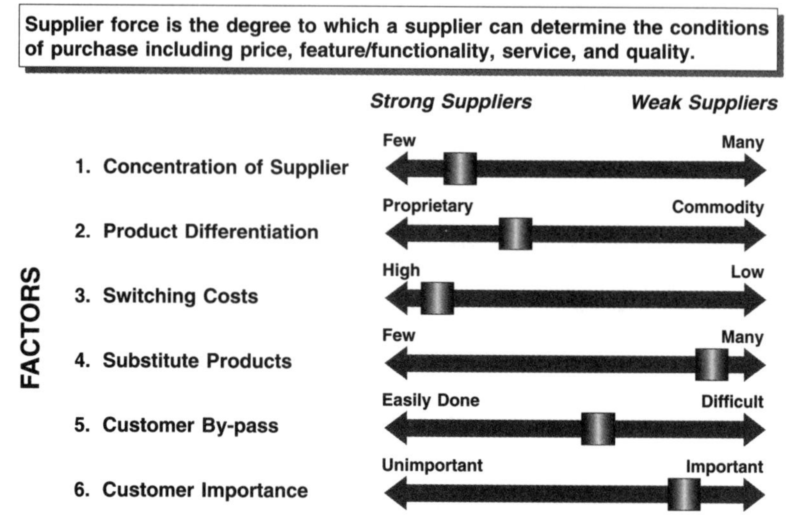

> **Supplier force is the degree to which a supplier can determine the conditions of purchase including price, feature/functionality, service, and quality.**

Figure 3.19   Five Force Positioning Example. The position of a business relative to a five force factor can be done by qualitatively plotting the evaluation against each factor.

Table 3.11
Supplier Power. Supplier power is a function of six variables.

Supplier Power Is the Degree to which Suppliers Can Determine the Conditions of Purchase	
Factor	**Definition**
Concentration of suppliers	The number and equality of suppliers
Product differentiation	The degree of commodity or proprietresses of the product
Switching costs	The total costs incurred by the buyer to switch to a different product
Substitute products	The existence of alternative products providing equal or better feature/functionality at equal or better price/performance
Customer by-pass	The degree to which the supplier can by-pass the customer and sell directly to the customer's customer
Customer importance	The importance of the customer to the supplier

Table 3.12
Buyer Power. Buyer power is a function of seven variables.

Buyer Power Is the Degree to which the Buyer's Bargaining Position Can Determine the Conditions of Purchase	
Factor	**Definition**
Concentration of buyers	The number of buyers and size of purchase
Product is commodity	The degree of commodity of the product
Product as component of buyer's cost structure	The influence of the product on the cost structure of the customers product
Buyers profitability	The current financial performance of the buyer
Product's importance to buyer	The degree to which the product is important in adding-value
Product viewed as an expense	The degree to which the product is viewed as a cost and only a cost
Supplier by-pass	The degree to which the buyer can buy from the supplier's supplier or do it themselves

Table 3.13
Threat of Entry. The Threat of Entry Five Force is a function of seven variables.

Threat of Entry Is the Degree to which There Is a Viable Probability that New Entrants Will Join the Marketplace.	
Factor	**Definition**
Economies of scale	The costs associated with achieving the necessary economies of scale to achieve competitive pricing
Product differentiation	The differentiation of incumbent products and their associated customer loyalty
Switching costs	The total costs of switching products
Capital requirements	The amount of up-front investment required to enter the marketplace
Distribution channel access	The openness the distribution channels to a new player
Government policy	The degree to which government policy and laws control market entry
Retaliation of incumbents	The degree to which incumbents have demonstrated a willingness to protect their markets

Table 3.14
Substitute Products. Substitute Products is a function of four variables.

Substitute Products Constrain the Ability of an Enterprise to Control the Terms of Purchase Since at Some Point the Customer May Switch.	
Factor	Definition
Strong substitute	The degree of equal or better feature/functionality
Price/performance	The degree to which the substitute offers equal or better price/performance
Profitability of substitute industry	The degree to which the industry of the substitute product is profitable
Competitive rivalry of substitute industry	The degree to which the level of competition in the substitute industry encourages migration to new markets

Table 3.15
Rivalry of Existing Competitors. This Five Force is a function of eight variables.

Rivalry Is the Degree to which Existing Combatants "Battle" for Market Share.	
Factor	Definition
Number and equality of competitors	The number of competitors and their equality
Market growth	The market growth or decline
Product differentiation	The degree that competitor products can substitute for each other
Switching costs	The total expense a customer incurs in switching competitors
Fixed costs	The degree of fixed costs and/or perishability of the product
Unit of capacity increment	The amount of additional product produced per investment in unit capacity increase
Exit barriers	The degree to which all the competitors play by the established rules.
Diversity of corporate personalities	The degree to which all the competitors play by the established rules

What the Five Force model points out is the competitive primacy of being able to maneuver, adapt, and change.

IM&M Strategic Planning Impact: The key impact of the Five Force model on IM&M strategic planning is that by using it for each market segment competed in, the user can:

- Understand which competitive factors determine competitive balance. These are the drivers of competition.

- Develop the actions needed to take to achieve a more favorable position, and

- Develop blocking actions to prevent Five Force antagonists from achieving more favorable positions at their expense.

9. Supplier Position

Definition: Supplier position is used to illustrate the strategic status of the suppliers to the IM&M organization.

Description: The management of the relationship with suppliers is increasingly important as the IM&M organization moves toward network computing. The internal IM&M organization will increasingly operate as a systems integrator; consequently, the depth of vendor relationship will have a profound effect on the IM&M organization's ability to offer end-to-end network computing solutions.

The status of existing and candidate strategic suppliers can be identified by the following factors:

- *Common objectives*—The supplier and the IM&M organizations share specific measurable and dated objectives.

- *Common actions*—The supplier and the IM&M organization engage in shared and coordinated actions to achieve the common objectives. Examples of this might include electronic commerce (EDI, e-mail, video conferencing, database access), on-site inventory, exclusive distribution rights, cooperative multi-vendor support teams, dedicated support teams, guaranteed service levels, early access to new technology, best price agreements, and inter-firm employee rotation.

- *Shared commitment*—The supplier and the IM&M organization management engage in visible and substantive programs to demonstrate mutual commitment to the partnership.

- *Critical component*—The product provided by the supplier is a critical factor in the final product created by the IM&M organization in the eyes of the user.

- *Value chain improvement*—The supplier and IM&M organization value chains are interlocked to provide continuous improvement in productivity and value added.
- *Preferred status*—The supplier has a publicly avowed and demonstrated preferred status.

The essence of a preferred supplier is the overlapping of strategy to help each accrue superior future strategic positions. A strategic supplier is thus best understood from the dimensions of trust, durability of relationship, information sharing, and common governance.

IM&M Strategic Planning Impact: The crucial issue in selecting strategic suppliers is that they provide "critical components." In the 1990s, the strategic suppliers will be those who provide the building blocks of successful systems integration, i.e., DBMS, distributed transaction monitors, advanced user interfaces, middleware (bonding software), etc.

10. Internal Business/IM&M Economy

Definition: The business/IM&M economy is the explicit design of the intra-business processes for the production and exchange of IM&M services.

Description: An economic system includes the processes used for the production and exchange of goods and services. Any economic system must address three fundamental problems:

1. What will be produced? How much and when?
2. How will it be produced? Who will provide the products using what resources and technologies?
3. For whom will the products be produced? Who will receive the products and in what proportion?

At one extreme, some societies solve these problems by "command and control" central planning economies where the government takes all decision making responsibility upon itself. At the other extreme, *laissez-faire* market economies work through a system of prices, markets, profit and loss, and incentives.

A business, as a self-contained economic entity, has to define an economic system to govern intra-business production and exchange of services between organizational entities just as a society does. Historically, large host-centered computing shops leaned toward a monopolistic command system. The IM&M organization was granted by the government (the executive business decision makers) monopolistic market power to determine what technologies would be used, when they would be used, the price of the services, and who would receive the services (usually done through a priority setting council). As was explained in Chapter 2, competitive pressures have caused many businesses to re-evaluate their internal IM&M economy and begin to move it toward the free market model.

While some explain this movement as the evolution of the IM&M function from a cost center to a profit center, I think it is better stated as the movement from a monopolist to a competitor. It is better stated this way because what is really wanted is not so much that the IM&M organization make profits, but that the IM&M organization's behaviors reflect those of serving the customer. This is characteristic of a free-market system and is markedly different than insular behavior which is characteristic of an internal monopoly.

An appreciation of the current design of the internal IM&M economy and probable change is extremely important to the IM&M organization because the economic model used to govern intra-business IM&M services has massive realignment implications on competition, budgeting and chargeback, organization design, staff behaviors, etc. The pivotal economic design points are as follows:

1. *Allocation System*—How is market demand governed? Does a central planning council decide what will be maintained and developed, or do user organizations, individually and in consortiums, dictate their wishes by purchasing control of their own IM&M dollars?

2. *Market System*—Are the user organizations free to choose any supplier, or must they use the internal IM&M organization? Is the internal IM&M organization free to choose *not* to supply desired services? Is the IM&M organization free to sell its services to external customers? To what degree is the choice of technologies which may be used regulated?

3. *Resource (Budgeting) System*—Do the user organizations have control over their own IM&M budget, or does a central planning board allocate IM&M expense as overhead (a corporate tax)? Does the IM&M get its own budget, or does it receive revenue from its products and services (chargeback) from which it funds itself? Is the IM&M organization free to grow and contract based on demand for its services, or is the IM&M budget used as a way to throttle IM&M expenses?

4. *Supplier System*—How does the IM&M organization interact with their customers? Is it a sole supplier who is an order taker, or does it operate using the market processes of a competitive business, i.e., sales organization, distribution channels, contracts, etc.

The answers to these questions represents the intra-buisness/IM&M economy position.

An example of the redesign of an internal economy to stimulate competitive fervor was announced by DEC as part of its Fall 1992 reorganization. DEC announced that it would create independent business units free to buy technology from outside vendors if DEC's internally sourced products are not competitive. As autonomous units, they would have the ability to bypass DEC components when necessary and appropriate. Obviously, the internal engineering monopoly is being eroded. Similarly, by the end of 1993, IBM business units will be permitted to acquire IM&M services from other than IBM's internal information technology organization. The imposition of a free-market economy is a common strategic move of turn-around situations.

IM&M Strategic Planning Impact: The impact of the redesign of the intra-business IM&M economy is as follows:

- The full intensity and pressure of competition as the catalyst for entrepreunship, innovation, and productivity is being applied to the IM&M organization.

- It is being applied by the redesign of the internal economy from a command model to a market-system model.

- The importance and impact of this change cannot be overstated. All strategic business areas must be re-evaluated to deal with a free-market economy.

- Understanding, influencing, and anticipating movements of the economy is a new major point of strategic focus for the IM&M strategist.

Two arguments which immediately arise in reaction to a free IM&M economy are how will IM&M infrastructure investments be funded, and how will cross-functional systems be orchestrated. There are three answers to the first question. Infrastructure may be funded by:

1. Including in chargeback rates a sufficient margin to fund inrastructure investment,

2. Making a case to the corporate governing body for a corporate level I/T investment, and

3. Making a case to the corporate governing body for a loan.

Cross-functional systems are developed by a creation of consortia. Customers with common objectives form a consortium to fund a shared system. If consortiums can't be formed, then there is no customer for the cross-functional system.

So while endless arguments can be made for why the IM&M organization should maintain its historical economy privileges (some cynics would say self-serving arguments), it is best to mourn their passage quickly and get on with adapting to the new economic order.

The compelling need for competitiveness has lead the business decision makers to decide that:

1. Each individual business unit knows best what will meet their needs and maximize their satisfaction,

2. The aggregate of these individual satisfactions will provide the maximum IM&M benefit for the enterprise, and

3. The free-market system provides the best mechanism to make needs known and satisfied.

IM&M sovereignty has been passed to the user organizations.

11. Product/Service Position

Definition: A product/service position is a series of interlocking matrices and graphs which collectively illustrate the position of a product or service. Product/service positioning is an example of the recursive attribute of positioning whereby:

$$P_{Business} = (P_{Market}, P_{Competency}, P_{Human\ Resources}, P_{Strategy\ Progress}, P_{Products/Services}, P_{Others}), \text{but}$$

$$P_{Products/Services} = (\text{a set of 13 interlocking graphs and matrices}).$$

Description: While strategy strives to satisfy the customer, the locus of strategy is the product. Meeting customer needs, incorporating new and advantageous technologies, battling competition, attacking markets, capturing revenue, and planning new products all revolves around "the product." Figure 3.20 provides a relationship map for the 13 graphs and matrices. As a collective position, the product map begins with the customer need(s) being satisfied and progresses to competitive, technological, financial, resource, and customer satisfaction views of the product. Each element of the product map will be individually explained:

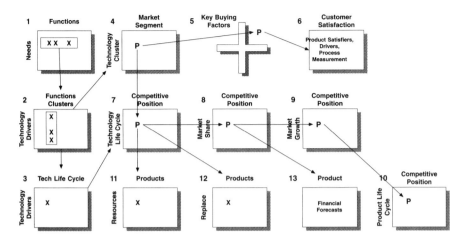

Figure 3.20   Product Map. The position of a product is best expressed through a series of interlocking matrices and graphs.

1. Customer Need/Function Matrix (Figure 3.21)

Purpose: The purpose of this matrix is to illustrate customer needs as a set of functions required to meet each need. A set of functions which satisfies a need is called a *function cluster*. Documenting customer needs in this manner separates transient products and technologies from understanding the functional requirements which have permanence. Products and enabling technologies have to be continually evolved to better meet the needs of the function clusters.

Cell Content: An "x" in a cell indicates that the function is required to meet the selected need.

2. Function Cluster/Driving Technology Matrix (Figure 3.22)

Purpose: The purpose of this matrix is to illustrate the current set of technologies which are being used to satisfy a function cluster. A function cluster is satisfied through a set of driving technologies. Driving technologies are the primary technologies which deliver the required function. The set of technologies which delivers the requirements for a function cluster is call a *technology cluster*. The IM&M organization must continually upgrade and evolve its driving technologies so that it maintains a rich portfolio of technologies from which to build technology clusters to ever better satisfy functional needs. This is why all IM&M technologies are inevitably tactical; they are destined to be replaced as soon as a superior substitute is available.

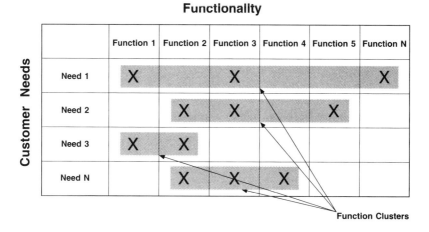

Figure 3.21   Customer Need/Function Matrix. Customer needs are best expressed as a set of functions.

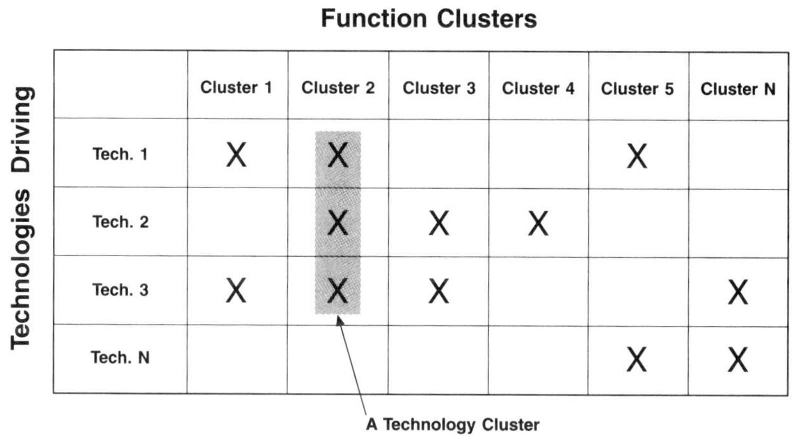

Function Clusters

	Cluster 1	Cluster 2	Cluster 3	Cluster 4	Cluster 5	Cluster N
Tech. 1	X	X			X	
Tech. 2		X	X	X		
Tech. 3	X	X	X			X
Tech. N					X	X

A Technology Cluster

Figure 3.22   Function Cluster/Driving Technology Matrix. A set of technologies, a technology cluster, meets the requirements of a function cluster.

Cell Content: An "x" in a cell indicates that the technology is required to meet the function cluster requirements.

Map Trace: A customer need is documented through a function cluster which is satisfied through a technology cluster.

Table 3.16
Driving Technology/Technology Life Cycle Matrix. Using this matrix,
one can assess the state of each of the driving technologies and the
composite state of each technology cluster.

Technology Drivers	Technology Life Cycle Stage					
	Embryonic	Development	State of the Art	State of the Market	Mature	Decline
Technology "1"						
Technology "2"						
Technology "3"						
Technology "4"						
Technology "5"						
Technology "N"						

3. Driving Technology/Technology Life Cycle Matrix (Table 3.16)

Purpose: The purpose of this matrix is to assess the technology life cycle position of each driving technology and the collective life cycle position of each technology cluster. All of the driving technologies are plotted against the technology life cycle. From this one can get a picture of the evolutionary state of each of the key technologies. For each technology cluster (from "2" above), a technology life cycle position should be assigned as the composite life cycle position of each technology cluster. A common rule is to assign the technology life cycle position of the dominant technology in fulfilling the function cluster requirements.

Cell Content: An "x" in a cell identifies the life cycle position of the selected technology.

4. Product Position Matrix (Table 3.17)

Purpose: The purpose of this matrix is to position a product as the intersection of a market segment and a technology cluster. We interpret this matrix as meaning that a given product is targeted to a given market segment and is composed of a given technology cluster.

Cell Content: The contents of a cell is a product or service.

Map Trace: A given product, P, is targeted for a market segment. The product is composed of a technology cluster which satisfies the needs defined by a function cluster which documents a customer need.

Table 3.17
Product Position Matrix. A product serves a market using a given technology cluster.

Technology Clusters	Market Segments					
	Segment 1	Segment 2	Segment 3	Segment 4	Segment 5	Segment N
Technology cluster "1"						
Technology cluster "2"						
Technology cluster "3"						
Technology cluster "4"						
Technology cluster "5"						
Technology cluster "N"						

5. Key Buying Factors (Figure 3.23)

Purpose: The purpose of this graph is to illustrate the positioning of a product against key purchase decision parameters. A product is designed to satisfy certain key buying factors. As many "Key Buying Factor" charts are developed as required to illustrate how the product was designed along each key purchase decision making dimension.

Graph Content: A product, P, is positioned along the axis to illustrate the positioning.

6. Customer Satisfaction

Purpose: The purpose of this entry is to illustrate the level of customer satisfaction with a product. Customer satisfaction is measured through a Customer Satisfaction Measurement System (CSMS) as illustrated in Figure 3.24. The CSMS defines a product-specific set of measurements as follows:

1. The major customer satisfiers for a product are identified, i.e., quality, value, service, etc.

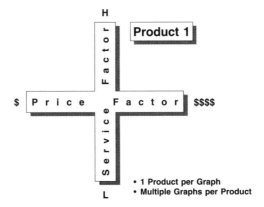

Figure 3.23   Key Buying Factors. A product is positioned by the factors which are key to the customer's purchase decision.

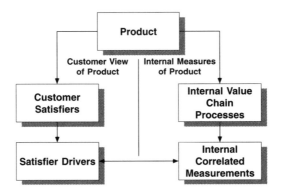

Figure 3.24   Customer Satisfaction Measurement System (CSMS). The CSMS defines customer satisfaction with a product from the customer's view and relates those drivers to internal measurements which can be positively influenced to continuously further customer satisfaction.

2. For each of the satisfiers above, a set of satisfier drivers are identified, i.e., for value it would be cost. Both item one and two are done from a customer view of the product.

3. The internal value chain processes (capabilites) that support the product are identified.

4. Measurements are identified by value chain process and correlated to a satisfier driver, i.e., by improving this measurement, we can

positively influence the driver and thereby improve customer satisfaction. Items three and four are done from an internal perspective.

The net result of this approach is the installment of a measurement system that directly correlates internal system measurements to customer satisfaction.

The customer satisfaction entry in the product map would structurally look as follows:

I. Customer Satisfier 1	II. Customer Satisfier 2	N. Customer Satisfier N
A. Satisfier Driver 1	A. Satisfier Driver 1	A. Satisfier Driver 1
a. Internal Value Chain Process 1	a. Internal Value Chain Process 1	a. Internal Value Chain Process 1
1. Measurement 1	1. Measurement 1	1. Measurement 1
2. Measurement 2	2. Measurement 2	2. Measurement 2
N. Measurement .n	N. Measurement .n	N. Measurement .n
b. Internal Value Chain Process 2	b. Internal Value Chain Process 2	b. Internal Value Chain Process 2
1. Measurement 1	1. Measurement 1	1. Measurement 1
2. Measurement 2	2. Measurement 2	2. Measurement 2
N. Measurement N	N. Measurement N	N. Measurement N
n. Internal Value Chain Process n	n. Internal Value Chain Process n	n. Internal Value Chain Process n
1. Measurement 1	1. Measurement 1	1. Measurement 1
2. Measurement 2	2. Measurement 2	2. Measurement 2
N. Measurement N	N. Measurement N	N. Measurement N
B. Satisfier Driver 2	B. Satisfier Driver 2	B. Satisfier Driver 2
a. Internal Value Chain Process 1	a. Internal Value Chain Process 1	a. Internal Value Chain Process 1
1. Measurement 1	1. Measurement 1	1. Measurement 1
2. Measurement 2	2. Measurement 2	2. Measurement 2
N. Measurement .n	N. Measurement .n	N. Measurement .n
b. Internal Value Chain Process 2	b. Internal Value Chain Process 2	b. Internal Value Chain Process 2
1. Measurement 1	1. Measurement 1	1. Measurement 1
2. Measurement 2	2. Measurement 2	2. Measurement 2
N. Measurement N	N. Measurement N	N. Measurement N
n. Internal Value Chain Process n	n. Internal Value Chain Process n	n. Internal Value Chain Process n
1. Measurement 1	1. Measurement 1	1. Measurement 1
2. Measurement 2	2. Measurement 2	2. Measurement 2
N. Measurement N	N. Measurement N	N. Measurement N
N. Satisfier Driver n	N. Satisfier Driver n	N. Satisfier Driver n
a. Internal Value Chain Process 1	a. Internal Value Chain Process 1	a. Internal Value Chain Process 1
1. Measurement 1	1. Measurement 1	1. Measurement 1
2. Measurement 2	2. Measurement 2	2. Measurement 2
N. Measurement .n	N. Measurement .n	N. Measurement .n
b. Internal Value Chain Process 2	b. Internal Value Chain Process 2	b. Internal Value Chain Process 2
1. Measurement 1	1. Measurement 1	1. Measurement 1
2. Measurement 2	2. Measurement 2	2. Measurement 2
N. Measurement N	N. Measurement N	N. Measurement N
n. Internal Value Chain Process n	n. Internal Value Chain Process n	n. Internal Value Chain Process n
1. Measurement 1	1. Measurement 1	1. Measurement 1
2. Measurement 2	2. Measurement 2	2. Measurement 2
N. Measurement N	N. Measurement N	N. Measurement N

An example of this for production operations would be as follows:

- *Customer Satisfier*—quality,
- *Satisfier Driver*—availability,
- *Value Chain Process*—production operations,

- *Measurement 1*—mean time between failures,
- *Measurement 2*—mean time to repair, and
- *Measurement 3*—95% response time.

A product must be measured periodically to measure the change in customer satisfaction over time and the changes in internally correlated measurements. An important strategic implication of the CSMS is that process improvement should be justified based on how the investment will improve the correlated measures; not just the traditional cost and benefit analysis. Customer satisfaction is of primary importance and must be included in all product maps.

7. Technology Life Cycle and Competitive Position Matrix (Table 3.18)

Purpose: The purpose of this matrix is to illustrate the relationship of the competitive position of a product with the collective technology life cycle position of the product's technology cluster.

   Cell Content: Each product, P, is positioned in the cell which reflects the intersection of the collective technology life cycle position of the product (from "3" above) and its competitive position.

8. Competitive Position and Market Share Matrix (Table 3.19)

Purpose: The purpose of this matrix is to illustrate the relationship of the competitive position of a product with the market-share position of a product and its competitors.

   Cell Content: The product and all its major competitors are placed in the appropriate cell of the matrix.

Table 3.18
Technology Life Cycle/Competitive Position Matrix. Each product is
positioned to reflect the relationship between its competitive position
and its technological position.

| Competitive Position | Technology Life Cycle Stage | | | | | |
	Embryonic	Development	State of the Art	State of the Market	Mature	Decline
Strong						
Medium						
Weak						

Table 3.19
Competitive Position/Market Share Matrix. The product and each of its
competitors is positioned by the relationship between market share
and competitive position.

Market Share	Competitive Position		
	Strong	Medium	Weak
High			
Medium			
Low			

9. Competitive Position and Market Growth Matrix (Table 3.20)

Purpose: The purpose of this matrix is to illustrate the relationship of the competitive position of a product with the market growth for the targeted market segment.

Cell Content: Products are placed in the appropriate cell of the matrix.

10. Competitive Position and Product Life Cycle Matrix (Table 3.21)

Purpose: The purpose of this matrix is to illustrate the relationship of the competitive position of a product with the life cycle position of the product.

Cell Content: Products are placed in the appropriate cell of the matrix.

Map Trace: This matrix, together with the prior three matrices, provides a comprehensive competition view of the product.

Table 3.20
Competitive Position/Market Growth Matrix. Products are positioned
to indicate the relationship between competitive position and market
growth.

Market Growth	Competitive Position		
	Strong	Medium	Weak
High			
Medium			
Low			

Table 3.21
Competitive Position/Product Life Cycle Position Matrix. Products are
positioned to indicate the relationship between competitive position
and product-life cycle stage.

Competitive Position	Product Life Cycle Stage			
	Introduction	Growth	Mature	Decline
Strong				
Medium				
Weak				

11. Product/Resource Matrix (Table 3.22)

Purpose: The purpose of this matrix is to illustrate which capabilities and core competencies support the product.

Cell Content: An "x" in a cell indicates that the selected core competency or capability support the corresponding product,

12. Product Replacement Matrix (Table 3.23)

Purpose: The purpose of this matrix is to identify which products are in development to replace the current product set.

Cell Content: A "x" in a cell indicates that the selected current product will be replaced by the indicated future product.

Table 3.22
Product/Resource Matrix. An "x" in a cell indicates that the core competency or capability supports the indicated product.

Capabilities and Core Competencies	Product 1	Product 2	Product 3	Product N
Capability 1				
Capability 2				
Capability 3				
Core Competency 1				
Core Competency 2				
Core Competency N				

Table 3.23
Product Replacement Matrix. An "x" in a cell indicates the currently
planned replacement product for each existing product.

Future Product	Product 1	Product 2	Product 3	Product N
Future Product 1				
Future Product 2				
Future Product 3				
Future Product N				

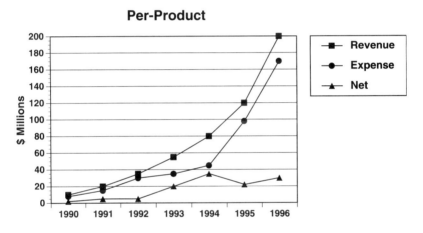

Figure 3.25   Product Financial History/Forecast. Associated with each
product is its financial history and forecast.

13. Product Financial History and Forecast (Figure 3.25)

Purpose: The purpose of this graph is to illustrate the historical and projected financial results for the product.

IM&M Strategic Planning Impact: These 13 matrices and graphs provide a comprehensive picture of the current state of a product. Starting from any perspective of interest, the analyst can move through the product map to understand the overall state or position of the product. The strategy team is responsible for designing a product map appropriate to their situation. All the graphs and matrices illustrated here need not be included, and others may be added (critical success factors, cost structure, method of sales and distribution, benchmark results, sustainable competitive advantage, and supplier relationships). Using this map, one can address the crucial question: Are my products meeting my customers needs?

As an aside, product maps provide an excellent tool for developing a meaningful picture of core competencies. Core competencies is one of the emerging leading strategic paradigms, but there is little guidance in developing the model. A product map-based approach would be as follows:

1. Develop product maps for all the products.
2. Work the core competency model backwards from the product maps by identifying
    *   your markets,
    *   your end products,
    *   the core products that enable those end products, and
    *   the competencies that enable the core products.
3. Repeat step two as many times as necessary and synthesize the result.

This technique replaces struggling with core competencies which is usually unfamiliar to the assigned team with products which are usually much more familiar and intuitive. If one performs this activity with the current product maps and the future product maps, the required evolution of core competencies for the organization can be ascertained.

Summary

Sun Tzu says:

> In ancient times, those known as good warriors prevailed when it was easy to prevail. Their victories are not flukes. Their victories are not flukes because they *position* themselves where they will surely win, prevailing over those who have already lost.[11]

Sun Tzu goes on to state that the greatest warriors are unknown. They are unknown because they positioned themselves with such daunting superiority over their opponents that the opposition always surrendered or retreated without battle. They surrendered or retreated because they recognized the gross inferiority of their position and that victory in combat was forlorn. The acme of skill, therefore, is not to engage in combat but "...it is best to win without fighting."[12]

The most appropriate metaphor to express this intent and purpose of positioning is chess. Among grandmasters, the loser is seldom defeated by an explicit checkmate; rather, she resigns. Though checkmate may take many more moves to occur and its inevitability is not clear to most game observers, the resigning player foresees that her board position is hopeless and, unless the opponent makes a gross error, defeat is the only end.

What has occurred is that the victor has achieved a fundamentally superior board position along a winning strategic dimension. Through control of the center of the board, control of key rows or diagonals, or piece advantage, the victor achieves a winning position which precedes the anticlimatic winning of the game. The opponent, recognizing the inevitability of defeat by virtue of an inferior position, resigns, and the actual act of checkmate is not required.

This is the exact notion and understanding of strategic business positioning that is sought. The objective is to position strategic business areas along their strategic dimensions in such a formidable way that the marketplace battle becomes anticlimactic. By focusing and concentrating on those strategic areas which decide victory, "…you will surely prevail over those who have already lost." Repetitive success is not the consequence of wishful thinking, good luck, magic, prayer, or chance. It is the consequence of creating and nurturing winning positions.

So those who embrace positioning as the path to success have more in common with the political strategist than the military strategist. The military strategist surmounts that the objective of war is to eliminate the opponent's military capability to resist. The political strategist views the purpose of war to be the creation of a better and more enduring peace; a political strategist takes "the long view." Similarly, a mundane business view of strategy would suggest that the purpose of strategy is to improve margins, rectify weakness, parry threats, etc. A positioning strategist would view the purpose of strategy to be creation of an enduring set of business positions which will sustain business success over an extended period.

3.4 Situational Analysis

Situational analysis is the collection and analysis of information about the business, from both an internal and external perspective, for the purpose of developing conclusions about the state of the business. It is performed by applying a robust set of analytical methods which aid in structuring the process of insight and discovery. Situational analysis is both a data intensive and process intensive activity.

This section will explain 11 analytical methods. These are not the only methods available, but they do represent a popular and strong sampling. As was the case with positioning, we analyze the business in the dimensions of current situation, competitive situation, and futures situations.

1. Strength/Weakness/Opportunity/Threat (SWOT) Analysis

Purpose: SWOT analysis is the analysis of the state of the business from the dimensions of:

- *Strength*: a collective organizational competency, asset, capability, etc., for which the organization has achieved a high level of proficiency,
- *Weakness*: a collective organizational competence, asset, capability, etc., which is competitively inferior and, consequently, provides a vulnerability for competitors to exploit,
- *Opportunity*: a trend or event that could lead to a positive change in position if addressed by a strategic response, and
- *Threat*: a trend or event that could lead to a negative change in position if not addressed by a strategic response.

Sun Tzu says:

The considerations of the intelligent always include both harm and benefit. As they consider benefit, their work can expand; as they consider harm, their troubles can be resolved.[13]

Description: The approach to performing SWOT analysis is illustrated in Table 3.24. The process is as follows:

1. Information is collected about a business area or resource.
2. Implications are developed which interpret what the information means.
3. The implications are summarized as a strength, weakness, opportunity, or threat.

The results of multiple individual SWOT analysis are summarized in a SWOT table which provides a composite picture (see Table 3.25).

IM&M Strategic Planning Impact: SWOT analysis findings provide the basis for conclusions; one should leverage strengths, eliminate weakness, exploit opportunities, and deflect threats.

Table 3.24
SWOT Analysis. Information about a business area or resource is analyzed and placed into one of the four classifications.

Information	Implications	Strengths	Weaknesses	Opportunities	Threats

Table 3.25
SWOT Table. The results from multiple SWOT analysis is summarized in a SWOT Table.

Strengths	Weaknesses
1.	1.
2.	2.
3.	3.
4.	4.
Opportunities	**Threats**
1.	1.
2.	2.
3.	3.
4.	4.

2. Critical Success Factors (CSF)

Purpose: Critical Success Factors identify specific competencies, capabilities, processes, etc., which an organization must do well to be successful. CSFs often focus on customer requirements and competition.

Description: Development of CSFs is similar to SWOT analysis (see Table 3.26). Information is collected about a subject area. This information is analyzed to extract key implications. The implications are then summarized as CSFs.

Table 3.27 illustrates a typical set of CSFs for a DBMS vendor from the dimensions of customer satisfaction and competition. Not surprisingly, what satisfies your customers and blocks your competitors often overlaps, and one could argue over the placement of any one factor. What is important is not where the factor is placed, but that actions are taken to assure that all CSFs are met.

Table 3.26
Critical Success Factors. Critical success factors identify what must be done well to successfully compete.

Information	Implications	Critical Success Factors

Table 3.27
CSF Example. DBMS vendors must do all these CSFs well to successfully compete.

Critical Success Factors	
Competition	**Customer Requirements**
1. Price/Performance	1. Developer productivity
2. Name recognition	2. Developer flexibility
3. Support	3. Portability
4. Training	4. Scalability
5. Distribution channels	5. Standards adherence
6. Feature/Functionality	6. Vendor viability
7. Market presence	7. Architecture robustness

It should be noted that CSFs do not equate to SCA. CSFs identify what must be done well. SCA identifies what you have decided to focus on to provide distinct advantage. While certainly related, they do not equate.

IM&M Strategic Planning Impact: CSFs can be viewed as encapsulating the "ante" for competing. If you satisfy your customers and block your competitors, you certainly are well on the road to sustained success.

3. Root Cause Analysis

Purpose: Root Cause Analysis is a methodology used to uncover the underlying etiology of a problem.

Description: Figure 3.26 illustrates this analytical method. The process proceeds as follows:

1. The complaints of interviewed people are viewed as symptoms or signs of a problem. They describe the most external manifestation of a problem but do not necessarily indicate or externalize the underlying cause.

2. Analysis of the symptoms and signs leads to the identification of the "operational problem" i.e., the malfunctioning object.

3. Further analysis is then undertaken to identify the "root cause" of the malfunction.

This type of analysis is important because the enduring effect of the strategic actions undertaken have very different efficacy depending on where in the root cause chain they are targeted. Actions which address signs and symptoms only offer temporary relief. Actions which target the operation problem are curative of this instance of the problem, but it can reoccur. Actions which address the root cause correct the problem systemically and prevent reoccurrence.

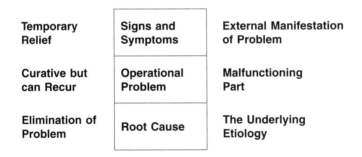

Figure 3.26   Root Cause Analysis. Root cause analysis is used to discover the fundamental etiology of a problem.

IM&M Strategic Planning Impact: Actions should be carefully designed to attack problems at the root cause level. Attacking problems at the other two levels provides temporary satisfaction but does not contribute to developing sustainable advantage for the organization.

4. Matrix Analysis

Purpose: Matrix analysis is a generic analytical method whereby one attempts to develop insight and understanding by analyzing the intersection (relationship) of two strategic business areas or between a strategic business area and its attributes.

Description: Matrix analysis is used to better comprehend relationships. Table 3.28 can be used to clarify which core competencies (a major strategic positioning framework) are put in motion by which capabilities (another major strategic positioning framework). Table 3.29 illustrates how matrix analysis could be used to assist in understanding the state of organizational alignment which was discussed in Section 3.1. We would populate the cells which are not in alignment with a statement of why they *are not* in alignment (the root cause) and what possible actions could be taken to move toward alignment. Note in Table 3.29 that business areas are aligned both with each other and the business scope.

This example raises the general problem of analytical depth of decomposition. In this example, the analysis is done at the macro organizational entity level. It is perhaps the case that better insight would be developed by doing the analysis at subunit levels. The general rule is to do the analysis at the highest possible level without sacrificing understanding. Experience, judgement, and operational problems in doing the analysis all contribute to help identifying when a further decomposition may be advantageous.

IM&M Strategic Planning Impact: Matrix analysis is simple but powerful. Both the absence of intersections or the existence of intersections provides opportunities for insight.

Table 3.28
Core Competency vs. Capability Matrix. An "x" in a cell indicates that the capability supports the indicated core competency.

	Capability 1	Capability 2	Capability 3	Capability n
Core Competency 1				
Core Competency 2				
Core Competency 3				
Core Competency n				

Table 3.29
Alignment Analysis. Matrix analysis may be used to analyze the state of organizational alignment.

	Business Scope	HR	Technology	Marketing	Sales	Engineering	Other
HR		Not applicable					
Technology			Not applicable				
Marketing				Not applicable			
Sales					Not applicable		
Engineering						Not applicable	
Other							Not Applicable

5. Technology Forecasting

Purpose: Technology Forecasting is the construction of models of possible futures with associated insights into those futures.

Description: A quality forecast contains:

- A statement of the forecast,
- The rationale of the forecast,
- Dates, values, and probabilities of occurrence,
- Opportunities and threats presented by the forecast, and
- Impact of the forecast on strategic positions.

Forecasting has earned a generally negative reputation. It is often characterized as error prone, not more than a guess, and suffers from historically poor track records and a mindless "law of upward motion." The etiology of this infamous reputation is as follows:

- Forecasters often become more concerned with the elegance of the mathematical models they are creating than the subject of the forecast.
- Forecasters become seduced by a technology high. Their enthusiasm for new technology overshadows the use of common sense and business sense in making realistic forecasts.
- Due to the above, forecasters ignore the basics of market success:

    What is the customer need being meet?

What is the cost/benefit of the technology?

How will the established technologies defend themselves?

Is the value added of the new technology worth the additional cost?

Is the need being addressed enduring or a fad?

What are the switching costs to adapt the new technology?

- Forecasters talk too much to each other; creating and reinforcing a "heads in the clouds" club.
- Being optimistic to a fault, forecasters ignore the practical issues of product commercialization, product diffusion, and creation of supporting and enabling infrastructures.

While all of these caveats are of concern, it is impossible to develop strategy in a dynamic area such as IM&M and ignore the future. A prudent approach to utilizing forecasts would be as follows:

- Be primarily concerned with the direction, degree of magnitude, and probability of occurrence of the forecast. Do not be concerned with the precision of the dates and values.
- Look for inter-forecast synergy, and determine if independent forecasts confirm each other.
- Test the forecasts against the market basics itemized above.

It is interesting, as an aside, to note that Dante shared an extremely negative view of forecasters. In the *Divine Comedy: Inferno*, fortunetellers are sentenced to Circle VIII, Malebolge, the center of Hell, where according to the law of retribution, by antithesis, they are to spend eternity with their heads turned backwards so as they walk forward they see only the past. This gross distortion of the human body is just punishment for those who sinned by trying to foretell the future which is known only to God. IM&M pundits, gurus, oracles, and other assorted coven members may wish to take this information into account when developing their own career plans.

Forewarned, but not dissuaded, we will now review five representative methods of forecasting.

1. Multivariate Analysis Methods

This refers to a set of mathematical methods where one or several variables are functions of some other known variables. Since we know the mathematical relationship, the values of the unknown variables can be computed. Typical multivariate forecasting methods include conjoint analysis, discriminant analysis, automatic interaction detection, canonical analysis, and simple relationship trending.

2. "S" Curve Technology Models

Pragmatic experience has indicated that technologies frequently follow "S" curve life cycles. For a given performance parameter, a technology evolves through predicable steps of initial commercialization, proliferation, standardization of design, and consolidation, as shown in Figure 3.27. The trick with "S" curve forecasting is to jump to a replacement technology with a better performing "S" curve at the right point. Figure 3.28 illustrates the application of "S" curves to human interface and DBMS technology. Multiple "S" curves may be summarized in a technology life cycle chart as shown in the bottom of Figure 3.28. "S" curve modeling is a powerful approach to understanding the evolution of technologies and their replacements. In building "S" curves, exact values are not critical. The technique is of particular value as a way to illustrate for a large community the technology shifts which are occurring.

3. Time-Line Monitoring

Time-line monitoring is a technique used to construct snapshots of possible future product configurations and definitions. Table 3.30 is a typical time-line forecast provided by market research firms. A PC is viewed as a collection of individual technologies, i.e., microprocessor, memory, secondary storage, etc. By maintaining individual time-line forecasts for each element, one can then "join" the individual time-line forecasts to create a snapshot picture of the future composite product. Time-line monitoring can be used very effectively to anticipate emerging technology clusters which may be used to better meet the functional requirements of a customer need. By doing this type of technology forecasting, you can better plan for the introduction of new technologies which will more effectively and efficiently solve customer needs. Performing timeline monitoring to create still frame snapshots of the future and coupling those snapshots with projections of future customer needs and functional requirements provides a way to directly link technology investments to customer requirements.

4. Delphi Technique

The objective of the Delphi Technique is to develop a consensus forecast of the future by asking experts, while at the same time eliminating the familiar problems of face to face communication. The technique algorithm is as follows:

1. Develop a questionnaire.

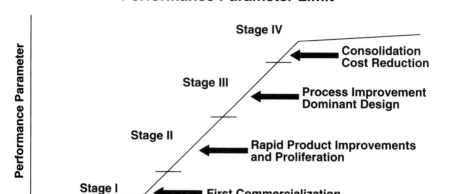

Figure 3.27   "S" Curve Technology Model. Technologies progress
through predictable stages.

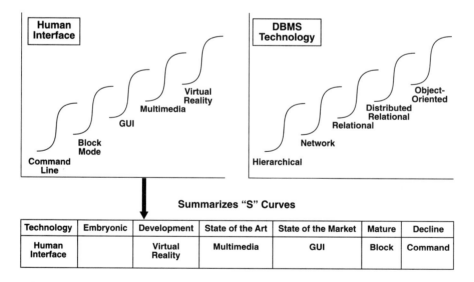

Figure 3.28   "S" Curve Example. DBMS technology and human interfaces can be tracked using "S" curves.

Table 3.30
1996 PC Forecast. Composite future product forecasts can be produced
by monitoring the individual timelines of each element technology.
Source: **The Gartner Group.**

	Size/ Weight	Processor	RAM	DASD	Comm	Video	I/O
Desktop $5000	N/A	150+mips SMP 64 bit	128 mb to 1 gb	Magnetic Optical	100 mbps Fiber	Multiple screens	Keyboard Voice
Notebook $2500	<4 lbs 6-8 hr battery life	100 mips 32-bit	64 mb	Flashflash Optical	10 mbps Cellular Wireless Rf Infrared Docking Station	Flatscreen Color Hi-Res-Megapel HDTV, 3D-Full Form 24 bit	Pen Keyboard Color Pen Glove/ Voice Eye
Handheld $500	Pocket size 1 lb	15 mips (up to 50 mips @ $1000)	16 mb	Flash Optical	Cellular RF Infrared	Color	Virtual Keyboard Pen Voice

2. Select renown subject matter experts.
3. Circulate the questionnaire and encourage exposition on opinions.
4. Analyze the results and structure them into quartiles.
5. Repeat step (3) but with the opinions from step 3.
6. Repeat steps (4) and (5) until a consensus is reached.

This method gathers the opinions of the most qualified experts while eliminating the problems (badgering, shyness, group-think) of focus groups.

5. Scenarios

Scenarios are a structured way to define possible futures, understand the causation chain for each possible future, and develop options to deal with the uncertainties. Figure 3.29 illustrates the essential character of a scenario. The following definitions help explain Figure 3.29:

- *Start state*—a summary of the current industry situation,

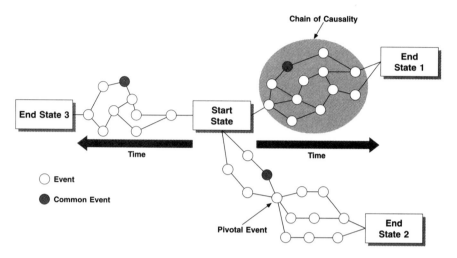

Figure 3.29   Scenario Structure. A scenario illustrates a possible chain of events which moves an industry from its current state to a future state.

- *End state*—the culmination of a set of events (causality chain). The state of the industry is now different because the chain of events has altered the industry structure.
- *Event*—something that is controllable by people. We are not at the mercy of an uncontrollable future.
- *Causality chain*—a set of interlocking events,
- *Pivotal event*—an event which makes or breaks a scenario, and
- *Common event*—an event which is common to multiple scenarios.

A good scenario has the following attributes:

1. It postulates plausible but divergent futures.
2. The futures are deterministic; driven by controllable events.
3. It captures strong biases and different points of view.
4. It stimulates debate, perpetuates learning, questions long-held assumptions, and challenges embedded "mental models" of the industry.
5. It includes, at minimum, three end states, including a "risk free" conventional wisdom end state.

Scenarios will necessarily overlap in their future description of the industry but should markedly differ in some dominant theme.

Scenarios provide fertile ground for insightful analysis. Alternatives could include:

- For a desired end state, what actions could be taken to make it happen,
- For an undesirable end state, what actions could be taken to prevent its occurrence,
- How you could position for common events,
- Whether you should do a complete assessment of each end state and compare required competencies, capabilities, etc., and
- Whether you should position for pivotal events.

Scenarios promote deep creative thinking, broad understanding of what drives an industry, development of horizontal thinkers as opposed to vertical thinkers, and preparation of a management team to recognize futures as they emerge (vigilance). As a consequence, scenarios stimulate development of strategic moves such as:

- *Hedge bets*—actions taken which prepare you for multiple futures,
- *Stagger*—development of strategic moves which can gradually be committed to,
- *Reserves*—plans to have resources in reserve to exploit the occurrence of a pivotal event, and
- *Vigilance*—implementation of a set of watching systems to provide early warnings of emergence of a particular chain of events.

Given the dynamic nature of the IM&M industry, it is obvious that scenarios can be particularly powerful in developing the strategic thinking capabilities of a management team. Two examples of IM&M scenarios are as follows:

A. IBM Futures Scenario[14]

- *Big Blue Never Learns*

    IBM continues to muddle along through the early 1990s, cutting its work force and making token gestures toward serious corporate reform. Eventually, shareholders force a change in management demanding a top-to-bottom overhaul of IBM's operations.

- *IBM Doomsday*

    A weak U.S. economy forestalls IBM's recovery. Consequently, anemic market demand leads to failures in the new product lines.

Before 2001, IBM is forced into U.S. Chapter 11 bankruptcy protection laws.

- *The Post-Industrial IBM*

    After a decade of radical change, IBM becomes a holding company for dozens of highly-specialized subsidiaries, each with autonomous management and independent development teams. The era of top-heavy bureaucracy ends as IBM enters the 21st century.

B. IM&M 1997 Industry Scenarios[15]

- *Scenario 1: A Future Dominated by Standards*

    Proprietary processing and communication architectures have faded. Internationally uniformed standards have made multi-vendor solutions practical and popular. Technology development has been restrained, however, by the need to preserve compatibility with a large installed base of equipment. The adoption of standards has allowed EDI, distributed databases, and electronic mail to significantly reduce the paper content of business. The open market fostered by standards has brought prices down and shifted competition to the application software level. Being small, specialized, and responsive or large with production scale advantages are the key means of surviving as margins erode.

- *Scenario 2: A Future Driven by New Technology*

    Information technology remains on fast forward. Flat screens, speech recognition, image processing, superb color, expert agent software, and multimedia have redefined the way users interact with computers and networks. Fiber-optic networks have made image transfer fast and inexpensive. Parallel processing and radical new computer architectures provide high-performance solutions. Embedded computers have infiltrated products of everyday life and go unnoticed. Object-oriented technology has significantly boosted software productivity. Large segments of the population become first-time users. Aggressive start-ups fuel most of the innovation while the big vendors remain bogged down in supporting their installed base.

- *Scenario 3: Distributed Objects Everywhere*

    The concept of discrete computers has faded as the network computing model takes hold. With LAN and bus speeds roughly equivalent, network machines function as distributed parallel processors.

Location independent data access and distributed processing are major software design paradigms. Groupware applications allow distributed teams to work on common projects. Major changes are taking place in business as networks allow direct interaction between producers and consumers. Public network operators offer all forms of processing and storage with tremendous economies of scale. Small firms use the highly interconnected global internets as a market place for new applications and information services offering instant knowledge at the point of need.

- *Scenario 4: Multi-Everything*

Capital spending on information technology has been declining steadily for the past five years as users re-think their investments. The economic logic of moving most applications to inexpensive distributed platforms is now inescapable. At least three generations of equipment are now maintained in most environments. Decentralized purchasing has led to a morass of incompatible configurations. End user generated applications account for most new software. Low cost, ease of use, and flexibility are key attributes of winning products. Economies of scale in production and effective market distribution are key competitive advantages.

- *Scenario 5: The Big Players Own the Future*

Intense consolidation on a global scale has reduced the number of broad line information technology suppliers to six international giants. Large differences between vendors persist as the need for return on large R/D investments drives strategies. Large vendor's *defacto* standards stay ahead through advanced technology, risk-free integration, and broader functionality. Users prefer packaged solutions that work over the confusion of standards-based do-it-yourself solutions. After painful experience with user generated applications, most critical systems are centrally developed and operated. The architectures that dominate the installed based have left the vendors with the dominant position, and have blocked the entrance of significant new players outside the big six alliance structures.

Management team discussions of scenarios such as these will clearly improve the collective understanding of what the future may be like. It will also help develop more "renaissance" thinkers within the organization. To deal with change, you require horizontal thinkers who are able to understand a subject from a wide variety of perspectives. Scenarios liberate people from tunnel vision.

IM&M Strategic Planning Impact: Forecasting techniques provide a robust set of analytical methods to sharpen the strategy team's view of the future. The key to properly using forecasting techniques is to constrain one's enthusiasm and excitement of technological possibilities and test all forecasts against the caveats which are listed at the beginning of this section. In analyzing forecasts, the IM&M strategist should be particularly vigilant in searching for technology discontinuities. It is difficult to surpass one's competitors when the *status quo* changes incrementally with everyone muddling along, more or less, at the same pace. Discontinuities, however, provide precious opportunities to improve one's advantage. So in analyzing forecasts, one must always be asking: Does this fundamentally change how things are done and create a new basis for advantage?

6. Theory/Hypothesis

Purpose: Theory/hypothesis is a way of developing explanatory arguments by developing a general theory of events and then proving that theory by proving derivative hypotheses. This method was described and applied in Section 2.2 to explain the radical shift occurring in IM&M technology.

Description: In using this method, it is important, as it is in all strategy work, to argue logically. Logical reasoning permeates the entire strategy process, and any strategist must be cognizant of basic concepts of logic. The two basic forms of logical arguments are:

- *Deductive argument*—The relationship between the statements (premise) and the resulting conclusion is a logical necessity. If you grant the truth of the premise, you must accept the truth of the conclusion.

- *Inductive argument*—The relationship between the statements (premise) and the resulting conclusion is not necessarily true. If you concede the truthfulness of the premise, the conclusion is highly likely, of extreme probability, but there is a "leap" to reach the conclusion.

Most strategy arguments are inductive; we are postulating future activities. Figure 3.30 illustrates the key building blocks of deductive or inductive arguments. The following definitions assist in understanding Figure 3.30:

- *Premise*—a set of statements which are true or false,
- *Conclusion*—the "therefore" from a true premise,

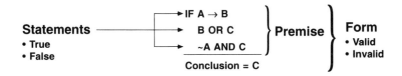

Figure 3.30   Argument Structure. Deductive and inductive arguments fit into a standard structure.

- *Form*—the structural relationships of the premise and the conclusion; may be valid or invalid,
- *Sound argument*—the form of the argument is valid and the premise is true,
- *Cogent argument*—a sound argument known to be sound, and
- *Convincing argument*—a cogent argument in which the truth of the conclusion is not known apart from the argument. The argument itself convinces us of the conclusion.

In proving hypotheses in support of a theory, we strive to develop convincing arguments.

Table 3.31 summarizes some of the key fallacies that people make in composing an argument. An argument is fallacious when there is something structurally wrong with it which inherently prevents a rational person from accepting the argument. The fallacies illustrated in the table are only too common in the information technology literature, debate, and rhetoric. The criterion for truth and action should be reason as opposed to custom, tradition, time, feelings, hunch, revelation, majority rule, or political consensus.

The following is an example of a fallacious argument taken from a letters to the editor column of an industry magazine in which the writer argues against the shift to network computing:

...I am doubtful, however, that the opportunities in the PC programming area are really very great. It is unclear to me how many corporations are actually moving production systems to PC LANs on more than a small experimental basis, and it is unclear to me that there is a compelling reason to do so.

Why, in principal should hundreds of small computers connected by cables be less expensive than one large computer? If anything, a LAN seems to be far more complex than a mainframe and includes far more possible points of failure.

Table 3.31
Fallacious Arguments. Strategists need to recognize fallacious arguments.

Fallacy Classification	Fallacy Type	Explanation
Argument is fallacious even if form is valid	Suppressed evidence	The deliberate omission of known relevant evidence from the argument
	Doubtful evidence	The use of unsupported or questionable evidence to support and argument. This includes: a. Acceptance as evidence of a fact which is not known nor can be known b. Acceptance as evidence of a doubtful evaluation c. Acceptance of contradictory or inconsistent arguments
	False charge of inconsistency	An argument based on an invalid charge of inconsistency. Often exemplified by changes in position over time without regard to changing circumstances that justify change in position.
Argument is fallacious because the form is invalid	Ad hominem	An attack on the arguer rather than the argument. This includes guilt by association.
	Two wrongs make a right	It's not wrong because the other side did it too.
	Strawperson	Attacking a pseudo position similar to but not the one that your opponent took
	False dilemma	An improper reduction of the possible alternatives
	Tokenism	Arguing an insufficient sample to prove the overall point
	Begging the question	Arguing the conclusion to prove the conclusion
	Improper appeal to authority	Appealing to an authority who is not an authority on the matter at hand
	Provincialism	An unchallenged assumption that your way is correct
	Irrelevant reason	Inclusion of evidence irrelevant to conclusion
	Ambiguity	Use of ambiguous terms to deliberately mislead

Table 3.31 *continued*

Fallacy Classification	Fallacy Type	Explanation
Argument is fallacious because the form is invalid	Slippery slope	Arguing that one step inevitably must lead to other steps without providing evidence
	Hasty conclusion	Jumping to a conclusion on insufficient evidence
	Questionable classification	Incorrectly classifying something and then proceeding erroneously based on that classification
	Questionable cause	Establishing an invalid cause/effect relationship
	Questionable analogy	Applying an analogy without establishing its likeness
	Equivocation	The use of a term in more than one sense in an argument while the impression is given that it is being used to express one and the same meaning throughout the argument
	Amphibology	The use of a statement which permits two interpretations
	Composition	Asserting that which is true of a part is true of the composite
	Division	Asserting that which is true of the composite is true of the part
	Compound question	Combining several questions into one which places the opponent in a logical dilemma
	Genetic error	Asserting something is false because of its origin
	Contrary to fact conditional error	Altering historical evidence and then drawing conclusions
	No true Scotsman	Denying the validity of a counterexample because it's a counterexample, i.e., declaring that contradictions are impossible

Is the tremendous cost-savings potential of LANs really more than the marketing hype of certain technology vendors?

The first paragraph suffers from the fallacy of provincialism, the second paragraph suffers from the fallacy of doubtful evidence, and the third paragraph suffers from the fallacy of *ad hominen*.

The following letter to the editor, in defense of Mr. John Akers, chairman of IBM, is fallacious because of the fallacy of suppressed evidence:

> Despite the criticism you level at IBM Chairman John Akers, under him IBM has:
>
> - Built its desktop computing business to $8.5 billion in worldwide sales in 1991—giving it 19% market share among the top 100 global information technology suppliers,
> - Remained the worldwide leader in information technology revenues—garnering $62.8 billion in computer related revenues in 1991. That's up nearly 30% from $48.5 billion in 1985, the year Mr. Akers became chairman, and
> - Avoided the worse crisis that could have befallen it—which would have been to sacrifice investments in research and development for the sake of a fast buck. In 1991, IBM's R&D expenditures totaled $6.6 billion, including product engineering investments. In 1985, R&D outlays amounted to $4.7 billion.

That's why John Akers still calls the *big shots at Big Blue*.

Unfortunately, Mr. Aker's defender failed to mention (for example) that *also* during Mr. Aker's watch:

- The credit rating services of Phelps-Dodge and Moodys lowered IBM's credit rating and Standard and Poors put IBM on the watchlist.
- Employee headcount has dropped by about 25%.
- IBM experienced a 1991 lost of $1.38 billion and a third quarter 1992 loss (alone) of $2.7 billion.
- IBM is an also ran in the high growth markets of lan operating systems, PC software, x-terminals, workstations, and portable PCs.
- IBM, while still the largest im&m company, has seen its dominance of IM&M shrink from a 67% market share in 1970 to about 18% in 1992.
- While IBM is losing money, companies like Novell, Microsoft, Adobe, Autodesk, and Cabletron are all making margins of greater than 20%.
- Companies like UNIX Systems Laboratories, SAS institute, and BGS spend three times as much as a percent of revenue on research and development as IBM does.

- The value of US shipments of IBM's cash cow, mainframes, has declined by about 10% from 1990 through 1992.

Fallacious arguments based on suppressed evidence are probably the most common type of poor reasoning in the IM&M community due to their self-serving nature. These types of arguments are often the easiest uncovered. The day following the publication of this letter in defense of Chairman Akers, 16 December 1992, IBM announced another $6 billion charge, the elimination of 25,000 jobs, and a further reduction in R/D of $1 billion, the specter of layoffs and the likelihood of a reduction in the dividend. IBM stock closed at an 11 year low of $51.875 and its stock valuation tumbled to $29.63 billion. As recently as 1990, IBM had the highest stock valuation of the Standards and Poors 500. At the end of 1991, IBM's stock valuation stood at $52.92 billion. So during Mr. Aker's shift, IBM stockholders have seen their stock value decrease by 40% in one year. Hopefully, it has been demonstrated that arguments based on suppressed data, while making you feel temporarily good, can ultimately prove quite embarrassing.

So the rules of admissible evidence are as follows:

- The evidence must be material, relevant, and probative.
- The evidence must be true.
- The evidence must be complete.
- The evidence must come from a qualified source.
- The evidence must be authentic.
- The evidence must be assembled into a valid argument form.
- The argument form must create a convincing argument.

No compromise of this is acceptable.

IM&M Strategic Planning Impact: Understanding and applying the rules of logical reasoning is critical to the strategist from two perspectives:

- As the developer of arguments we must develop convincing arguments.
- As a listener to the arguments of others, we must insist that they provide convincing arguments and analyze them from a convincing argument perspective.

Since the long-term well being of the business hinges on the strategic decisions that are to be made, whim, prejudice, emotion, and "I want to" must be replaced by sound logic. It is worth noting that this entire book is one large inductive argument. The conclusion is that IM&M organizations must adopt strategic business planning methods, and the rest of the book provides the premise of the argument.

There remains, however, one problem: How is the dilemma of rational decision making and vision resolved? The acme of strategic success occurs when you foresee what has not yet occurred ("…seize victory when there is no form"). The truly aware individual is one who knows what has not yet taken shape (see Appendix A under foresight and vision for quotes). It has been asserted that what will be believed and acted upon should be provable or, at minimum, be provable to be highly probable. A belief or opinion for which a convincing argument cannot be provided should be discarded. But how then is it possible to suggest that we proceed based on unprovable foresight and expect acquisition of truth and success?

There is no dilemma. There is, however, an order. People are given different faculties in different degrees. Most are given the faculty of reason, and reason, the highly available ingredient, provides the normal method for developing strategy. Vision and foresight, however, are a faculty of a higher order and much rarer. Visionaries can provide an organization with simply extraordinary and unlimited possibilities. Of course, since foresight is less demonstrable, it is difficult to know whether you being given advice from a "good witch" or a "bad witch." So it is usually riskier to follow a visionary, and to follow one requires commitment and courage. This is not a contradiction. It is just that reason and foresight are different from one another, and this must be kept in mind when proceeding from either.

You ask, "What does the visionary see?" Imagine the progression of a business as an endless parade. The typical proletariat member of the organization stands at the parade barricade looking straight ahead at "what is" with minimal peripheral vision. The visionary perches on the top of the highest building. From this vantage point, she can see all of what has come, what is, and what shall be. The choreography of business change is clearly displayed before her eyes. From the vantage point of foresight, the constraint of seeing the future is transcended. How different the consequences of strategy based on what the visionary foresees versus what the barricade standee sees.

Strategy is to the strategist as clay is to the potter. How much greater the result when the strategist can shape the strategy, her clay, from clearly seeing the formless. An organization which has visionary employees has a distinct and truly fortunate advantage. The perennial problem of believing and acting on their insights, however, remains irresolvable.

7. New Product Position

Purpose: A future product or service position is a series of interlocking matrices and graphs which collectively illustrate the anticipated position of a prospective product. This is the same concept as introduced in Section 3.3 when "Product/Service Position" is analyzed, except here the concept is applied to products or services in development.

Description: Figure 3.31 provides a global relationship map for the set of graphs and matrices which collectively define the position of a prospective product or service. The graphs and matrices numbered 1 through 13 coincide with the identical graphs and matrices on Figure 3.20 and are explained in Section 3.3. Only the tense has to be changed. The four new matrices required for future product positioning will now be explained.

14. Future Product Position (Table 3.32)

Purpose: The purpose of this matrix is to position prospective products by the dimensions of technology cluster and type of market. This positioning illustrates how our technology set and target markets are changing, if at all.

Cell Content: The content of a cell is a prospective product or service.

15. Remaining Product Development Cost (Table 3.33)

Purpose: The purpose of this matrix is to illustrate the remaining development budget for each prospective product and the anticipated time until product announcement.

Cell Content: The content of a cell is a prospective product or service.

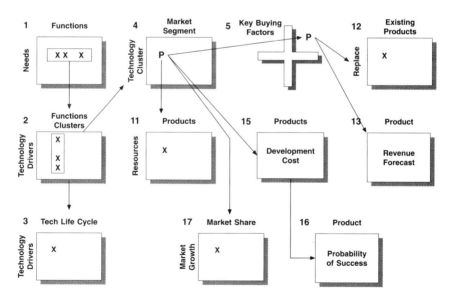

Figure 3.31   Future Product Map. Products in development can be analyzed through a series of interlocking matrices and graphs.

Table 3.32
Future Product Position. Future products should be positioned by the intersection of markets and technology clusters.

		IncreasingTechnology Newness -->		
		No technological change	Improved existing technological clusters	New technology clusters
Increasing Market Newness (Down)	Existing markets	N/A	Reformulation	Replacement
	Strengthen market	Remerchandising	Improved product	Product line extension
	New market	New use	Market extension	Diversification

Table 3.33
Remaining Product Development Cost. Future products may be positioned to illustrate both the time remaining until product announcement and the anticipated remaining development cost.

		Time Remaining Until Product Announcement		
		< 6 months	6 months–1 year	> 1 year
Remaining Development Budget $M	> 2M			
	1M–2M			
	< 1M			

16. Probability of Success (Table 3.34)

Purpose: The purpose of this matrix is to illustrate the probability of success for the product. Together with the prior matrix, "Remaining Product Development Cost," and the following matrix, "Year 1 Market Share/ Growth," this matrix is used to assess risk.

Cell Content: The content of a cell is a prospective product or service.

Table 3.34
Probability of Success. The probability of success in the context of
anticipated payoff provides an important criteria for evaluating future
products.

		Probability of Market Success		
		<50%	50–75%	> 75%
Payoff	High			
	Medium			
	Low			

17. Year 1 Market Share and Growth (Table 3.35)

Purpose: The purpose of this matrix is to illustrate the market-place projection for the product one year after its introduction.

Cell Content: The content of a cell is a prospective product or service.

IM&M Strategic Planning Impact: Map element 12, Table 3.23 in both
Figures 3.20 and 3.30, bridges the product set "that is" with the product
set "that will be." It is extremely powerful to place both maps on a wall
and, probably for the first time, get a comprehensive picture of the evolution of the product line. With this global picture of the product set, decisions can be made about adding, changing, or deleting products. A final
point: The power of the product maps is not the individual graphs or
matrices but the complete picture of the state of a product or service that
the set of graphs or matrices provide. A combined review of the current
map with the future map amplifies this benefit.

Table 3.35
Year 1 Market Share/Growth. This matrix is used to illustrate the anticipated market position of the product 1 year after introduction.

		Market Share		
		High	Medium	Low
Market Growth	High			
	Medium			
	Low			

Since it has now been discussed both how to position current products and how to analyze future products, it is an ideal time to address an obvious question: What kinds of products and services will the IM&M organization have to sell in the 1990s to remain viable? Historically, the IM&M organization has sold:

- Computing resources (MIPS, storage, etc.), and
- Business applications—life cycle development and maintenance services.

Growth for the IM&M organization will center around the following types of products and services:

1. Professional services such as systems integration, business solutions consulting, business re-engineering consulting, and project management,
2. Distributed processing platform and application production support services,
3. Information sharing applications (global team and meeting support),
4. Electroinc commerce with customers and suppliers,
5. Support services for increasingly mobile and global computing,
6. Information brokering services, and
7. Sales to customers outside the business to demonstrate competitiveness to those inside the business.

The locus of products and services will shift from renting capacity on mainframes to selling solution-oriented services.

Additionally, services will have to be packaged to meet the fragmented needs of different customers. Rather than one size fits all, as illustrated in Figure 3.12, not a service, but a family of services built around one product theme will have to be provided. One should imagine that for a given service there would be, at minimum, a low cost Spartan solution, a high-value solution, a high-end solution, and a customizable solution.

So the successful IM&M organization of this decade will have to hit with power from both sides of the plate. They will have to be ambidextrous. On one hand, they will have to maintain, nourish, and extend the large embedded base of host-based systems which were built over the past 20 to 30 years. On the other hand, they will have to move aggressively to offering solutions for highly mobile and networked users deploying ever more application-specific information technologies as a result of re-engineering. Such a situation is a challenge to manage, but is to be expected during a paradigm shift.

8. Value Chain Analysis

Purpose: Value chain analysis is a method for classifying, analyzing, and understanding the translation of resources through processes into final products and services.[16] It is used as a mechanism to analyze how to improve cost structure (productivity) and value-added (product differentiation).

Description: Figure 3.32 provides two popular illustrations of the value chain concept. The basic notion is that one can trace a product or service as it moves from your supplier's value chain to your value chain to your distributor's value chain to your customer's value chain. As it moves through the value chains, opportunities arise to improve productivity and value-added. Figure 3.33 illustrates the interrelationships of value chains.

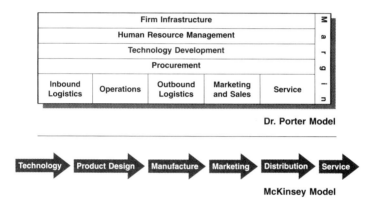

Figure 3.32   Value Chain. The value chain illustrates how value is added to a product as it moves through your internal business processes.

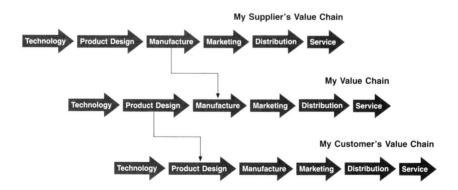

Figure 3.33   Value Chain Interlock. Cost savings and value-added can be accomplished by interlocking value chains.

Value Chain analysis proceeds as follows:

- Value chain analysis to improve cost (productivity)

    1. Disaggregate the chains into discrete activities.
    2. Establish relative weight of each activity as cost contributor.
    3. Identify for each activity the drivers (i.e., what drives costs, productivity, time, etc.).
    4. Identify links to previous and following value chains.
    5. Improve cost structure by redesign, re-engineering, better linkage, outsourcing, etc.

- Value chain analysis to improve value-added (differentiation)

    1. Disaggregate the chains into discrete activities.
    2. Identify for each activity the drivers (i.e., what adds value at each step).
    3. Select the most advantageous drivers for the product.
    4. Link drivers to customer value chain to validate value-added.
    5. Invest in value-added drivers.

In analyzing value chains for productivity or value-added improvements, it is often advantageous to think in terms of a "perfect" value chain. How should my value chain be designed so it operates flawlessly?

A special form of value-chain analysis is called *Bottleneck Analysis*, (Figure 3.34). Bottleneck analysis suggests that it is profitable to trace the flow of products across the value chains and look for bottlenecks. You should then take actions to alleviate the bottlenecks. This method emphasizes speed as the focus of attention.

What are the major bottlenecks inhibiting the IM&M services value chain as we enter the mid 1990s? In addition to those itemized in Figure 2.3, there are three major bottlenecks to IM&M success:

1. *Application development*—The true value of IM&M is in its application not in the raw resources. The rapid creation and amending of applications is a major bottleneck.
2. *Configuration management*—The migration to network computing puts the IM&M organization in the role of managing the integration of components from multiple vendors. The orderly evolution of the network components is a major bottleneck to successful network computing.

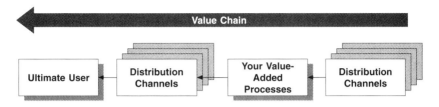

Trace the flow of a product from your suppliers to the ultimate user and look for "bottlenecks." Take strategic actions to eliminate bottlenecks.

Figure 3.34   Bottleneck Analysis. Take strategic action to eliminate bottlenecks throughout the value chain.

3. *Network computing operations, administration and maintenance (OAM)*—The daily end to end operations (trouble shooting, help desk, repair, software distribution, node administration, backup and recovery, performance tuning, etc.) of client/server computing architectures. OAM must be managed at two levels:

- *platform*—the technology infrastructure that provides the operational environment for a business application,
- *application*—the business software that solves a specific transaction processing, decision support, or information sharing problem for the user.

Table 3.36 identifies the primary functions that need to be performed in the network computing environment at both of these levels. Breaking these bottlenecks provides the basis for advantage.

IM&M Strategic Planning Impact: Value chain analysis and bottleneck analysis provide structured ways in which to analyze the process flows of an organization for productivity improvement and value-added opportunities. The bottlenecks and value-added activities selected for attention must, of course, relate to a product need or requirement of direct importance to the customer. Specifically, they should be understood in the context of improving the results from the customer satisfaction measurement system (Figure 3.24). Of particular concern to the IM&M strategist is how to apply IM&M throughout the value chain to accomplish these objectives.

In designing and analyzing value chains to support network computing environments, it will be important to focus on lateral ability rather than vertical specialization. Historically, value chain productivity has been optimized through decomposition and specialization. Capital is

Table 3.36
OAM Functions. Industrial grade operations, administration, and management of the network computing environment is a major bottleneck.

OAM Level	Function	Examples
Application	Software release management	Distribution, installation, testing, change control, backout, intersite coordination
	Monitoring	Component connectivity, message movement, file transfer completion
	Performance management	Proactive prevention, trend analysis, tuning, bottleneck resolution, trending
	Change management	Application movement, topology management, directory maintenance
	Backup/restore	Full/Incremetnal backup and restore, media management, off-site archival storage
	Database administration	Space management, permissions, restart, sizing
	Security administration	Userid and password administration, incident tracking
	Help desk	User-query resolution
	Job management	Batch job startup, scheduling, monitoring, output distribution
Platform	Configuration management	Provisioning, system software distribution, installation, directory management, name management, change management
	Fault management	Help desk, trouble identification and tracking, tiered support, problem isolation, and resolution
	Performance management	Measurement, tracking, turning
	Security management	Access permissions, violation monitoring, permission levels
	Accounting	Billing identifiers, billing, asset utilization

substituted for labor, and automation is applied to maximize component throughput. Since the notion of network computing is best encapsulated by the phrase "end-to-end," the horizontal capability of the IM&M organization to architect, design, and operate network computing environments will be critical. Especially until the real needs of network computing environments are well understood, it may prove advantageous to expedite the migration to network computing by assembling renaissance teams of staff to nurse network-computing through the life cycle rather than initially attempting to automate and optimize. These teams of people with broad-based lateral capabilities should be supplemented by artificially intelligent "counselors and advisors" to assist them with detailed knowledge. The success of network-computing value chains may well prove to be the ability to manage the horizontal complexity and not the vertical component optimization.

9. Benchmarking

Purpose: Benchmarking is a process for measuring and comparing products, and services, competencies, capabilities, etc., against those recognized as best in class. Machiavelli summarized the essential motivation for benchmarking when he said:

> Men nearly always follow the tracks made by others and proceed in their affairs by imitation, even though they cannot entirely keep to the tracks of others or emulate the prowess of their models. So a prudent man must always follow in the footsteps of great men and imitate those who have been outstanding. If his own prowess fails to compare with theirs, at least it has an air of greatness about it.[17]

Benchmarking permits you to profit from the experiences of many rather than the more limited and expensive experiences of your own.

Description: There are three basic types of benchmarks:

1. *Analogous*—used to compare specific processes, competencies, etc., against industry leaders,
2. *Competitive*—used to compare oneself against specific competitors, and
3. *Strategic*—used to understand the parameters of a major new initiative.

The basic benchmarking process is a nine step process as follows:

1. Define what you want to benchmark.
2. Define the purposes and objectives of the benchmark.
3. Define the subjects and metrics of comparison.
4. Define whom to benchmark against (see Table 3.37).
5. Develop data collection method.
6. Execute data collection.

Table 3.37
Whom to Benchmark. Companies with similar product and a high market overlap are the best benchmark candidates.

Product/Services Similarity	Market Overlap	
	Low	High
High	Parallel—second-best candidates	Clones—high candidates
Low	N/A (but what about their strategic intent?)	Potential—third-best candidates

7. Summarize the findings and results.

8. Define gaps.

9. Perform a root cause analysis identifying the underlying reasons for the gaps.

The gaps provide ripe opportunity for drawing conclusions about both what needs to be addressed and how to address it .

IM&M Strategic Planning Impact: Benchmarking is an extremely powerful analysis tools because it replaces opinion and wishful thinking about the state of resources with concrete comparisons. The key areas for benchmarking are those strategic areas you have put under position management (see Section 3.3). By definition they are the most strategic dimensions of your business and therefore must be most successfully and aggressively managed. You may then determine, apart from your own internal (and biased) opinions, whether they are noncompetitive, competitive, very competitive, or world class in comparison to the competition (see Table 3.38).

10. Competitor Analysis

Purpose: Competitor analysis is the strategic analysis of a competitor so that you can take actions to foil their strategy.

Description: Sun Tzu says:

What is valued is foiling the opponent's strategy, not pitched battle. A skillful strategist ruins plans, spoils relations, cuts off supplies, or blocks the way and hence can overcome people without fighting. Use strategy to thwart the opponents causing them to overcome themselves and destroy themselves. Overcome the opponent psychologically. Destroy their countries artfully, do not die in protracted warfare.[18]

Table 3.38
Benchmark Results. Benchmarking enables you to clearly assess
whether you are performing below, at, or above sea level.

Benchmark Area	Benchmark Results			
	Non-Competitive	Competitive	Very Competitive	World Class
Core Competencies				
Capabilities				
Cost Structure				
Customer Satisfaction				
Supplier Relationships				

To accomplish this, it is necessary to do a parallel strategic analysis of each competitor, a composite competitor, or a "perfect" competitor. Figure 3.35 illustrates the components of the strategic planning process that needs to be executed for selected competitors. While this is difficult to do, there is a surprising wealth of public information available through financial reports, market research reports, trade journals, marketing literature, etc. Some companies create "competition departments" whose objective is to create a staff which thinks and acts as the competitors would.

By understanding our competitors strategically, we can develop conclusions which can lead to elegant strategic moves to block them, change the rules of the game, disable alliances, date capabilities, and obsolete competencies. We design actions which increase our opponents levels of friction and drag, making it ever harder for them to execute their strategy. In doing so, we create strategic paralysis and avoid pyrrhic victories which leave us an exhausted winner.

IM&M Strategic Planning Impact: As explained in Section 2.3, many companies are moving to a free-market economy for IM&M services. One can compete with the outsourcers, system integrators, or facilities managers by engaging in "warfare" or by heeding the admonition of Sun Tzu. The goal of competitive analysis in this case is to devise strategies which preempt an approach by a competitor or motivate them to abandon an attempt. A stubborn willingness has to be demonstrated to protect markets. Ways of doing this could include:

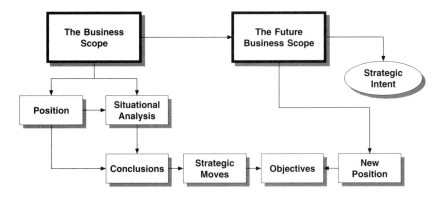

Figure 3.35   Understanding Competitors Strategically. Competitor analysis requires doing a strategic analysis of the competition.

- First and foremost, demonstrate through benchmarking that you are, in fact, highly competitive.
- Leverage advantages of being an internal supplier, i.e., concern for security, knowledge of applications, political connections, flexibility as opposed to commercial contractual obligations, etc.
- Use alliances with friendly vendors to fill gaps in product line, i.e., if you are weak in business consulting, form an alliance with a consulting company that only does business consulting.
- Attack your competitor where they will have to defend, i.e., case studies of failures, inexpereinced staff, lack of industry knowledge, etc. If possible, involve the highest levels of the competitor as possible, draw out the decision making process, create distractions, and keep raising the cost and time of geting the account.

Defense is normally the stronger partner of conflict. Change in this context raises fear, uncertainty, and doubt on the side of those who would outsource. All of this can be used to raise the perceived risk of such actions. So one can defend first through merit and then by raising the ante so that the reward is not worth the risk or efforts (time or cost) to both the outsourcer and internal promoter.

The limited objective of the IM&M organization to maintain the *status quo* conveys advantages over the acquisitive intentions of the outsourcer. Sun Tzu says:

> What motivates competitors is profit…what restrains competitors is harm…. Wear enemies out by keeping them busy and not letting them rest…make them rush about trying to cover themselves,

they will not have time to formulate plans.... To keep them from getting to you, attack where they will surely go to the rescue.[19]

So the strategy of defense is to first frustrate and then exhaust your adversary's commitment.

11. Pivot Position Analysis

Purpose: Pivot position analysis is a method of analyzing possible future positions to determine what positions will provide the organization with flexibility and maneuverability to deal with an unknowable future.

Description: A pivot position is a position, as was defined in Section 3.3, which has the additional attribute of having to sit at a crossroads. As illustrated in Figure 3.36, a pivot position allows one to go in multiple directions. The classical definition of strategy places the strategist on the horns of a dilemma. Concurrently, strategy is to provide both focus and flexibility. Paradox often sits at the center of strategic problems and their resolution is a key aspect of strategic thinking. To resolve this dilemma, it is necessary to design both specific future positions (in the sense of Section 3.3) to provide focus and pivot positions to provide flexibility. A pivot position is the same as a specific position except its definition would focus on the maneuverability attributes of its definition. Since the future specific position embraces the pivot position, if and when necessary, one can "back up" and set off in a new direction with minimum disruption.

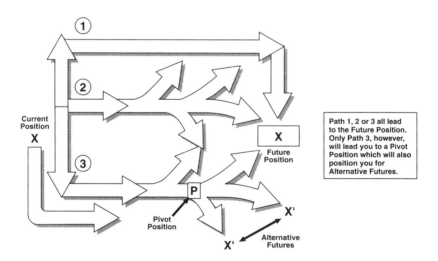

Path 1, 2 or 3 all lead to the Future Position. Only Path 3, however, will lead you to a Pivot Position which will also position you for Alternative Futures.

Figure 3.36   Pivot Analysis. Pivot analysis identifies a position to be obtained which is a point of maneuverability.

Sun Tzu says:

In battle, confrontation is done directly, victory is gained by surprise.[20]

Pivot positions are therefore required to deal with the fact that our desired and designed future is, at best, probabilistic. Time and circumstances will bring surprises. Competitors may surprise you, customers may surprise you, or you may wish to surprise others. Pivot positions allow for this flexibility and are mandated by the definition of strategy. The Reach/Range/Maneuverability Architecture discussed in Section 2.1 is an example of the IM&M architecture elevated to a pivot position.

A methodology for developing pivot positions would be as follows:

1.   Using the scenario methodology previously presented, develop a set of information technology scenarios.

2.   Using the scenario methodology previously presented, develop a set of customer futures scenarios. Customer needs and technology possibilities are the two primary drivers of future positions.

3.   Create a scenarios matrix, Table 3.39, matricing the technology futures against the customer futures.

4.   Select those strategic areas for which you desire to develop pivot positions. Typical candidates would be core competencies, capabilities, IM&M architecture, supplier relationships, and alliances.

5.   For each selected area, test the continued viability of your current position for that area against the matrix cells. In which cells will your current position remain viable? This tells you the staying power of your current positions.

Table 3.39
Scenario Matrix. Pivot positions can be developed by analyzing what future positions may be required.

		IM&M Futures			
		Scenario 1	Scenario 2	Scenario 3	Scenario N
Customer Futures	Scenario 1				
	Scenario 2				
	Scenario 3				
	Scenario N				

6. For each selected area, complete the matrix identifying what position is necessary to deal with that intersection of scenarios. Based on the positions developed, lay them out into a combination of end states and enabling states (those positions that lead to an end state) analogous to Figure 3.36. If natural pivot positions do not emerge, design in a pivot position that leads to these end states.

As is the case with all positions, pivot positions must be designed to be extensible, i.e., one must always be able to imagine that having achieved a position, an ever better position is achievable.

IM&M Strategic Planning Impact: In Section 3.3, it was asserted that one must decide which strategic areas will be put under position management. This notion has to be extended to a decision concerning which strategic areas will be placed under specific position management, pivot position management, neither, or both. We will develop this idea in Section 4.1.

Summary

Situational analysis is the application of analytical methods for the purpose of developing insight and understanding about the state of the business. Situational analysis aids in effective and efficient data reduction. It assists in developing the agenda of what needs to be focused on in a given planning cycle. Without the use of the various analytical methods, the quantity and unstructured nature of the data about the business would prohibit meaningful analysis. Situational analysis is not a prescription for detached analysis, but a prescription for the use of structured inquiry tempered by sensitivity and intimate understanding of the business. It is a prescription for intense and focused strategic thinking about the business.

In this section, we have tried to cull the most advantageous methods from the wide assortment of techniques available. It is not at all improbable that although we have tried to present this information in a manner to minimize misunderstanding, it may nevertheless be understood to convey a meaning different from that which is intended. It is my view that these methods are equally important and of utility whether you engage in formal but expedited strategy formulation or engage in a more dynamic *ad-hoc* method. In both cases, what is of prime importance is to have aids to focus the analysis of the information. This is exactly what situational analysis techniques provide.

3.5   Conclusions

Conclusions are explicit statements describing the state of the business. They are descriptive and demand exploitative or remedial actions. They are not an exhaustive "health check," and only conclusions requiring action need be itemized. Conclusions are the culmination of assessment and provide the focus of attention for the strategy step. Conclusions must be succinct, clear, and demand attention. They are the composite statement of what management must focus strategic attention upon. A conclusion:

1. Identifies which issues are vitally important,
2. Identifies what drives each issue,
3. Identifies the relationship of each issue to the whole, and
4. By absence, identifies which issues are not vitally important.

It is in reaction to conclusions that creative and innovative strategy must be developed.

Table 3.40 illustrates the format of a conclusion. The elements are as follows:

- *Conclusion*—a succinct statement of the opportunity or problem uncovered,
- *Description*—a brief explanation of the conclusion,
- *Etiology*—an explanation of the root cause of the conclusion,
- *Possible actions (Strategic moves)*—a speculative list of actions which could be taken to deal with the conclusion, and
- *Supporting evidence*—detailed or summarized information from the positioning and situational analysis to support the validity of the conclusion. The evidence should provide a "convincing argument." The amount of evidence required is a function of the credibility of the creators of the conclusion and the controversy which the conclusion may invoke, i.e., how big a change would the conclusion imply and how politically upsetting would that be.

The description or etiology should identify the explanatory strategic framework which governs the conclusion, i.e., misalignment, five-force shift, value chain, etc. By identifying the explanatory strategic framework, all the knowledge of the framework is associated with the conclusion.

Table 3.40
Conclusions. Conclusions identify the imperative items that demand
strategic attention by management.

Conclusion Attribute	Definition
Conclusion	A short explicit statement that succinctly and clearly identifies a situation requiring strategic attention
Description	A one to three paragraph explanation of the conclusion
Etiology	An explanation of the root causes of the conclusion
Possible actions (strategic moves)	Examples of what actions may be taken to deal with the conclusion
Supporting evidence	Convincing arguments to support the conclusion

3.6   Summary

Assessment is the process of deciding what to focus attention upon. Figure 3.37 illustrates the thrust of assessment which is to perform a comprehensive review of the business from multiple dimensions in order to uncover gaps. Gaps may be gaps of performance and execution (cost, quality, logistics, cycle time, productivity, profitability, etc.) or gaps of opportunity (markets, customer satisfaction, growth, leverage, new products, etc.).

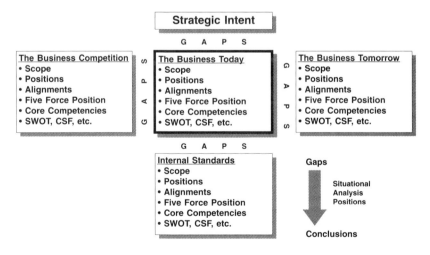

Figure 3.37   Assessment Summary. Gap analysis is the driving analytical methodology.

Gaps identify the Achilles heels of yourself and your competitors. Sun Tzu says:

> Attack what can be overcome, do not attack what cannot be overcome.… To advance irresistibly, push through their gaps.… So when the front is prepared, the rear is lacking, and when the rear is prepared the front is lacking. Preparedness on the left means lack on the right, preparedness on the right means lack on the left. Preparedness everywhere means lack everywhere.… Attack where there is no defense.[21]

The gaps should not only identify the deltas between the current position and a desired one, but also explain the reasons for the difference. This provides initial hints for developing first cut strategies. Table 3.41 illustrates how the gap perspective makes problems and opportunities visible. Gaps drive the identification of conclusions which clamor for management attention and action.

Table 3.41

IM&M Organization Economic System. Through gap analysis, conclusions can be drawn on what changes are required in the design of the economic systems which govern both commerce with the customers and within the IM&M organization.

Key Economy Design Questions (Examples)	Economic System Between IM&M Organization and Other Business Organizations				Economic System Within the IM&M Organization		
	Current State	Customer Desired	External Bench mark	IM&M Desired	Current State	External Bench mark	IM&M Desired
1. How is market demand governed?							
2. Are customers free to choose suppliers?							
3. Are suppliers free not to supply?							
4. Are technologies regulated?							
5. Who controls budgets?							
6. What is the relationship between supplier and customer—free market or monopoly?							

While gap analysis drives the identification of conclusions, conclusions are often the synthesis of multiple individual analyses and therefore of complex origin. The receptivity of the conclusion by the corporate community is enhanced by graphical presentation. As has been demonstrated throughout this section, diagrams, graphs, matrices, etc. are far superior tools for visualization and communication. Conclusions may be summarized using a *conclusion map* (see Figure 3.38). The conclusion map presents the primary logic chain that was followed to reach the conclusion and diagrams in the "Supporting Evidence" part of the conclusion (see Table 3.40). As shown by the legend of Figure 3.38, a piece of evidence leads to other pieces of evidence. The relationship between distinct items of evidence is indicated by a pointed arrow. A plus sign on the arrow indicates that the first piece of evidence had a "positive impact" in leading to the linked item. Conversely, a minus sign indicates that the first piece of evidence had a "negative influence" in leading to the linked item. The conclusion is stated in the octagon symbol. A conclusion map may be appended to each conclusion to enhance its validity, and it serves as an excellent means of presenting the conclusion to an audience. It is advisable to keep the maps straightforward, limit them to one page per conclusion, and not decompose them. The objective is to summarize the essence of the convincing argument as simply as possible. Obviously, at a summary or detail level, conclusion maps may be used as working documents to help develop as well as document the conclusions.

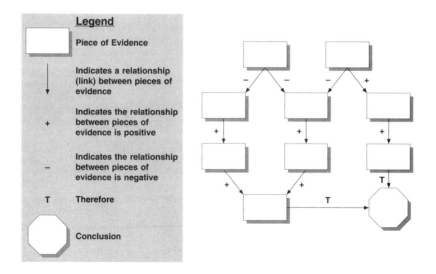

Figure 3.38 Conclusion Map. This diagramming technique may be used to summarize the logical deduction which was made to adduce the conclusion.

Assessment is based on understanding the current and projected future states of multiple strategic variables. When assessment is limited to only competition or only customers or only products, etc., the seeds of future problems are sown. They are sown because misalignment is created and problems are not forestalled. A strategist must view the business as a polyphony; each function performing its individual function in perfect harmony with all others.

Table 3.41
IM&M Organization Economic System. Through gap analysis, conclusions can be drawn on what changes are required in the design of the economic systems which govern both commerce with the customers and within the IM&M organization.

Key Economy Design Questions (Examples)	Economic System Between IM&M Organization and Other Business Organizations				Economic System Within the IM&M Organization		
	Current State	Customer Desired	External Bench mark	IM&M Desired	Current State	External Bench mark	IM&M Desired
1. How is market demand governed?							
2. Are customers free to choose suppliers?							
3. Are suppliers free not to supply?							
4. Are technologies regulated?							
5. Who controls budgets?							
6. What is the relationship between supplier and customer—free market or monopoly?							

Footnotes

1. Sun Tzu, *The Art of War.*
2. Based on the work of C. K. Prahaldad and G. Hamel.
3. Sun Tzu, *The Art Of War.*
4. B. Tregoe and J. Zimmerman, *Top Management Strategy.*
5. Sun Tzu, *The Art Of War.*
6. Sun Tzu, *The Art Of War.*
7. Sun Tzu, *The Art Of War.*
8. Based on the work of C. K. Prahaldad and G. Hamel.
9. G. Stalk, P. Evans, and L. Shulman, *Competing on Capabilities.*
10. Based on the work of Dr. Michael Porter.
11. Sun Tzu, *The Art Of War.*
12. Sun Tzu, *The Art Of War.*
13. Sun Tzu, *The Art Of War.*
14. Northeast Consulting Resources, Inc.
15. Ibid.
16. Based on the work of Dr. Michael Porter.
17. Machiavelli, *The Prince.*
18. Sun Tzu, *The Art Of War.*
19. Sun Tzu, *The Art Of War.*
20. Sun Tzu, *The Art Of War.*
21. Sun Tzu, *The Art of War.*

4

Strategy

The purpose of this chapter is to explain the strategy step of the strategic planning process. *Strategy* is the definition of both what is to be accomplished and the means of accomplishment. As the assessment step filters the environment to determine what to focus on, the strategy step sieves through the alternative objectives and actions to determine what is to be done. Figure 4.1 is an enlargement of the strategy step. It will be explained in the following manner:

- Section 4.1: *The Future Business Scope and Position*

    This section will explain the notion of a future business scope and set of strategic positions. In the assessment step, the current businsss scope and strategic positions are defined. Future improvements and adjustments to these are defined in this step.

- Section 4.2: *Objectives*

    This section explains the development of objectives. *Objectives* are specific measurable results to be accomplished during this planning cycle.

- Section 4.3: *Strategic Moves*

    This chapter explains how to develop strategic moves. *Strategic moves* are coherent and purposeful actions taken to achieve an objective. They are the prescriptive actions that move the organization form its current positions to realizing its objectives and future business scope and strategic positions.

- Section 4.4: *Change Management Plan*

    This section will explain the development of specific actions to deal with the problems of organizational change. Strategic actions are designed and intended to cause change and movement. Inevitably, resistance occurs within the organization due to multiple motivations. This section will analyze the cause of the resistance and actions to be taken to overcome change barriers.

- Section 4.5: *Commitment Plan*

  This section will explain issues surrounding the development of a commitment plan. A *commitment plan* is a specific set of actions taken to establish the creditability of the overall plan. A strategic plan can only succeed with wide-ranging organizational commitment to its success.

- Section 4.6: *Summary*

  This section will summarize the major ideas of this chapter.

Sun Tzu says:

When your strategy is deep and far-reaching, then what you gain by your calculations is much, so you can win before you even fight. When your strategic thinking is shallow and near-sighted, then what you gain by your calculations is little, so you lose before you do battle. Much strategy prevails over little strategy, so those with no strategy cannot but be defeated. Therefore it is said that victorious warriors win first and then go to war, while defeated warriors go to war first and then seek to win. [1]

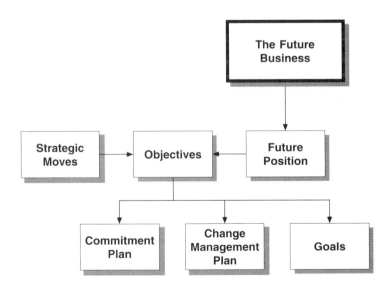

Figure 4.1 Strategy. The Strategy Step identifies both what is to be accomplished and the means

Consistent with the business scope notion of strategic intent, the intent of the strategy step is to develop a strategy that is "deep and far-reaching."

4.1   The Future Business Scope and Position

The future business scope and position defines the desired future state of the business in terms of a new business scope and a new set of strategic positions. It is this new business scope and set of positions that are to be achieved during the planning cycle. As illustrated in Figure 4.2, the intent is to move the business from its current scope and positions, which are documented in the assessment step (Chapter 3), to a new scope and set of positions closer to our strategic intent. We wish to transform the business from $P_{\text{current business scope and positions}}$ to $P_{\text{future business scope and positions}}$.

The definition of the Future Business Scope and Positions requires the most intense strategic thinking on the part of the strategy team. This is the definition of what the business is to be; it may be incrementally different from the present or it may be radically different. In either case, it is the "end zone" for the planning period and requires the most intense thinking. It is to this future that all strategic actions will be targeted, therefore it calls for careful definition and measured forethought.

Any change in the business scope will motivate realignment actions throughout the organization. Gaps between the current positions and desired future positions will require actions to close. The future business scope and positions coupled with the conclusions from the assessment step provide the playing field for developing objectives and strategic moves for the planning cycle.

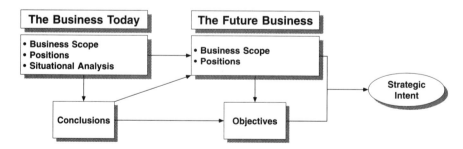

Figure 4.2   Future Business Scope and Positions. The future business scope and positions define the desired future state of the business at the completion of the strategic planning period.

Two types of future positions must be defined: specific positions which provide focus for the organization and pivot positions which allow for flexibility in order to address any future surprises. There are five choices to select from:

1. *You cannot define any future positions.* In this case, you have abandoned the responsibilities of leadership because you provide neither focus nor flexibility for the business.

2. *You can define only specific future positions.* In this case, you meet the responsibility of focus but neglect the equal responsibility of flexibility.

3. *You can define only pivot positions.* In this case, you meet the responsibility of flexibility but neglect the equally important responsibility of focus. Nevertheless, this may be prudent to do if you are one who believes setting fixed objectives is meaningless.

4. *You can define both specific positions and pivot positions.* In this case, you meet the classical definition of strategy.

5. *You can mix and match, as appropriate, based on time and circumstances.* This option may be best of all.

Your choice must balance the need to provide a clear target for the organization while permitting the organization to maneuver with minimal difficulty in the event of surprises.

The statement of positions and pivot positions can therefore be modulated and calibrated to be in conformity with the degree of stability or turbulence of the business environment. For highly turbulent times, pivot positions may be defined to posture for mobility in the face of certain uncertainty. In times of stability and predictability, fixed positions can be defined to provide a precise target for the business. As required, fixed positions only, pivot positons only, or both may be defined by strategic area to be sensitive to the distinct condition of volatility of each area. In this manner, the future positions of the business may be defined in accord with the times and circumstances.

4.2   Objectives and Goals

Objectives define specific measurable states to be accomplished. A good objective is measurable, achievable, explicit, succinct and clear, dated, and consistent with all other objectives. Measurement may be defined in any of three modes:

Table 4.1
Objectives. The definition of objectives and goals is the same, except
goals usually do not require a contingency plan.

Objective Attribute	Definition
Objective	A precise and concise statement of the objective
Date	By when the objective is to be achieved
Measure	The measurement(s) to be used to assess whether the objective has been accomplished
Contingency plan	A plan to deal with a low-probability but high-risk event whose occurrence would jeopardize realizing the objective

- *Existence*—Something which didn't exist now exists (or the converse),
- *Effectiveness*—A quantifiable measure of satisfaction, or
- *Efficiency*—A quantifiable measure of productivity.

Objectives are realized incrementally in the form of serial goals which are dated interim positions of accomplishment on the way to realization of the objective. Table 4.1 defines the format of an objective. The format of a goal is identical except a contingency plan is often not required.

Objectives often overlap and in many cases will equate to future positions, i.e., the objective is to achieve the desired future strategic position. One could eliminate the notion of objectives and use the future positions as the direct targets for the strategic moves. The reason for not doing this, adding a level of indirection, is that most companies will not position everything; rather they will put a relatively small number of strategic areas under "positioning management." Nevertheless, it may be desirable to set objectives for the planning period for non-positioned items. By structurally separating positions from objectives, one does not need to completely position everything that one may wish to set an objective for. Conversely, if one either positions all strategic areas or only wishes to achieve positioned items, objectives become redundant. They can be eliminated and their additional attributes (contingency plan and goals) can be associated with future positions. This discussion assumes that relatively few areas are positioned and that objectives need to be set for non-positioned items.

Objective Setting

Objective setting is an art. As shown in Figure 4.3, objectives represent the resolution of conclusions and the realization of the desired future business state (business scope and positions). While analytical techniques can provide assistance, especially in forecasting future financial and market-share objectives, objective setting is more characterized by vision, insight, and business feel and savvy than rigorous techniques.

As previously stated, good objectives are rigorously defined, explicit, dated, and measurable. Some theorists recommend an alternative called *regimen objectives*. Regimen objectives focus on doing the right things; a healthy regimen will lead to success. Consequently, they focus less on objectives and more on strategic moves. Regimen objectives are an interesting but minority approach.

Objective Relationships

Objectives have important relationships with other strategic planning outputs. As shown in Figure 4.4:

- A conclusion is satisfied through the accomplishment of multiple objectives. Multiple objectives, collectively, satisfy a conclusion.
- The future business scope and positions are realized by accomplishing multiple objectives. Multiple objectives, collectively, accomplish the realization of each future position and the business scope.
- Multiple strategic moves, collectively, enable the accomplishment of an objective. Multiple objectives are realized by each move.

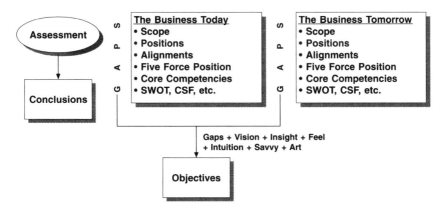

Figure 4.3   Objective Setting. Objective setting is an art driven by the need to close future position gaps and resolve existing conclusions.

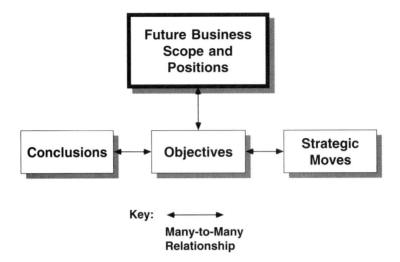

Figure 4.4   Objective Relationships. Objectives exist in complicated many-to-many relationships with other key strategy outputs.

Objectives exist in a pivotal and complicated state of many-to-many relationships with the other strategic planning outputs of conclusions, strategic moves, and future business scope and positions.

Standing Objectives

Normally three standing objectives exist, i.e., objectives which are always automatically defined. These objectives are:

1. *Financial*—define profitability, ROI, cash-flow, etc.,
2. *Market share*—define market share objectives for each market segment, and
3. *Customer satisfaction*—define customer satisfaction objectives per product or product group.

The logic of this is that continued success in these three critical areas is always mandatory to preempt business decay. At minimum, failure in these crucial areas leads to inadequate margins to fund reinvestment in new products, staff development, customer satisfaction, competencies, capabilities, etc. The consequence is a vicious downward cycle. Consequently, standing objectives represent the minimum set of objectives for the strategic plan.

Contingency Plan

A contingency plan is a plan to deal with a possible event that could pre-vent achieving an objective. Contingency plans cover high-risk but low-probability situations. By anticipating and planning for such events, responses may be designed which can contain the problem based on an identified trigger event.

Table 4.2 provides a decision aid to use in considering when a contin-gency plan is warranted. Contingency plan development consists of six steps:

1. Define the set of possible high-risk but low-probability situations for each objective.
2. Identify trigger mechanisms.
3. Define consequences to objectives of each event.
4. Define responses. What actions would be taken and what alterna-tive objectives would be set?
5. Test the plan (walk-through, simulation, devil advocacy, expert opinion, etc.).
6. Interlock the plans.

Sun Tzu says:

Those who are good at getting rid of trouble are those who take care of it before it arises.[2]

Contingency planning eliminates uncertainty, confusion, and delays in reacting to potentially catastrophic events and minimizing the damage. The contingency plan helps assure that either the original objective is still obtainable or that a substitute but acceptable objective is realized.

Table 4.2
When Contingency Plans. Contingency plans are used for events which pose high risks but have low-probabilities.

		Probability of Occurrence	
		High	**Low**
Risk	**High**	Include for in strategic plan	Contingency plan
	Low		Deal with it when and if it occurs

Setting Goals

Goals are interim points of accomplishment on the path to achieving an objective. They share the same attributes as objectives in that they should be succinct, clear, measurable, and dated. As shown in Figure 4.5, goals may be developed by working backward from the objective and answering the question: Where must I be and when must I be there to achieve the objective by the stated date?

Summary

Leadership requires providing the organization with a clear definition of what is to be accomplished. How can alignment take place if the desired future state is fuzzy and ambiguous? Objectives coupled with the future business scope and positions define an unambiguous target for the organization. This is vitally important for an IM&M organization during such turbulent times.

4.3   Strategic Moves

Strategic moves are purposeful and coherent actions taken to achieve one or more objectives. Strategic moves are prescriptive; they identify exactly what is to be done. They are purposeful in that they directly act to achieve

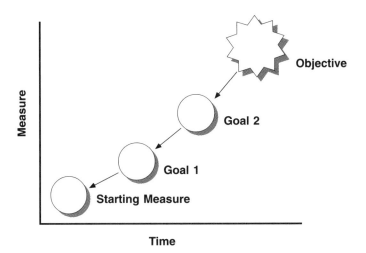

Figure 4.5   Setting Goals. Goals are normally set by working backward from the objective.

an objective. They are coherent in that there is synergy between them. They do not block, retard, or contradict each other, rather they complement and support each other. Strategic moves identify what is to be done, but they do not tell how. As was shown in Figure 4.4, a move may provide leverage by helping to realize multiple objectives.

There is a great deal of ambiguity with regard to the use and meaning of the word *strategy*. We use the word strategy to mean the second step of the strategic planning process which embodies a future business scope, future strategic positions, objectives, strategic moves, a change management plan, and a commitment plan. We use the label *strategic move* (used interchangeably with *strategic action* or *initiative*) to mean a specific action undertaken to achieve an objective. The word strategy is often used to mean strategic move and, sometimes in the same article, it is also used to mean both our meaning of strategy and strategic move based on usage context. As this can become very confusing, we use the phrase strategic move to denote specific strategic actions and the word strategy to denote the second step of the strategic planning process with all the components that it implies. Strategy is more than just actions. It is the robust definition of what is to be and how it is to be achieved.

Elements

Table 4.3 summarizes the format of a move. Each element is explained as follows:

- *Move*—A brief, succinct, and clear statement of the action. A strategic move should contain an action verb and prescribe what is to be done.

- *Description*—A brief elaboration of the strategic move. An important part of the design of a strategic move is *leverage*. Leverage is the amplifier, multiplier, and accelerator of the benefits of an action, i.e., leverage = (strategic move x multiplier x payoff). Typical multipliers are reusability, sharing, open accessibility, linkage, replicability, duplicability, layering, economies of scale, maneuverability, economies of scope, synergy, dispersion, cascading, and modularity. However beneficial a strategic move may be, it can be made an order of magnitude better by designing leverage into it. Leverage gives the strategic action "muscle."

  The Core Competency framework which was presented in Section 3.3 is an excellent example of leverage. Multiple core competencies are combined into multiple core products which serve multiple business units which contribute to multiple end products. Through this layering approach, core competencies are multiplied and reused to leverage their benefits.

- *Owner*—The individual in the organization who is responsible for implementing the strategic move. Owners are individuals throughout the business; remember, strategic actions are horizontal in magnitude. There is only one owner per action, and that should be an individual, not an organization, so accountability can be pinpointed.

- *Champion*—The strategy team member charged with "championing" the move. Champions are alternatively referred to as managing partners, change managers, and executive sponsors. While the owner "owns" the direct problem of implementing the initiative, the champion has the ancillary responsibility of providing continual high-level support, counsel, and focus for the effort.

- *Rationale*—Explains the business justification for the action: Exactly why should we take this action? Table 4.4 summarizes common approaches to justifying actions. Not surprisingly, many strategic moves are justified based on strategic importance, i.e., in order to realize the future business scope and future strategic positions, this action is required. The other methods, particularly the economic justification set, are used by the implementation teams to choose how best to implement the action.

- *Priority*—All strategic moves are, by definition, important. Priority should be understood as relative importance among the very important. A typical priority classification scheme would include labels of imperative, high, medium, and low.

- *Measurement*—Defines by the criteria of existence, effectiveness, and efficiency the manner in which success will be measured.

- *Date*—Defines the specific time by when the initiative is to be concluded.

- *Implementation program parameters (IPP)*—Strategic moves define what is to be done but not how. IPP provide directions and boundaries of action for the implementation owner. IPP are used to force alignment of actions and to explicitly state that not only does an action need to be done, but it needs to be done within certain constraints. Figure 4.6 illustrates this concept. It is interesting to observe that IPP serve the same function, albeit at a lower strategy level, that directives and assumptions serve to the assessment step.

Strategic moves should be designed to encourage experimentation, trial and error, and continuous learning and adaptation in their implementation. Sun Tzu says:

> Test them to find out where they are sufficient and where they are lacking. Do something for or against them, making opponents turn their attention to it, so that you can find out their patterns of aggressive and defensive behavior.[3]

No matter how carefully formulated the strategy is, it is still conjecture. Mixing in experimentation as an integral component first tempers and then guides our actions by the sobering effects of reality. Strategic moves, therefore, must also include sponsoring experiments, prototypes, trial and error, etc. to provide proof-of-concept and generate convincing evidence to support a full commitment. In this way, endless cycles of experimentation and reason complement each other. The results from experiments provide evidence to evaluate whether or not full strategic commitment is warranted. Conversely, the actual results from monitoring strategic moves in progress provide feedback so moves can be accelerated, modified, or abandoned. In a sense, the sense of learning and adaptation, all moves are experiments, but experiments with widely varying degrees of expectations, maturity, and commitment.

Figure 4.6 Implementation Program Parameters. Implementation program parameters define explicit conditions to be followed by the implementation owner in implementing the strategy.

Table 4.3
Strategic Moves. A well defined strategic move consists of nine elements.

Strategic Move Attribute	Definition
Move	A brief and clear statement of the action
Description	A few paragraphs elaboration of the action.
Owner	The individual in the organization responsible for making the action happen.
Champion	The executive in the organization responsible for assisting the owner.
Rationale	The business logic of the action
Priority	Relative importance of the action
Measurement	The way to measure that the action has been completed.
Date	The date by which the action is to be concluded
Implementation program parameters	Rules, guidelines, boundaries, etc. That the implementation owner should follow in implementing the action

Table 4.4
Justification Methods. Strategic moves may be justified in a variety of ways.

Justification Methods	
Portfolio Views actions as contributing to building a balanced portfolio	*Analytic* Analytic techniques which balance risk against value
Economic Estimate cost savings and revenue growth and incorporate the time value of money Examples: 1. Cash flow 2. Discounted cash flow 3. Net present value 4. Payback 5. Accounting ROI	*Strategic* Justification based on meeting strategic requirements Examples: 1. Strategic intent 2. Alignment 3. SCA 4. Competitive parity 5. Maneuverability

Tactics

Strategic moves are executed through the development of *tactics*. Tactics are the detailed actions taken to implement the initiative. They are formulated by the implementation owner together with her project team. Tactics need to be responsive and sensitive to the evolving environmental situation. Sun Tzu says:

> Adaptation means not clinging to fixed methods, but changing appropriately to events…those who can face the unprepared with preparation are victorious. The ability to gain victory by changing and adapting to the opponent is called genius.[4]

Tactics provide the malleable part of the strategic plan to allow for adaptation to the constantly changing reality. Objectives define what is to be accomplished. Strategic moves define the ways. Tactics define the explicit "how," but do so in a flexible and dynamic manner in accord with events.

Formulation

The formulation of strategic actions is a difficult task. It is difficult because of the risk, uncertainty, and consequences of the actions. In addition to the ideas generated during the assessment step and the candidate actions proposed as part of the conclusions, there are six common approaches to developing moves. *Art* is clearly the dominant approach. Each will be explained individually.

1. Formula

Formula methods represent codified experience which has proved successful in the past. Table 4.5 and Table 4.6 are examples of this approach. The former defines actions in terms of the intersection of competitive position and market growth. The latter defines actions as a function of product-life cycle position. Strategic action equates to locating the position of a product on the respective matrices and executing the indicated actions.

While helpful as a starting point, these approaches are transparent, easily decoded by competitors, and do not suggest novel or creative actions. Unfortunately, your competitors have access to the same formulas and may consequently anticipate your actions. Strategy is to be "…deep and far-reaching," not ritualistic or fill-in-the-blanks.

Table 4.5

Competition/Market Growth. This formula matrix can be used to decide major actions for a given product.

Market Growth	Competitive Position		
	Strong	**Medium**	**Weak**
High	*Protect* 1. Invest to grow at maximum rate 2. Maintain strengths 3. Expand business	*Invest to build* 1. Challenge for leadership 2. Build on strengths 3. Eliminate weaknesses 4. Expand business	*Build selectively* 1. Specialize around strengths 2. Build on strengths 3. Eliminate weaknesses 4. Expand business
Medium	*Build selectively* 1. Invest to grow at maximum rate 2. Maintain strength 3. Expand business	*Manage for earnings* 1. Protect 2. Focus on high profitability segments 3.Low risk	*Limited expansion* 1. Low risk expansion 2. Minimize investment
Low	*Protect and refocus* 1. Manage for current earnings 2. Defend strengths 3. Milk product	*Manage for earning* 1. Protect 2. Minimize investment 3. Milk product	*Divest* 1.Sell 2. Avoid investment

Table 4.6

Product Life Cycle. This formula prescribes strategic actions as a function of the product life cycle position of the product.

Strategic Dimension	Product Life Cycle Stage			
	Introduction	**Growth**	**Maturity**	**Decline**
Overall thrust	Market establishment	Market penetration	Market defense	Milk
Customer	Innovative	Mass market	Mass market	Laggards
Channels	Few	Many	Many	Dwindling
Advertising	Awareness	Mass market benefits	Differentiation	Minimum
Price	High	Lower	Lowest	Rising
Configurations	Basic	Constant improvement	Sophisticated	Slow change

2. Analytical Methods

Analytical methods are a set of frameworks, models, analysis techniques, etc., which assist in formulating actions. They are similar in nature to those applied during the assessment step. Three representative methods are as follows:

1. Strategic Thrust (Figure 4.7)—The purpose of this method is to develop a repositioning goal for each product and define the means of attainment. The process is as follows:

   - Position each product by the dimensions of competitive position and market share.
   - Select a "strategic thrust" for the product, i.e., expansion, explosion, continued growth, slip, contraction, or consolidation.
   - Define the actions needed to accomplish the thrust.

     Strategic thrust is particularly powerful because of the way it can individually and collectively show the intended movement of the product portfolio.

2. Market Opportunity Analysis—*Market Opportunity Analysis* is the use of a set of analytical and positioning methods to assess both the attractiveness of a market opportunity and the necessary actions that need to be taken in order to succeed. Typically included in a market opportunity analysis would be market segmentation, competitor analysis, SWOT analysis, critical success factors, core competencies, FiveForce analysis, new product positioning, and market-entry analysis.

   All these techniques have been explained except market entry analysis which is illustrated in Table 4.7. *Market-entry analysis* provides a structured framework to analyze the alternative paths of entering a market. Most of the market-entry alternatives require in one form or another the selection of a partner. In choosing the suitability of a partner, one must consider:

   - What would be the form of the partnership governance?
   - How will participation aid each partner in reaching their distinct strategic intents, future business scopes, future strategic positions, and objectives?
   - What would be the shared objectives and strategic moves of the partnership?
   - How would commitment be demonstrated?

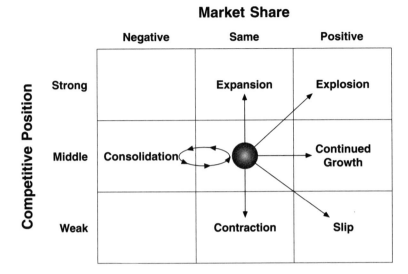

Figure 4.7   Strategic Thrust. Strategic thrust provides a vehicle to visualize the intended repositioning of a product during the planning cycle.

Table 4.7
Market-Entry Analysis. Each of the ways to enter a market needs to be considered.

Market Entry Options	Critical Success Factors	Risks	Leverage	Advantages	Disadvantages
Reseller					
Subcontractor					
Acquisition					
Strategic alliances					
Joint venture					
Start-up					
Existing product-line extension					
Franchise					

- What leverage does each partner bring to the partnership?
- How do distinct competencies and capabilities provide superior value when joined?
- What will be learned from each other?
- How will the economy of the joint effort be designed?
- When the partnership expires, will there be a net gain or a net loss in terms of transfer of capabilities, competencies, knowledge, etc.
- Partnerships are very serious undertakings which require careful strategic forethought.

As the complexity of IM&M increases, IM&M organization will increasingly need to enter into joint arrangements with other suppliers. Sun Tzu says:

> If you carry on alliances with strong countries, your enemies won't dare plot against you... Make informed alliances... compete for alliances... If you do not compete for alliances and helpers, then you will be isolated with little help.[5]

Given the technology turbulence and the shift to a free-market economy for IM&M services in many corporations, strong and competent friends are to be welcomed. Table 4.8 illustrates how Novell, which dominates the LAN network operating system market, has built a network of alliances.

3. Strategy Coherence—*Strategy coherence* is an algorithm to force alignment. Its objective is to test the proposed moves set iterativiely against each other and the business areas to discover additional actions which are required. Strategy coherence has four steps:

   1. The complete list of actions, however generated, is assembled.

   2. The actions are cross-checked for synergy. As a set, are they in alignment? If not, the actions are adjusted to force alignment. Recursively, this step is continued until alignment is achieved. Remember, when an action is adjusted it may cause new misalignment.

   3. The aligned actions are tested, set against all the business areas. Since the actions will change the positions of the immediately impacted business areas, adjoining areas may also need modification. Again, when an action is adjusted or added, new misalignments may be inadvertantly created.

4. Repeat the third step until perfect alignment is achieved.

This technique is time-consuming and meticulous, but it discovers missing actions during the strategy development phase rather then the implementation phase when shortcomings are more disruptive, embarrassing and expensive to fix.

Table 4.8
Novell Allies. Novell is an excellent example of a firm that builds a variety of alliances.

Type of Alliance	Other Party	Date	Objective
Joint Ventures	Next Inc	3/89	Netware on Next computers
	NCR Corp.	7/89	Netware for UNIX
	Apple	11/89	TCP-IP Support
	IBM	2/91	Netware for OS/2 and AIX
	Gupta	3/91	Netware with Gupta DBMS
	Borland	4/91	SQL DBMS access
	Sun	10/91	Netware for Sun
	HP	12/91	Netware for HP RISC Workstations
	USL	12/91	Univel joint venture
	Stratus	12/91	Netware for Stratus
	Compaq	2/92	Network management
	DEC	2/92	Netware for DEC product line
	3Com	2/92	Joint marketing
	Ing. C. Olivetti	3/92	Joint product development
	Lotus	4/92	Notes over Netware
	Ungermann-Bass	5/92	Netware/intelligent wiring hubs
	WordPerfect	6/92	WordPerfect over Netware
	CA	8/92	Netware/Mainframe management
	Memorex Telex	8/92	Netware with host SNA

Table 4.8 *continued*

Type of Alliance	Other Party	Date	Objective
Investments	Dayna Comm.	6/88	Macintosh connectivity
	Gupta	4/90	SQL DBMS Technology
	Indisy Software	10/90	IBM host-messaging software
	USL	4/91	Unix development
	Da Vinci Systems	7/91	E-mail software
	Serius Corp.	12/91	Objected-oriented technologies
	Cooperative Solutions Inc.	12/91	Client/Server transaction processing
Acquisitions	Microsource	11/85	Distribution company
	Cache data products	5/86	Distribution company
	Santa Clara systems	10/86	Storage subsystems
	CXI	3/87	LAN to host software
	Softcraft	3/87	Database tools
	Excelan	6/89	Unix and Macintosh networking
	Digital Research	7/91	DOS OS
	International Business Software	4/92	Virtual server technology
	Annatek systems	6/92	Automated software distribution
	Unix System Laboratories	12/92	Unix OS

The rational for performing this technique is best understood by analogy to chess. If you understand that a king may move one space in any direction, you know a little about the king and the moves of chess but not very much. If you are told additionally that a king may not move into a check, you know more, but still very little. If you wish to truly understand the consequences of moving the king, then you must understand all the moves and rules of the game. You must see and understand the king's moves in the totality and context of the whole game. The same is true of strategic moves. If you truly wish to understand the consequences of a strategic move, it must be tested and understood in the totality of the strategic game board.

4. *Principles*—Principles are general rules or maxims which have repeatedly proven successful when followed. The most interesting set of principles for business strategy do not come from the field of business but from the sphere of military strategy. Since warfare is the primal metaphor used in describing business competition, this is not completely surprising. A set of military strategic principles that have direct application to business strategy development are as follows:[6]

    1. Adjust you ends to your means.
    2. Keep your object in mind (focus).
    3. Choose the line of least expectation (surprise).
    4. Choose the line of least resistance—it is better to win through indirection than by direct confrontation.
    5. Choose a line of operation that offers alternative objectives (adaptability).
    6. Ensure that both dispositions are flexible and adaptable to circumstances (maneuverability).
    7. Do not throw your weight into a stroke while your opponent is on guard.
    8. Do not renew an attack along the same line or in the same form after it has once failed.

These principles provide a formula for developing moves that let you "thrive on chaos," but not in the popular meaning of the phrase. The popular meaning of the phrase suggests that one should accept, come to terms with, the chaos of the business environment and prosper by living with it. The eight principles would suggest that a better definition for "thriving on chaos" would involve taming chaos, creating order, purpose, and intent for yourself while perpetuating and extending chaos for your opponents. With the popular definition of "thriving on chaos," it is not possible to build deep and far reaching strategies because chaos invalidates any and all long-term plans. With the newer definition, not only can you build deep and far reaching strategies, but you can concurrently position yourself to win and your opponents to lose. The higher rung on the strategic ladder is mastery and exploitation of chaos rather than resignation to chaos and living by your wits.

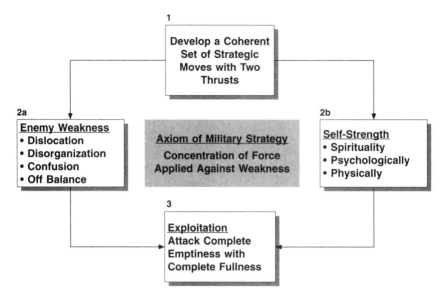

Figure 4.8 Military Strategy. The Military Strategy Model shows how to create dislocations to defeat an adversary.

Figure 4.8 illustrates how these principles are to be applied. The law (axiom) of military strategy is to apply "concentrated force against weakness." This is done as follows:

1. Develop a coherent set of strategic moves with two thrusts. Use the principles to guide the development of the actions.

2a. The first thrust is to create enemy weakness. Through strategic actions, cause confusion, dislocation, paralysis, fear, etc., in the enemy camp. Throw the opponent off-balance.

3b. Concurrently, take strategic action to strengthen and prepare yourself.

4. Exploit the strategic opportunity created by (2a) and (2b). Take advantage of the opponents dislocation and your own strength and "attack complete emptiness with complete fullness."

This model is very appropriate for understanding the true strategic significance of IM&M technology to the business. IM&M technology will achieve its optimum strategic value when the business can use it to create chosen dislocations in the marketplace and concurrently develop its own strength to exploit the consequences.

Viewed in this way, IM&M is not just administrative and record keeping systems; rather IM&M is the cutting edge of business conflict, permitting the business management to choose the time, place, and terms of competitive engagement.

The use of this method to design strategic moves is richly illustrated by use of what is called the *Kano methodology*. If you will recall from the discussion on product positioning in Section 3.3, an integral component of a product map is the customer satisfaction measurement system (see Figure 3.24). Following the Kano methodology, customer satisfaction drivers should be partitioned into three categories (see Figure 4.9):

1. *Threshold attributes*—Basic and important but quickly reach a saturation point. Added investment after a point results in a decreasing marginal benefit.

2. *Performance atrributes*—Very important; the more and better you do it, the more satisfied the customer. There is a linear effect between investment and customer satisfaction.

3. *Excitement drivers*—Extraordinary impact on customer satisfaction. The customer is satisfied far beyond expectations. There is a high leverage effect between added process investment and customer satisfaction.

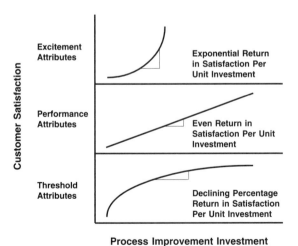

Figure 4.9   Kano Diagram. A Kano Diagram illustrates that superior customer satisfaction can be obtained by dividing customer satisfiers into three categories.

The relationship between added process investment and customer satisfaction is illustrated by the three rectangles in Figure 4.9.

One would then manage the Kano attributes as follows:

1. Invest in threshold attributes only to the point of saturation and no more.

2. Invest in performance attributes until they decay into threshold attributes.

3. Invest heavily in excitement drivers. Invest in them to the point that you have them mastered. Then reposition them in customer perception as threshold attributes. As shown in Figure 4.10, you will then have a basic set of customer satisfiers which you can fully meet that your competitors can't. By design, you will have created both a market dislocation and a large strategic distance between your ability to meet this basic customer requirement and that of your closest competitor.

By following the path of least expectation and least resistance, you concurrently create a difficulty for your competitors and a method of exploitation for yourself. There is no head on competition; to the contrary, you win by creating a far superior position for

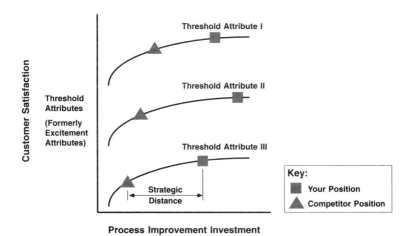

Figure 4.10   Excitement to Threshold. By driving excitement attributes to threshold attributes, you create a favorable dislocation in the marketplace.

yourself while creating an inferior position for the competitor. And, best of all, you vastly increase your customer's satisfaction in the process. Of course, this algorithm for dislocation and exploitation must be continuously re-executed, or else a competitor will catch you, or worse, turn the tables and do it to you.

The Kano methodology is exactly what farsighted developers did in adopting prototyping as a superior requirements definition strategy.[7] Recognizing that simplicity, speed, and visuality of requirements definition combined to form an excitement attribute, they developed robust application prototyping capabilities to replace incredibly slow and even more boring structured techniques. Users then flocked to those developers that could build requirements through prototyping. Developers, who could only do rigorous pre-specification methods, were left behind with a large strategic distance to overcome.

5. Key Findings—*Key findings* are learned during the assessment step, and are of particular important value. Examples of key findings are five force drivers, capabilities, core competencies, SWOTs, critical success factors, bottlenecks, and value chain drivers (cost and value-added). Key findings-based formulation focuses on using the key findings as the basis for developing actions to achieve the objectives.

6. Art—The book is called *The Art of War,* not *The Analytical Methods and Formulas of War.* Sun Tzu says:

> There are only five notes in the musical scale but the variations are so many that they all can't be heard. There are only five basic colors but the variations are so many, that they all can't be seen. There are only five basic flavors, but the varieties are so many that they can't all be tasted. There are only two basic charges in battle, the unorthodox surprise attack and the orthodox direct attack, but the variations of the orthodox and the unorthodox are endless. The unorthodox and the orthodox give rise to each other like a beginningless circle—who can exhaust them.[8]

The heart of strategy is surprise: the sewing together of a unique set of actions, unanticipated and unsuspected by the opposition for *this* encounter.

The formulation of strategic actions remains an art. All of the other methods help but deep and far-reaching actions are not the product of repetition. Instead, they spring from deep understanding of the situation. This is why strategy formulation is entrusted to the highest levels of the business. Through experience and demonstrated success, these individuals are best prepared to deal with the problem of developing a mixture of orthodox and unorthodox actions.

Organization Structure

Organization structure should follow strategy and should be crafted to facilitate the realization of the strategy. Reorganization alone is not strategy, and developing strategy with the constraint of a frozen organizational structure is not good strategy. Sun Tzu said:

> Structure depends on strategy. Forces are to be structured strategically based on what is advantageous.[9]

Organizational structure is a function of strategy; not the reverse. Figure 4.11 illustrates the relationship between structure and strategy.

IM&M organizational design, while always complex, is now even more challenging due to the technology shifts explained in Section 2.2. While organizational design must enable strategy, it must also take into account the pragmatic issues of culture, management style, reward systems, etc. So while design is peculiar to each, a starting point does exist. Figure 4.12 provides a starting point for designing an IM&M organization to deal with the challenges of the 1990s. The primary functions are as follows:

- *Operations*—experts in running the IM&M services,
- *Technology support*—experts in selecting, supporting, and integrating IM&M technologies,
- *Architecture and standards*—development and consensus building for an IM&M architectural blueprint for the firm,

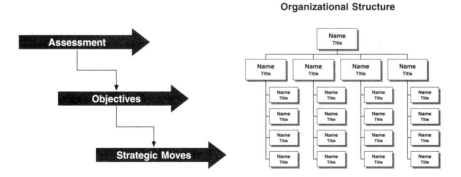

Figure 4.11 Structure Follows Strategy. Organizational structure is designed to facilitate the realization of the business strategy.

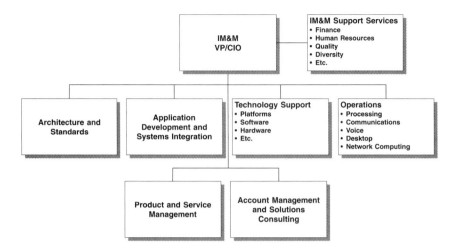

Figure 4.12   IM&M Organization Structure. While the exact organization design is unique to each business, these major functions would most likely be needed.

- *Product/service management*—overall product management responsible for all IM&M products and services,
- *Application development and systems integration*—experts in the design development and life cycle evolution of complex business applications,
- *Account management and consulting*—responsible for account management and providing business solutions consulting, and
- *Support services*—non-direct value chain functions such as finance, human resources, etc.

These seven functions would appear to be the building blocks for most IM&M organizations.

On top of this functional organization, an internal IM&M economy must be imposed to incent desired behaviors and decision making. Given the shift to network computing (and its requirement for horizontal end-to-end solutions), the presence of growing competition to the internal IM&M organization, the importance of process to success (capabilities and value chain strategic frameworks), and the primacy of alignment, the following is suggested:

1. Budget control should be given to the product management function.

2. Product management should buy processes form process owners throughout the organization. Process owners, not functional managers, sit on the product teams.

3. Process owners buy needed functions from the various functional organizations. The functional organization, analogous to object servers, advertise what services they can perform, and process owners string the services together to provide the end-to-end services needed to deliver the products.

Figure 4.13 illustrates this approach. Customers buy products. Product managers deliver products throughout their life cycle by contracting for horizontal process with internal process owners. Process owners subcontract with functional organizations to do required services. Functional organizations consume resources (expense elements) in delivering the services. This approach imposes a proper customer and supplier relationship within the IM&M organization, incents desired cooperative behaviors, and forces alignment through the funding of horizontal capabilities as opposed to vertical functions. Product managers can measure (cus-

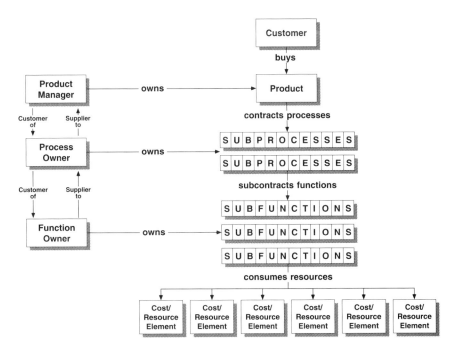

Figure 4.13 Internal IM&M Customer and Supplier Relationship. By imposing a proper economy on top of the organization structure, desired behaviors can be incented.

tomer satisfaction measurements) and negotiate for required processes. Process owners can measure and negotiate for needed functions. Function owners compete for usage and focus on controlling expense. As a by-product of imposing this type of economy on the organization, the organization is well positioned to perform value chain anlaysis to improve productivity, time, or value added. By organizing in this manner, product managers would not only fund research and development (R/D) for their products, but they would also fund R/D for their processes; both product and process would be subject to continual improvement.

Figure 4.14 illustrates how this concept may be applied to developing new client and server environments. A core systems integration group of the technology support organization contracts to engineer a new network computing platform. It then subcontracts to OAM, application support and application enabling specialist, to clip-on their respective pieces. This arrangement provides a proper customer and supplier relationship, encourages leverage, and assures that complete solutions will be developed. Once completed, multiple business applications can then be built on top of this reusable platform. A federation of developers, traditional centralized I/T, the users themselves, and

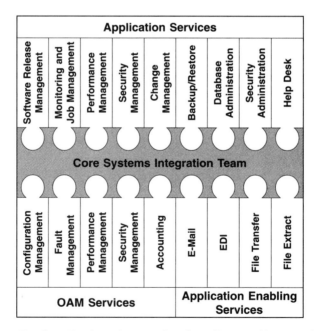

Figure 4.14 Product Engineering. To develop client and server platforms, it would be advantageous for the systems integration organization to organize in terms of a master systems integrator who implements the core capability and subcontracts to functional specialist who clip on their specific piece.

consultants can all attack the bottleneck of application development by standing on the common shoulders of the engineered client/server environment.

Imposing a customer and supplier market economy on the IM&M organization represents "big change," and "big change" often requires radical restructuring. The largest IM&M suborganziation (if not by head-count then by budget) is often the operations group. Understandably, they are often the most conservative; after all they have to make it work everyday. For large IM&M shops, it may be prudent to break the operations organization into multiple internally competing "factories" which bid to win work. This drives competition to the largest expense item on many IM&M organization balance sheets, dismantles the operations hegemony, and encourages free-market entreupreunship behaviors.

Figure 4.15 summarizes the economic problems of organization design. The organizational design must facilitate the efficient functioning of two economic systems, one between the IM&M organization and the other enterprise customers and one internal to the IM&M organization. Machiavelli coldly summed up the problem as follows:

> There is simply no comparison between a man who is armed (we read "armed" as budgetary control) and one who is not. It is unreasonable to expect the armed man should obey the one who is unarmed....This is how we can distinguish between innovators who standalone and those who depend on others; that is between those who to achieve their purpose can force the issue and those who must use persuasion. In the second case, they always come to grief having achieved nothing. Whenever they depend on their own resources and can force the issue, then they are seldom endangered.[10]

It is therfore impossible to properly do an organization design without proper consideration of how the economic system will provide gentle (and not so gentle) incentives to force alignment to serve the customer.

Summary

Strategic moves are the purposeful and coherent actions taken by the organization. Sun Tzu said:

> Go forth without having determined strategy and you will destroy yourself in battle.[11]

The development of strategy is not an optional extra.

With this broad understanding of strategy now accrued, what constitutes a strategic action can be clearly understood. An action is strategic when its successful execution, alone or in collaboration with other actions (serially or in parallel), will:

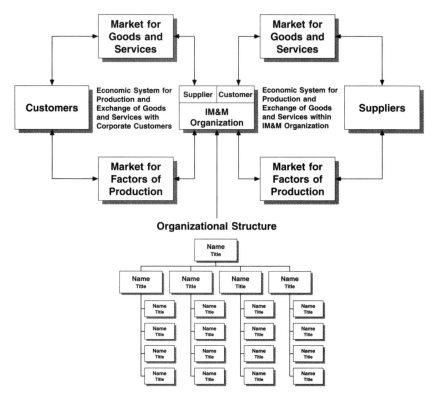

Figure 4.15   Organizational Structure and the Economy. The IM&M organization must be designed to support effective commerce both with the external corporate customer and within the IM&M organization.

1. Positively and materially alter one or more strategic position, or
2. Prevent a negative and material alteration in one or more strategic positions.

We refer to (1) above as an offensive action and to item (2) as a defensive action. If a move, an action, a push, an initiative, etc., can't do that, it may of value and worth doing, but it is not strategic.

4.4   Change Management Plan

A *change management plan* is a subplan to infuse the strategic plan with premeditated actions to preempt resistance to change and enroll the organization in the change effort. Strategy is change; movement from the a current set of (mis)aligned positions to a new set of positions. Many in the organization, for a wide variety of reasons, will resist. Resistance can be anticipated and planned for. The change management plan performs this function.

Frozen Mental Models

Table 4.9 uses the *root cause analytical method* to present an analysis of the causes of resistance. At the root of resistance is often a *frozen mental model*.[12] A mental model is a deeply held internal image of how the world works. It defines what is seen, how one sees, and how one comprehends and interprets what she sees. It provides a very personal framework for coping and dealing with the complex world. Mental models become "frozen" when one fails to adapt the mental model to a changing environment; though the world around is changing, the individual persists in the old comfortable and complacent view in denial of the emerging new reality. One becomes hermetically sealed to new information.

Mental models are deeply embedded and reinforced in close knit communities. They provide a familiar view of the world, "group think", which has been confirmed through shared experiences and successes. The underlying assumptions of how the world works are rarely stated or surfaced but shared by the community. Never subject to challenge or debate, the model freezes over time and automatically rejects new ideas which are considered threats rather than opportunities.

The genesis of many change problems is that a new idea is at variance with the "absolutely" correct mental model. Change threatens both the individual and community's mental model as they strive to reassert the "correct" view of the world. Given the tremendous personal investments and comfort it provides, individuals and organizations will fight hard and long to defend their mental model.

Table 4.9
Why Resistance. Resistance to change is often rooted in a frozen mental model.

Symptoms	Job status loss, loss of opportunity, limited mobility, loss of security, loss of relationships, loss of power, threat to skills, end of monopoly of knowledge or power, change of behavior and attitudes required, violation of implied covenant, likes the world as it is, devaluing of personal and career investment
Problem	Fear of change
Root cause	Frozen mental model

In Section 3.2, examples of two frozen mental models were provided; one being the Navy's resistance to shifting to steam-powered Man-of-Wars in the 1800s and the other being a heroic defense of traditional mainframe computing circa 1992. Both provided the classical symptom of a frozen mental model when the defender used the word "never." The Navy admirals said, "A steamer would *never* do as a sea going Man-of-War. The mainframe defender said, "Our mainframe will *never* die." Imagine, the current mainframe computing model of presentation, processing, and data manipulation all occurring on a centrally operated, proprietary-based environment which originated in the late 1960s remaining more or less as is *forever*. "Never" is the revealing clue of a frozen mental model. One can almost picture those with frozen mental models standing confidently inside their ice palace, impervious to the growing pools of water around their feet.

People with frozen mental models generally engage in the reasoning fallacy of "No True Scotsman" (see Table 3.31). They confuse and substitute an instance of a universal idea (human race, justice, mankind, etc.) for the universal. Mainframe computing is but an instance of the universal "business computing." The frozen mainframe partisans argue fallaciously as follows:

1. Mainframe computing is and only is business computing.
2. All other forms of computing are not mainframe computing.

   Therefore, all other forms of computing cannot and never will be business computing.

A counterexample to mainframe computing is not possible since mainframe computing has been made equivalent to business computing. A parallel set of reasoning explains the erroneous conclusions of the Navy Admirals.

Change strategy must focus on altering mental models, the root causes of the resistance problem. To accomplish this, a change management plan must:

1. Take actions to explicitly surface the embedded models and externalize the deeply held but unstated assumptions about how the world works,
2. Demonstrate the forward invalidity of the assumptions.
3. Unfreeze the model; get the community to concede that their model could be dated (the use of scenario sessions is a beneficial technique to accomplish this),
4. Provide convincing arguments that formulate a new mental model, and
5. Assist the community in understanding their changed roles and value in the new mental model.

It is not the intent to "refreeze" the organization in the new model. The staff must learn that especially in the IM&M field change will remain fluid. The enduring value of the staff members is in their professionalism, not their tactical expertise in a particular technology at a particular time. The creation of an adaptive organization which can gently switch mental models in accord with events has to be a linchpin of any IM&M strategy.

So the problem of frozen mental models is a problem of insight, or more accurately, the absence of insight. *Insight* is the ability of an individual to fully comprehend the true cause, meaning, and implications of a situation. There are multiple levels of insight:

- *True insight*—an understanding of the objective reality of a situation coupled with the motivation to take positive actions to master it,
- *Intellectual insight*—an understanding and acceptance of the objective reality of the situation but an inability and unwillingness to take actions to master it, and
- *Impaired insight*—a diminished ability to understand (for whatever reason) the objective reality of the situation. There is a wide range of impairment states:

  - complete denial,
  - slight awareness but strong denial,
  - awareness, but rather than acceptance a state of anger and bargaining at the unjust situation, and
  - begrudging acceptance with no willingness to positively confront the situation.

It is therefore the job of the change agent to move the organization from a state of impaired insight (a condition of being technologically comatose) to a state of true insight where positive actions can be taken to reverse the situation for everyone's advantage.

Methods for Dealing with Change

There exists a rich, behavioral science literature on ways to manage change. It is impossible to do justice to such a rich source of information in this book, and it is suggested that you research the topic. We would like, however, to present two examples. Table 4.10 is an example of generic guidance. It provides a variety of approaches based on the situational parameters. Except for "explict coercion," they all attempt to weaken resistance before overcoming it. Direct assualts on ideas which have substantial intellectual, emotional, and temporal investments will almost always force increased resistance. It is much better to craft change methods around "indirection." So when you can find allies among the impacted, divide and conquer. Package the change as natural evolution rather than revolution. Let people change at their own pace (see Figure 4.16). Find ways to appeal to their selfish interests to force alignment with your strategic interests.

Table 4.10
Change Methods. There is a variety of approaches to managing change which can be used individually or in combination.

Approach	Used When	Advantages	Disadvantages
Education and communication	Lack of information is cause of resistance	Supportive persuasion	Time-consuming
Participation and involvement	Empowerment is best method to gain buy-in	Enrolls organization	Time-consuming and risky
Facilitation and support	Organization suffers from morale decline	Deals with adjustment problems	Expensive
Manipulation	Time is of the essence	Quick	Staff reaction
Explicit coercion	Time is of the essence and you have the power	It works	Long-term consequences

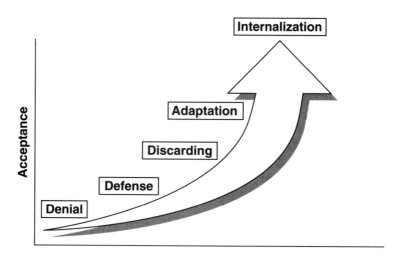

Figure 4.16   Stages of Change. People confronted with major change react in predictable patterns.

It is unfortunate, but not unusual, that the decisive change move must be to create a pseudo crisis to shock the organization out of complacency, smugness, arrogance, and misplaced confidence. As illustrated in Figure 2.52, time decays the degrees of freedom for strategic action. If the partisanship of "what was" is so severe as to preempt any possibilities of anticipatory change, the creation of a spurious crisis can be used to stimulate action. So if the organization will not be moved without acute pain, we will create artificial pain as preferable to real pain. A well designed forged crisis is built on six variables:

1. *Intensity*—The depth of the crisis will be such that it penetrates defense mechanisms. It cannot be ignored.

2. *Duration*—The length of the crisis will be sufficient to force attention. The discomfort will be enduring.

3. *Certainty*—The problem will not go away. There will be no remission; it must be dealt with.

4. *Immediacy*—It will definitely happen soon. The days of judgment are at hand.

5. *Shareability*—The crisis impacts everyone. There is no place to run; we're all in this boat together.

6. *Therapy*—The proposed change, however distasteful it was before the forgery, offers an acceptable escape from the crisis.

Sun Tzu says:

Confront them with annihilation, and they will then survive; plunge them into a deadly situation, and they will then live. When people fall into danger, they are then able to strive for victory.... When they have fallen into dire straits, they obey completely.[13]

Crisis elevates change from a matter of casual individual choice to a matter of urgent community necessity. Necessity is the prime mover of change.

A change agent must accept the axiom that it is possible to move a community from a state of hardened doubt and resistance to a state of new beliefs. A state of belief in the new order is the prerequisite for change. Belief is the pivot position for change. While creating forgeries has some ethical problems and a sham is normally not to be admired, it can pragmatically yield the desired result with minimal pain.

Figure 4.17 provides an example of a specific analytical method to be used to anticipate obstacles to each move and develop preempting strategies. *Barrier analysis* suggests that change agents will encounter three classifications of barriers:

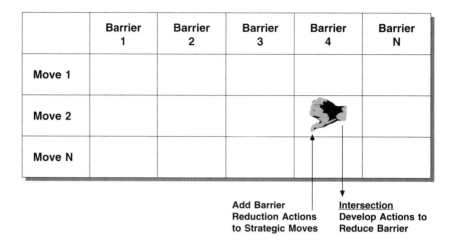

	Barrier 1	Barrier 2	Barrier 3	Barrier 4	Barrier N
Move 1					
Move 2					
Move N					

Add Barrier
Reduction Actions
to Strategic Moves

Intersection
Develop Actions to
Reduce Barrier

Figure 4.17   Barrier Analysis. Strategic moves should be incorporated into the strategy to preempt predictable obstacles. *Source*: "Implementing Client/Server Computing: A Strategic Perspective," Bernard H. Boar, McGraw-Hill, 1993 with permission of publisher.

1. *General*—organizational history, culture, style, etc.,
2. *Role*—specific incumbent positions in the organization will object, and
3. *Individual*—specific individuals will object.

As shown in Figure 4.17, the approach is to matrix the objectives against anticipated barriers. Whenever there is an intersection, barrier reduction actions should be developed and added to the strategic plan. Typical barriers are complacency, disbelief, fear of failure, expediency, culture, inertia, "it works" attitude, partisan warfare, and a "kvetch" culture. Sun Tzu says:

Those who face the unprepared with preparation are victorious.[14]

Anticipating and preempting barriers is not easy, but it is better than facing them unprepared.

Organization Politics

By far, the most difficult barrier to overcome is organizational politics. A business organization, like any social community, naturally divides itself into political interest groups. These groups are defined by division of work, allocation of resources, shared mental models, aspirations, training and skills, etc. Change will revise the partitioning of status, power, opportunities, resources, etc. Some political groups will perceive themselves as losers, and some will perceive a net gain. They all will be concerned about the threat of a change in the *status quo* and will prefer the known power equilibrium.

Political groups focus on the continued well being of their constituency. They will not be amenable to change which hurts their group regardless of merit (Who defines merit?). Preservation of group interests supersede organizational interests. Political groups will therefore intensely lobby during the change debate. They will attempt to control:

- What can be debated,
- How resources will be divided,
- How much commitment will be devoted, and
- The legitimacy of the proposed change.

Politics is a hard reality for the strategic change agent. Whatever their source of power, control of physical resources, control over or access to information, formal authority, reputation, charisma, or alliances, each political group will use their power to alter the strategy to their advantage.

Politics is not peripheral to the formulation of strategy; it is the threatening background against which all change plans and commitment plans must be designed. The veteran organizational politician is not opposed to change because they object to creation, they are opposed because they know that with creation comes complementary destruction. The laws of conservation and experience have taught the savvy politician that the change agent is both a creator and, though not advertised as such, an annihilator. So the rule of behavior is simple, better to protect and defend "what is" rather than be at the mercy of the change agent, or should we say the "annihilator."

The following quote from *Electronic News* (21 December 1992) in reference to the collapse of IBM's stock price and IBM's reactive initiatives provides an excellent example of politics at their worst:

> While analysts applauded IBM's de-emphasis of the struggling mainframe business, the move was characterized by many as a further sign of tenacious corporate inertia. A critical question was why the decision was deferred so long considering the popular view that areas identified by IBM as fast growing have been expanding at the expense of mainframes for some time. Long time IBM watchers, however, suggest that because the revenue base and manufacturing complex of the traditional mainframe business is so vast, *that partic-*

ular interest has had long standing political wherewithal to protect itself from internal machinations.

So having resisted the market realities for so long and protected its frozen mental model, IBM's mainframe business will now have to endure the trauma of crisis change rather than the evolutionary nature of proactive change. One can *never* overestimate political opposition to change which confronts a long-standing and powerful political group.

Table 4.11 is a useful aid in dealing with organizational politics. Change can only occur if coalitions can be formed to bring adequate political power to permit mobilization of resources and commitment. The matrix should be used to identify each political group, their agenda, anticipated reaction, and what actions can be taken to improve their reaction. Examine each political group to see whose vanity will expand and whose will be reduced; who will grow in power and who will shrink in power; whose budget will escalate and whose will contract; whose security will be enhanced and whose will be jeopardized; whose mental model will be validated and whose will be rejected; whose counsel will be sought and whose ignored; whose fortune will rise and whose will fall; whose competitive position will be increased and whose will be reduced; whose glory will become known and whose will be negated. In this manner, you will be able to foresee who will tentatively be an ally of change and who will resist. The likelihood of success can thereby be judged in advance.

Politics is an extremely important but often overlooked reason for the development of convincing arguments. A truth, once established by proof, does not gain added certainty by the amount of consent by others, nor does it lose validity by the quantity of dissent. To overcome politics and the inertia to action it causes, persuasive arguments that transcend the ability of the fractions to resist must be developed. It is kinder to overwhelm them with the need for change when change can still be managed in a prevenient manner than to debate until a point of crisis change is reached and everyone, finally but too late, appreciates the need.

Heritage

A barrier, second only to organizational politics, is the monopolistic mind-set and behaviors of the IM&M staff. Game theorists have developed a diagramming technique called a "payoff matrix" to illustrate the risk and reward payoffs for alternative actions and consequences. Table 4.12 shows a payoff matrix for introducing new technology by an organization which has prospered under little competition and control of all (almost all) IM&M resources. The columns depict behaviors, the rows

Table 4.11
Political Analysis. Change management planning must anticipate the development of an enabling political coalition.

Strategic Moves	Political Groups (PG)			
	PG1 Basis of political agenda	PG2 Basis of political agenda	PG3 Basis of political agenda	PG4 Basis of political agenda
Move 1	1. Reasons for support 2. Reasons for resistance 3. Actions to obtain support	1. Reasons for support 2. Reasons for resistance 3. Actions to obtain support	1. Reasons for support 2. Reasons for resistance 3. Actions to obtain support	1. Reasons for support 2. Reasons for resistance 3. Actions to obtain support
Move 2	1. Reasons for support 2. Reasons for resistance 3. Actions to obtain support	1. Reasons for support 2. Reasons for resistance 3. Actions to obtain support	1. Reasons for support 2. Reasons for resistance 3. Actions to obtain support	1. Reasons for support 2. Reasons for resistance 3. Actions to obtain support
Move "N"	1. Reasons for support 2. Reasons for resistance 3. Actions to obtain support	1. Reasons for support 2. Reasons for resistance 3. Actions to obtain support	1. Reasons for support 2. Reasons for resistance 3. Actions to obtain support	1. Reasons for support 2. Reasons for resistance 3. Actions to obtain support

depict possible consequences, and the cells depict the payoff (reward) for each intersection.

The individual game players, having been raised in a culture that does not reward risk, quickly conclude that:

- There is little to gain and much to loss through entrepreneurship, and that
- A "minimax" (minimize the maximum possible loss) strategy, while not exciting, results in a satisfactory payoff.

Game players will, consequently, almost always choose slow and conservative introduction as the optimum behavior. Although this worked while the IM&M organization had a hegemony over IM&M resources, as more and more companies move to a free market system, this risk and reward system is incompatible with being a viable competitor.

Table 4.12

Payoff Matrix. The payoff matrix for the typical IM&M employee does not reward risk.

Possible Consequences	New Technology Introduction Style	
	Slow/Conservative	Entrepreneurship
No problems	+10	+10
Problems	-10	-100

The change agent is thus confronted with a compound barrier:

1. The agent must deal with a technology revolution which is obsoleting the competencies of the IM&M staff; a staff whose frozen mental model doesn't believe it, and

2. The change agent must deal with an embedded behavioral system which rewards non-competitive behaviors.

Nobody said it would be easy.

Other Barriers

There are two other barriers to success that deserve special attention; they are the overwhelming desire of management to simplify and the problem of "worthiness."

- *Simplification*—While understandable, the desire to simplify is often taken to extremes. Some have suggested that had Einstein worked for corporate America, his famous formula, $E=MC^2$, would have been repackaged as $E = M + C$ since addition is so much simpler for everyone to understand than are multiplication and exponentiation. While this is an exaggeration, it does make the point. Concepts, actions, consequences, etc., should only be simplified to the point where the essence is not compromised. If one is going to engage in sophisticated strategy, there is a community level of understanding that must be achieved above the lowest common denominator.

  The demand to simplify strategy so that it is understandable by all, without any instruction in its fundamentals, trivializes it. Few would be expected to sysgen an operating system, repair a corrupted database, or interpret a memory dump without proper training, apprenticeship, tutoring, and graduated experience. There are distinct ideas, perspectives, and skills which surround strategy just like any other discipline. Shouldn't the process which commands all other processes insist on excellence?

Galileo in "The Assayer" says:

> ...The universe cannot be understood unless one first learns to comprehend the language of mathematics, and its characters are triangles, circles, and other geometric figures without which it is humanly possible to understand a single word of it.

The universe is written in the dialect of mathematics. Strategy, likewise, has its own distinct dialect that must be comprehended to effectively develop, communicate, and execute strategic programs.

- *Worthiness*—To develop strategies that are deep and far-reaching, the management community must be worthy, i.e., they must be literate in the ways of strategy. A management team uneducated in strategic planning will block initiatives because they don't understand the underlying frameworks that rationalize the actions. The community must raise themselves to be worthy of more than tactical muddling through, which always equates to taking too long and costing too much. The benefits of strategic planning are commensurate with, and proportional to, the state of preparation. Preparation effects a positive change in the ability of the management team to participate in and understand the consequences of the strategy process. Any benefits to be accrued through strategic planning are therefore contingent upon the management team achieving the requisite state of literacy, preparation, and worthiness.

  To achieve mastery of a discipline, preparation is either required or it is not. If it is not required and one engages in preparation, then one wastes time and effort; the activity of preparation is superfluous. It is superfluous because no benefit is derived from its execution. If it is required and one does not engage in it, then one commits a hoax. A hoax is committed because one proceeds with the persona of knowledge and skill while, in reality, one does not even have the ability of a novice. Strategy belongs to the class of disciplines that require preparation.

  The need of the management team to master the discipline of strategic planning is fundamental to success; it is not an arcane add-on. If you will recall Machiavelli's quote on the transitory nature of success (see Section 1.3) illustrated in Figure 1.10, you'll remember that the ideal end of strategy would be to escape the eternal tread-mill. By escape, we mean creating advantageous "time and circumstances" rather than being a victim of them. In Section 8.3, we will suggest how IM&M can contribute to accomplishing this, but it must be maintained that this will never be achievable without mastery of strategy.

Change Plan Structure

A change plan consists of *change objectives* which define what is to be accomplished and *change moves* which define the actions to be taken to achieve the change objectives. Table 4.13 and Table 4.14 summarize the elements which compose each.

Summary

Machiavelli understood best the challenge of being a change agent:

It should be borne in mind that there is nothing more difficult to handle nor more doubtful of success, and more dangerous to carry through than initiating change. The innovator makes enemies of all those who prospered under the old order, and only lukewarm support is forthcoming from those who would prosper under the new. Their support is lukewarm partly from fear of their adversaries; who have the existing laws on their side, and partly because men are generally incredulous, never really trusting new things unless they have tested them by experience. In consequence, those who oppose the changes attack vigorously and the defense made by the others is only lukewarm.[15]

Table 4.13
Change Objectives. Change objectives define what is to be accomplished.

Change Objective Attribute	Definition
Objective	A precise and concise statement of the objective
Date	By when the objective is to be achieved
Measure	The measurement(s) to be used to assess whether the objective has been accomplished

Jack Welch, the CEO of General Electric, provides the circa 1990s version of Machiavelli's insight in his new book when he says:

Change has no constituency. People like the *status quo*. They like the way it was.

Nothing is harder than being a change agent. The only thing harder than getting a person with a frozen mental model to accept a new idea, is to get them to give up their old idea. Every change agent shares the moment of horrific realization when they know what needs to be done but nobody cares. Imagine the ambivalent organization, hesitant and resistant, approaching the edge of a monstrously deep and wide canyon. Across the precipice is the objective, the desired future state of the organization. Imagine then, beyond the obstacles of frozen mental models, beyond the obstacles of organizational politics, beyond the obstacles of simplicity and unworthiness, beyond the obstacles of disincentive payoff matrices, and beyond the obstacles of delusional self-satisfaction rests a frail bridge that crosses the abyss, the bridge of change, and you are its sole guardian. Nothing is harder.

Table 4.14
Change Moves. The change moves define the actions to be taken to implement the change objectives.

Change Move Attribute	Definition
Move	A brief and clear statement of the action.
Description	A few paragraph elaboration of the action.
Owner	The individual in the organization responsible for making the action happen.
Champion	The executive in the organization responsible for assisting the owner.
Priority	Relative importance of the action
Measurement	The way to measure that the action has been completed.
Date	The date by which the action is to be concluded
Implementation program parameters	Rules, guidelines, boundaries, etc., that the implementation owner should follow in implementing the action

4.5   Commitment Plan

A *commitment plan* is a specific set of actions taken to establish creditability. A commitment plan is a set of actions designed to alter the beliefs, actions, and behaviors of others to motivate desired behaviors. You will wish to devise a commitment plan that will push the organization to voluntarily and enthusiastically reposition itself in harmony with the strategic plan.

This section will emphasize the need for strong (ironclad?) commitment and ignore the complimentary issue of flexibility. Few management teams have a problem with taking provisional steps towards an objective. The problem with strategy is not flexibility, everyone is willing to be provisional, but the demonstration of staying power. Since little assistance is required to develop the flexibility choice, this section will concentrate on the arguments to support the harder commitment choice.

It is unfortunate, but the reality is that many management teams have little credibility with the mass of workers. Each year, new programs are announced with tremendous fanfare and each year they die a slow death. The staff, understandingly jaded and cynical, reacts with a predictable maxim: "This to shall pass." They suspect that management believes deeply in little and is committed to less. Because of this and the reality that little is accomplished without the endorsement and efforts of all the people, the inclusion of a commitment plan to provide and sustain credibility in an expedient world is a necessary part of the plan to ease the implementation effort. The commitment plan explains how, both symbolically and substantively, management will convince the corporate community that objectives will be pursued to realization; that this time there will be staying power.

A credible approach to building commitment can be constructed on three principles as follows:

1.   Altering your own payoff[16]

   The objective of this approach is to rearrange the situation so that it is clearly not in your own interest to alter direction. It becomes clear to all that a reversal is not likely because a reversal is clearly contrary to the management team's own benefit. Two tactical ways to accomplish this are:

   • *reputation on the line*—put your reputation clearly and firmly behind the effort, and

   • *contractual obligation*—be subject to clear penalties for failure to carry through on the effort.

2. Make it difficult to back-out

The objective of this approach is to constrain your ability to change direction. It makes it visible that you won't change direction because you can't. Four tactical ways to accomplish this are as follows:

- *cutoff communication*—literally take yourself out of the loop and thereby prevent a reversal,
- *burn your bridges behind you*—commit an irreversible act that makes accomplishment of the effort mandatory,
- *leave the outcome to chance*—put in place a process that has a life of its own that you can't control, and
- *small steps*—proceed in many well defined and small steps with visible payoffs. Changing direction is deterred because of the remaining payoffs from just "one more step."

3. Use others to force and maintain commitment

The objective of this approach is to make it difficult to revise your direction because of the "others" involved. It alters the belief of the staff because they feel "while one person might change, all of them would never." Two tactical ways to accomplish this are as follows:

- *teamwork*—get many people in the boat with you. You all have to swim or sink together.
- *delegated agent*—delegate authority to someone who has a clear interest in accomplishing the effort. This makes a reversal highly unlikely.

The above are general actions and need to be customized to specific situations. The overall point, however, is clear. To be successful in implementation, it will be necessary for the staff to believe that the management team is thoroughly committed to the plan. There is a tremendous chasm to be crossed in repositioning an organization. The clear commitment of the management team to the effort significantly eases the passage. Nothing will be accomplished if the corporate community views the strategy as simply the current (and passing) "strategic *programme du jour*," but another instance of the recurring corporate attention deficit disorder.

Sun Tzu says:

When an army goes forth and crosses a border, it should burn its boats and bridges to show the populace that it has no intent of looking back.[17]

Commitment has the notion that once a strategic choice has been made, it is difficult to redeploy invested assets and resources. It is this difficulty of reallocation that convinces the staff of the seriousness of the action.

The problem of strategic commitment is similar to the problem of committing transactions when using a database management system. When an application program wishes to update a database, it creates a transaction of the following logical structure:

1. Start transaction,
2. 1-n data manipulation statements (insert, update, delete, select) and associated conditional return code checking statements, and
3. Commit transaction.

This structure assures the integrity of the database. The database management system guarantees that:

1. The update will be atomic; either all or none of the data manipulation statements are executed.
2. Concurrency control will be provided; two independent transactions will not concurrently update the same records.
3. The database will be moved from one state of consistency to another state of consistency.

If during the data manipulation statements a condition occurs which negates the desire to update the databases, the programmer may issue an "abort" statement which cancels all pending transaction updates. Conversely, once the commit has been issued, the database may only be restored to its prior state by applying before or after change journal images.

Following this archetype, strategy commitment would appear as follows:

1. Start strategy execution.
2. Execute 1-n strategic moves tempered by vigilance, learning, and monitoring.
3. Commit strategy.

The overriding problem is that the organization does not believe that the "commit" will ever be executed. Rather, based on the historical experiences that have formed their outlook, they anticipate that "aborts" are inevitable. Their collective jury verdict is that there is always significant up front rhetoric and hoopla but little else. Why waste time working diligently on the strategic moves when we are confident that there will come diversions and this strategy will also be aborted? Commitment is therefore necessary to unequivocally demonstrate that you will move the business from its current position to its future position; this time, no aborts.

An excellent example of where commitment will be required is the augmentation of service warranties to IM&M products. It is one thing to tell a customer that you are an excellent provider, it is another thing to measure services, but it is a whole different thing to agree to refunds and penalties for missing contracted service measurements. Warranting, which will inevitably be required by internal IM&M service providers to compete with outsourcers, will require an extended effort by IM&M management to put in place appropriate processes and a service culture. An action demanding commitment.

A commitment plan consists of commitment objectives which define what is to be accomplished and commitment moves which define the actions to be taken to achieve the commitment objectives. Table 4.15 and Table 4.16 summarize the elements which compose each. Commitment moves should be direct and highly visible to maximize receptivity. Unlike strategic moves and change moves, commitment moves are best when they directly assault the problem of building credibility.

The maxim of commitment would therefore be as follows: the challenge is not so much to design a perfect strategy (whether the selected strategy was the optimum will not be known for years, if ever), but to fully commit oneself to successfully implementing the one that was designed. Whether it's the best of strategies or the worse of strategies, it's the only strategy that you have. *You therefore devote your full energies to make it the right decision.*

Dr. Grove of Intel summed up this nature of commitment very well:

> The operative word is focus. You have to put all your effort behind the thing that you do better than the other people in the business, and then not hedge your bets. If you're hedging, you're more likely to lose; and even if you win, you win in a mediocre way. If you focus and you're wrong, you lose—but if your right, you win big time.[18]

So commitment is a synonym for courage. Without courage, how could one maintain perseverance in the face of the endless obstacles. This is why we choose to emphasize commitment. Flexibility, while a necessary and correct action, is nevertheless a relatively easy one to take. Commitment is a courageous and ever the rarer action. Courage and commitment are therefore both one in the same. Courage provides the energy to make and sustain commitments. Commitment provides visible instances of courage to the organization. As one demonstrates commitment and courage, a reputation is developed which results in needing to use less courage and less demonstrative commitments because credibility has been a priori established. So the long-term consequence of strong courage and commitment is not needing it; it is only compulsory for those who do not have it.

Table 4.15
Commitment Objectives. Commitment objectives define what is to be accomplished.

Commitment Objective Attribute	Definition
Objective	A precise and concise statement of the objective
Date	By when the objective is to be achieved
Measure	The measurement(s) to be used to assess whether the objective has been accomplished

Table 4.16
Commitment Moves. Commitment moves define the actions to be taken to make the commitment happen.

Commitment Move Attribute	Definition
Move	A brief and clear statement of the action
Description	A few paragraph elaboration of the action
Method	The type of commitment action, i.e., altering your own payoff etc.
Commitment domain	The individuals who need to demonstrate/make the commitment
Owner	The individual in the organization responsible for making the action happen
Champion	The executive in the organization responsible for assisting the owner
Priority	Relative importance of the action
Measurement	The way to measure that the action has been completed
Date	The date by which the action is to be concluded
Implementation program parameters	Rules, guidelines, boundaries, etc., that the implementation owner should follow in implementing the action

In Dante's "Divine Comedy: Inferno," the "uncommitted" are sentenced to spend eternity in the vestibule of hell. They are assigned neither to hell proper nor to paradise because being "uncommitted" they have not earned either through their actions. Having refused to make choices and be decisive in life, their punishment according to the law of corresponding retribution is to be eternally stung into movement. In strategy, the punishment for neglecting commitment is failure; if you will not make open choices and take decisive actions to demonstrate commitment to your strategy, neither will anyone else. Strategists who are unable to include commitment will see their strategies go nowhere.

4.6 Summary

Strategy is the most intellectually stimulating part of the strategic development process. With few formal methods of assistance, you are confronted with the crafting of future positions, objectives, and moves. Because it is not easy, when it is well done it offers the basis for building advantage. Since "...much strategy prevails over little strategy," the strategically focused organization is well rewarded. How else should we expect it to be?

Figure 4.18 provides a summary "big picture" of the strategy step. It should be understood as follows:

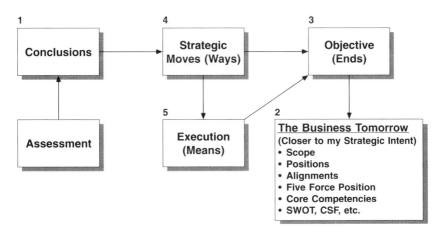

Figure 4.18   Strategy Summary. The strategy defines the "ends" and the "ways."

1. The assessment step culminates with the generation of a set of conclusions which itemize strategic imperatives for management attention.

2. A desired future state is defined for the business. It brings the business closer to its strategic intent.

3. Objectives are defined; they explicitly list what is to be accomplished.

4. Strategic moves are defined which itemize the ways to achieve the objectives.

5. The strategic moves are executed in the next step, execution, of the planning process.

The change management plan and the commitment plan posture the strategy for success.

The strategy step, as we have presented it, is in the form of a process model. Consequently, the outputs are organized by process type, i.e., all the positions, then all the objectives, and, finally, all the strategic moves. Some would prefer a functional presentation by strategic area. In this case, you would just sort the positions, objectives, and strategic moves and arrange them by strategic area, i.e., (market position, market objectives, market strategic moves), (human resource position, human resource objectives, human resource strategic moves), (core competency position, core competency objectives, core competency strategic moves), etc.

Now, a business must choose either to stay at rest or to move. If it chooses to stay at rest and its trading partners continue to evolve, then it will become increasingly irrelevant. *Hibernation* is a strategy of planned decline through complacency. If it chooses to move, then there are four alternatives:

1. It can define its strategic moves but not its objectives. In this case, anyone's and everyone's objectives are equal and the strategy is purposeless.

2. It can define its objectives but not its strategic moves. In this case, it leaves realization to the chance congruence of each organizational entity and the strategy is futile.

3. It can define neither its objectives nor its strategic moves. In this case, it abrogates its responsibility of leadership, participates in a hoax, and leaves the strategy to Divine Providence.

4. It can define both its objectives and its strategic moves. In this case it provides strategic leadership.

Movement requires a first mover and the first mover is strategy.

Objectives and strategic moves, however, are not alone sufficient. A strategist must overcome the challenges of lack of commitment and resistance to change. Like Odysseus in Homer's *Odyssey*, who had to navigate between the twofold horrors of Scylla and Charybdis, the strategy must navigate between failure because of lack of commitment and failure because of resistance to change. So a whole strategy must include a change management plan and a commitment plan.

The question is asked: Is there the notion of a perfect strategy? The answer is yes, and its character has been described by Sun Tzu and the means of testing by Machiavelli. The objectives of a perfect strategy are to achieve a set of vastly superior strategic positions The strategic moves would realize these positions by being deep and far-reaching. The test of this strategy would be its ability to breach the eternal challenge explained by Machiavelli (see Figure 1.10). If your strategy can command fortune rather than making you the victim of times and circumstances, then your strategy is perfect. What could be a greater accomplishment then being immune to misfortune and being assured that you can avert ruin.

So those who believe in a rational approach to strategy formulation do not believe that repeated successes are due to good fortune, the roll of the dice, Faustian pacts with the devil, magical incantations, prayer, or wishful thinking. Success is the consequence of strategy which make the success of execution inescapable and anticlimactic. Success is the consequence of creating a perfect score for the corporate orchestra to play. Each note perfect unto itself and in perfect harmony with all others. In summary:

> The successes of the IM&M organization may only be as grand as the foundation of strategy upon which they are built. Strategy may be of two kinds; it may be shallow and nearsighted or it may be deep and far-reaching. When it is shallow and nearsighted, all successes are temporary and isolated. This is because the foundation has been mixed with strategy which is weak and hollow. The foundation inevitably cracks and buckles under the load. When the strategy is deep and far-reaching, then successes compound and support each other. This is because the foundation has been mixed with strategy that is holistic and has the strength to support the business. The foundation easily holds the load. The priority of IM&M management is therefore obvious. The first priority of management is the mastery, internalization, and application of strategy, and then, and only then, the mastery and exploitation of IM&M technology. This is the only path to building, sustaining, and compounding competitive advantage through IM&M. There is no other path.

Such is the primary and enduring relationship between strategy and IM&M.

Footnotes

1. Sun Tzu, *The Art of War.*
2. Sun Tzu, *The Art of War.*
3. Sun Tzu, *The Art of War.*
4. Sun Tzu, *The Art of War.*
5. Sun Tzu, *The Art of War.*
6. B. H. Liddell-Hart, *Strategy.*
7. Bernard Boar, *Application Prototyping: A Requirements Definition Strategy for the 80s.*
8. Sun Tzu, *The Art of War.*
9. Sun Tzu, The Art of War.
10. Machiavelli, *The Prince.*
11. Sun Tzu, *The Art of War.*
12. P. Senge, *The Fifth Dimension.*
13. Sun Tzu, *The Art of War.*
14. Sun Tzu, *The Art of War.*
15. Maciavelli, *The Prince.*
16. A. Dixit and B. Nalebuff, *Thinking Strategically.*
17. Sun Tzu, *The Art of War.*
18. *Fortune Magazine.*

5

Execution

The purpose of this chapter is to explain the execution step of the strategic planning process. *Execution* is the act of putting the plan into motion. Strategies are operationalized through implementation programs under the leadership of a strategy owner and the sponsorship of a strategy champion. Figure 5.1 is an enlargement of the execution step. Execution confronts the strategy owners and champions with a wide assortment of problems, including:

- Inadequate project management skills,
- Discovery of unforeseen problems,
- Lack of organizational commitment,
- Lack of executive leadership,
- Churning strategy,
- Resistance to change,
- Demands for immediate results, and
- Cost containment efforts.

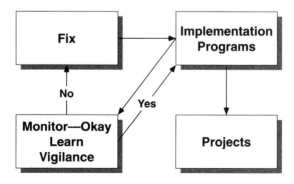

Figure 5.1   The execution step puts the plan into motion.

Execution can be anticipated to be extremely difficult or approached as a creative opportunity to imagineer, improvise, experiment, and prototype to discover the best way to accomplish strategic moves.

Execution Success

The success of the execution step must be positioned prior to beginning it. Sun Tzu says:

> ...A victorious army first wins and then seeks battle, a defeated army first battles and then seeks victory.[1]

Success is designed and prepared for by:

1. A thoughtful commitment plan,
2. A fully developed change management plan,
3. The selection of able strategy owners and champions,
4. The design of a human resource architecture which stimulates desired behaviors,
5. Wide strategy development participation (covered in Chapter 7),
6. Project management training and support,
7. A professional strategic planning process that earns the organization's respect,
8. A strategic intent worthy of extended individual effort, excitement, and commitment,
9. A "...deep and far reaching strategy" which captures the imagination of the staff,
10. The design of an internal IM&M economy that incents desired behaviors and decision making, and
11. A well-designed customer satisfaction measurement system.

Without such preparations, it is not surprising that the execution step can turn into a nightmare. Remember the admonition of Machiavelli, "...there is nothing more difficult or doubtful of success...." The depth and breadth of preparation performed in the prior steps determines the success of the execution step.

Implementation Programs and Projects

Implementation programs are the master projects to implement the strategy. Implementation owners develop tactical projects to operationalize the moves within the boundaries defined by the implementation program parameters. Each program is divided into manageable subprojects. Projects strive to achieve goals. Implementation programs and projects are done using the tools of professional project management for which there exists an abundant and rich literature.

As would be expected, everyone is anxious for rapid results. When actions are independent, a matrix such as exhibited in the top part of Figure 5.2 can be used to order projects. For interdependent actions (the most common type), PERT charts such as the example at the bottom of Figure 5.2 must be used to evaluate dependencies for ordering.

While implementation programs are divided between owners and champions and partitioned into projects, the implementation should be conceptualized as one unified grand project. Collaboration, inter-project coordination, and cooperation are required for the collective success of the individual efforts.

Execution is often cited as the most difficult step of the strategy process. Failures of strategy are routinely attributed to poor project management. I do not share this view. While undoubtedly the mechanics of project management can be poorly executed, the ability of the project managers to execute implementation programs is preordained during the strategy step by the design of the internal IM&M economy, the design of the human resource architecture, the assignment of owners and champions, the customer satisfaction measurment system, the commitment plan, and the change management plan. The etiology of execution failure is most often due to failures in the strategic plan,

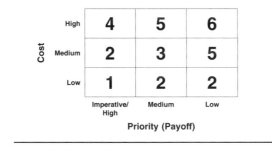

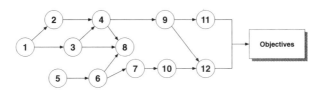

Figure 5.2   Implementation. Implementation order of strategic moves is a function of independence, dependency, and payoff.

not to incompetent project managment. The six items create an implementation environment on which change agents can effect change. Given what
has been learned about frozen mental models, organizational politics, management fickleness, and payoff matrices, it is amiss to assign the success of
execution to the discipline of project management. As Sun Tzu says:

> …A victorious army first wins and then seeks battle, a defeated
> army first battles and then seeks victory.[2]

Strategy execution is won or lost based on the depth, insight, and foresight of the strategic plan, not the procedures of project management. The
success of execution can be foretold at the completion of the strategy step.
Project management inadequacies are relatively easy to correct. It is the
prepositioning for success that is the challenge.

Monitoring, Learning, and Vigilance

Monitoring is the periodic formal review of the projects to assess progress.
Actions as well as tactics must be revised, adapted, and tuned based on
real-world experience. One can only be endlessly amused at the all too
human but vain efforts of bowlers to redirect their bowling balls once they
have been thrown. As the ball rolls down the alley, the bowler jumps up
and down and pushes the air in front of her face with her hands in a futile
attempt to redirect the ball's projection. Fortunately, this is not the case with
the monitoring of implementation programs. By careful and regular
review, purposeful actions can be taken to meaningfully redirect the course
of our strategies to be in accord with evolving times and circumstances.
Monitoring, however, must go beyond conventional project management
reviews. We are equally concerned with learning and vigilance.

By *learning* we mean actively seeking lessons from the practical experiences and incorporating those lessons into processes and programs. The
day to day experiences of the project teams are some of the best sources for
gaining insight into how to improve the strategy process. Learning answers
the question, "What can be done in the assessment and strategy steps of the
process to improve and simplify the execution step next time?"

Vigilance is continual proactive scanning of the environment for events
which may require a real-time strategic assessment and response. The strategic planning model presented is a "calendar model." Unfortunately, the
world does not always choose to evolve in synchronization with a given
planning schedule. One must be vigilant to recognize unforeseen events
which may change plans. The process that deals with unanticipated events
of a strategic nature is referred to as *Dynamics Issues Management*.

The need for vigilance raises an important question: Is the calendar
model a valid approach, or must strategy development be continuous
(dynamic and real-time)? A response to this is as follows:

- Strategy is by definition forward looking.
- Strategy, by definition, deals with the mega-issues. Mega-issues are long-term issues
- Strategists must anticipate.
- Strategic implementation programs may take years to realize. Sustainable competitive advantage, new organizational cultures, world class capabilities, and new core competencies are not developed overnight.
- Large organizations cannot change fundamental directions every day and overnight. The massive logistical issues make it impossible.
- If all strategy is dynamic, the organization will quickly learn the game and wait for the next change.
- Given the time to develop, productize, and diffuse new technologies, overall direction should be reasonably foreseeable. What state-of-the-art or state-of-the-market technology, now available, was not observable on the horizon five years ago? What technology which will be available five years from now is not currently being speculated about or in development or productization at some research lab or product house? Products are not created by spontaneous combustion.
- If it is necessary to continually change course, either one needs new strategist or the situation is so chaotic (in turbulent transition) that one must proceed tactically without strategy.
- Tactics, the heart of the implementation programs, provide an adaptable and fluid vehicle to deal with environmental changes.
- Pivot positions infuse the strategy with flexibility.
- A primary objective of strategy should be to develop a highly adaptive and maneuverable business so that the day-to-day business processes can maintain a strategic fit with the environment.

Consider what the notion of "real-time strategy" really means. A *real-time system* typically consists of two components: a regulatory (controlling) component which monitors and controls and a regulated (controlled) component which is monitored and controlled. Either periodically or event driven, the regulatory component evaluates the situation and sends corrective and adaptive instructions to the regulated component. The regulated component adjusts its state accordingly and the cycle continues indefinitely.

Strategy, as has been defined (future business scope, future strategic positions, objectives, strategic moves, change management plan, and commitment plan), is the corporate regulatory agent. The business is the regulated component. Now, if the analogy is followed, real-time strategy would require that as the strategy is event driven reformulated, that the business, the regulated component, could respond to a continual stream of strategic change messages; a stream of messages dictating major redirections. Is this doable or desirable? Is this not both practically impossible and definitionally incorrect? Strategy is suppose to be "deep and far reaching," not "shallow and nearsighted." It is therefore asserted that the calendar model as a strategy anchor is valid, but unanticipated events of significance do occur and they must be dealt with.

An unforeseen event of strategic import is an event which was not anticipated, was grossly incorrectly anticipated, or was anticipated and will not occur. Also, a change may occur in the directives and assumptions received or in the business scope *and* the event is of strategic significance. To be of strategic significance, the event alone or in collaboration with other events must have the potential to materially alter a strategic position. These events are discovered through vigilance.

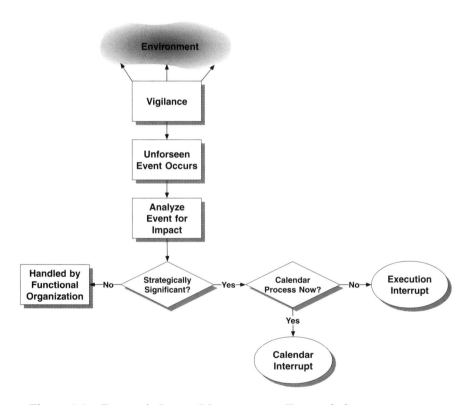

Figure 5.3   Dynamic Issues Management. Dynamic issues management is the process used to manage dynamic events of strategic import.

The process used to manage unforeseen strategic events is called *Dynamic Issues Management*. Figure 5.3 is an umbrella illustration of the process. Non-strategic events are directed to the appropriate functional organization for action. The method of handling strategic events is determined by whether one is in the strategic planning stage (Calendar Interrupt) or the execution stage (Execution Interrupt).

A calendar interrupt occurs when an unforeseen event happens during the current assessment or strategy step of the process (see Figure 5.4). Since this type of interrupt occurs during plan development, it can be handled fairly smoothly as illustrated in Figure 5.4. An execution interrupt occurs when an unforeseen event happens during the execution step (see Figure 5.5). If the interrupt does not alter the plan or handling it can wait, the event is incorporated into the next planning cycle. Otherwise, a partial or, in rare cases, a complete redo of the strategic plan is dictated.

When Dynamics Issues Management is included as part of the strategic planning process, a balance is achieved in the need for dealing with both strategy anchoring and environmental dynamics. The notion of a purely real-time strategy would whipsaw any large business. Conversely, you cannot stop the world until the time is convenient for your next planning cycle. The calendar process provides the necessary baseline of strategy. The dynamic process allows for incorporating new information when it appears. Together all the strategic planning needs are met. While dynamic issues have to be dealt with expeditiously, they must also be analyzed within the context of the whole business system for impact, and response actions must be disciplined or latent disorder will be created.

Summary

Execution is strategy in motion; the directed mobilization of resources toward a defined end. Through the use of Dynamic Issues Management, execution adapts the strategy to unforeseen strategic events. Tactics handle day-to-day melding of the implementation programs with the ever shifting environment. Figure 5.6 summarizes the essence of the execution step. Execution is the project management, monitoring, and vigilance required to move a business from the business of today to the business of tomorrow. Strategic moves are executed in parallel to achieve multiple objectives. On the path to reaching the objectives, strategic moves achieve serial goals. Execution is the process of organizational transformation; the transformation of the future business from a state of potentiality to a state of actuality.

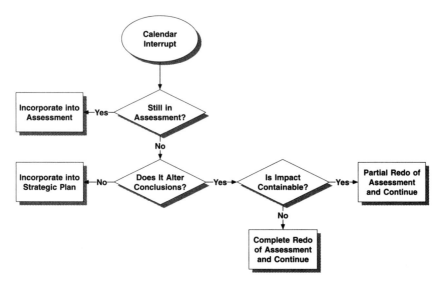

Figure 5.4   Calendar Interrupt. This process defines how to handle
unforseen strategic events when they occur during the assessment or
strategy steps of the strategic planning process.

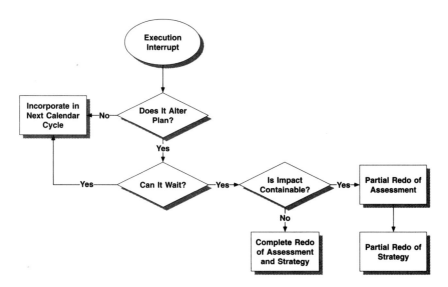

Figure 5.5   Execution Interrupt. This process defines how to handle
unforseen strategic events when they occur during the execution step
of the strategic planning process.

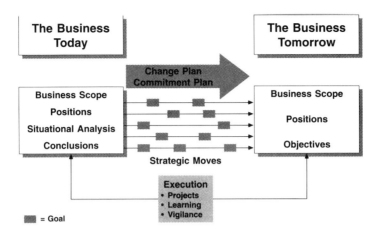

Figure 5.6   Execution Is Movement. Execution is the transformation of the business from its current business state to its new business state.

Project management is the primary tactical tool of execution. The strategic component of execution occurs in the prior strategy step. Implementation managers dispersed throughout the organization do not have the ability of a fairy tale Rumplestilskin, to weave gold out of straw; they cannot unilaterally overcome deeply embedded organization infrastructure obstacles. Eliminating such obstacles is the responsibility of the strategy team by virtue of the change plan, commitment plan, customer satisfaction measurment system, economy design, human resource architecture design, and assignment of "move" owners and champions. Table 5.1 summarizes why these items are so cardinal to positioning for execution success. An implementation phrase characterized by implementation owners thrashing wildly about in a tar pit of problems is most often a sign of poorly developed strategy; not poor project management. It is a sign that all efforts to implement it will be in vain.

The design of the internal economy, the measurement system, and the human resource architecture are critically important to incenting cooperation because, unlike most things, they are not easily ignored. The reaction of the obstructionist is often benign neglect; they do not directly challenge the strategy, they just simply ignore it, hoping it will wither away. It is much more difficult to ignore a new zero base budgeting system where product teams, at a level of detail they select, negotiate budgets. It is difficult to ignore customer satisfaction measurements which are used to monitor your processes. It is difficult to ignore new salary and bonus systems which are directly linked to budgetary goals and customer satisfaction measurements. If you are really committed to change, you must use

Table 5.1
Execution Enablers. The success of the execution step is determined by
the design of these key enablers in the strategy step which foster strong
organizational alignment.

Execution Enabler	Why Cardinal	Penalty for Absence
Change plan	Anticipate and minimize resistance to change	Overt and covert resistance to change
Commitment plan	Demonstrate management commitment to strategy	Collective attitude that "this to shall pass"
Customer satisfaction measurement system	People pay attention to what they are measured on.	Measurement system which is not linked to meeting customer satisfiers—gross misalignment
Economy design	Economic system pushes feel of competition throughout organization and prompts competitive reactions.	Monopolist behaviors
Human resource architecture	Convert values into desired behaviors	Misalignment of behaviors with strategy
Selection of "move"owners and champions	Both symbolic and substantive message of importance of strategy	Both symbolic and substantive message of unimportance of strategy

as the spearhead those things which get and keep everyone's attention. Usually, those things have a strong and personal financial attribute.

In considering the character of execution, one should always remember the following three points:

1. Project management, the management process of strategy implementation, is a strategic core competency. It is the tool for the coherent management of movement, learning, vigilance, and adaptation.

2. Execution is an integral component of strategic planning. It is a non-divisible part of the strategic planning triad of assessment, strategy, and execution. Assessment is the antecedent of strategy, strategy is the antecedent of execution, and execution is the antecedent of assessment. The essence of something includes those properties of it which cannot be removed without it losing its identity. All three, assessment, strategy, and execution compose the essence of strategic planning and must be understood as a unity of

one. It is therefore meaningless to discuss strategic planning without the intention of execution, and it is impossible to execute strategy without it being preceded (whether formally or informally) by assessment and strategy design.

It is not uncommon to attend strategic planning seminars and hear the speakers talk about the 1990s being "the era of transition from planning to execution." What are they babbling about? Sun Tzu says:

Some rulers are fond of words but do not transfer them into deeds.[3]

Up until now, could management engage in magical thinking, believing that simply writing down strategies equated to making them happen? Conversely, do actions now arise spontaneously without forethought? The only rational approach to strategic planning is to consider the three steps as sharing a unity which demands that each be executed in return. Each step has and always will be necessary since they share the same essence.

3. Execution is "the battle." As taught by Sun Tzu, it is won or lost before the actual engagement, based on how deep and far reaching your strategy is.

Such is the nature of execution.

Footnotes

1. Sun Tzu, *The Art of War.*
2. Sun Tzu, *The Art of War.*
3. Sun Tzu, *The Art of War.*

6

Quality Control

The purpose of this chapter is to provide a robust set of tools which can be used to improve the quality of the assessment and strategy steps of the strategic planning process. Quality is not appended at the end of the process as an afterthought nor is it done by a separate group. Quality control is interleaved throughout the process and is as important a responsibility for the strategy team as all other activities.

Infusing quality into the planning process will be explained from three perspectives:

- Section 6.1: Logical Relationship Checks

   This section will explain a set of checks which can be applied to insure the logical consistency of the plan.

- Section 6.2: Completeness Checks

   This section will explain a set of checks which can be applied to insure that the strategy is comprehensive.

- Section 6.3: Correctness Checks

   This section will explain a set of techniques which can be used to evaluate the value and validity of the strategy.

- Section 6.4: Summary

   This section summarizes the major points of the chapter.

Together, the three types of checks provide a system for evaluating the strategy. The logical checks assure that the logical flow of the strategy is correct, i.e., it is a valid format. The completeness checks assure that "all the bases" have been covered. The correctness checks answer the bottom line question: Is it good strategy?

6.1   Logical Relationship Checks

Logical relationship checks provide a way to trace the forward and backward logical flow of the strategic move. These checks answer the question: Is the strategy structurally sound? Figure 6.1 provides the overall framework for tracing logical validity. It may be understood as follows:

- A conclusion is addressed through multiple objectives. An objective meets the needs of multiple conclusions.
- An objective is realized through multiple strategic moves. A strategic move enables the realization of multiple objectives.
- A strategic move has one and only one owner. An owner may own multiple strategic moves.
- A strategic move has one and only one champion. A champion may champion multiple strategic moves.

Figure 6.2 illustrates a forward and backward trace.
The logic may be traced forward as follows:

- Conclusion "a" is addressed by objectives "b" and "c."
- Objective "b" is realized through strategic moves "d" and "e."
- Objective "c" is realized through strategic moves "e" and "f."
- Strategic move "d" is owned by owner "g" and championed by champion "h."

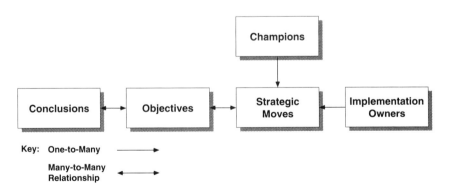

Figure 6.1   Logical Relationship Checks. There are distinct relationships between conclusions, objectives, moves, owners, and champions that should be validated.

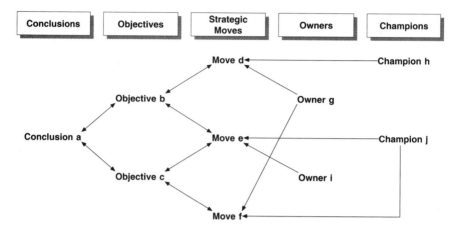

Figure 6.2   Logical Relationship Example. There should be a logical flow between conclusions, objectives, strategic moves, champions, and owners.

- Strategic move "e" is owned by owner "i" and championed by champion "j."
- Strategic move "f" is owned by owner "g" and championed by champion "j."

A partial backward trace would be as follows:

- Champion "j" champions strategic move "f" which is owned by owner "g."
- Strategic move "f" is used to realize objective "c."
- Objective "c" addresses the problems identified in conclusion "a."

The analysis of the relationships are managed through four matrices as follows:

- Conclusion/Objective Check (Table 6.1)

    Conclusions are matrixed against objectives. An "x" in a cell indicates that the objectives address the requirements of the conclusion. Except for standing objectives, all objectives must support at least one conclusion. This check may be performed once objectives have been formulated.

Table 6.1
Conclusion/Objectives Check. At least one objective should address each conclusion.

Objectives	Conclusions				
	Conclusion 1	Conclusion 2	Conclusion 3	Conclusion 4	Conclusion N
Objective 1					
Objective 2					
Objective 3					
Objective 4					
Objective N					

- Objectives/Strategic Move Check (Table 6.2)

  Objectives are matrixed against strategic moves. An "x" in a cell indicates that the selected objective is realized through the corresponding strategic move. All objectives must have at least one enabling strategic move. This check may be performed once strategic moves have been formulated.

Table 6.2
Objectives/Strategic Move Check. At least one strategic move should address each objective.

Objectives	Strategic Moves				
	Strategic Move 1	Strategic Move 2	Strategic Move 3	Strategic Move 4	Strategic Move N
Objective 1					
Objective 2					
Objective 3					
Objective 4					
Objective N					

Table 6.3
Owner/Strategic Move Check. Each strategic move has exactly one owner.

Owners	Strategic Moves				
	Strategic Move 1	Strategic Move 2	Strategic Move 3	Strategic Move 4	Strategic Move N
Owner 1					
Owner 2					
Owner 3					
Owner 4					
Owner N					

- Owner/Strategic Moves Check (Table 6.3)

  Owners are matrixed against strategic moves. An "x" in a cell indicates that the designated owner owns the corresponding strategic move. Each strategic move must have one and only one owner. This check may be done once strategic moves have been formulated. This check may also be used to provide an owner view of the strategic moves which will assist in assessing whether or not ownership is balanced and if it has been properly assigned.

- Champion/Strategic Moves Check (Table 6.4)

  Champions are matrixed against strategic moves. An "x" in a cell indicates that the designated champion champions the corresponding strategic move. Each strategic move must have one and only one champion. This check may be done once strategic moves have been formulated. This check may also be used to provide a champion view of the strategic moves which will assist in assessing whether or not championship is balanced and if it has been properly assigned.

Though not illustrated, checks similar to those shown in Tables 6.2, 6.3, and 6.4 may be done to assure the logical correctness of both the commitment plan and the change management plan.

Table 6.4
Champion/Strategic Move Check. Each strategic move has exactly one champion.

Champions	Strategic Moves				
	Strategic Move 1	Strategic Move 2	Strategic Move 3	Strategic Move 4	Strategic Move N
Champion 1					
Champion 2					
Champion 3					
Champion 4					
Champion N					

Logical checks confirm validity of a strategic move structure, but they do not assure that a strategic move is complete or correct. For these items, other checks are required.

6.2 Completeness Checks

Completeness checks are used to test the plan for completeness; complete meaning that all areas of importance have been considered. This is accomplished through a series of analytical techniques as follows:

- Strategic Areas Check (Table 6.5)

  The business areas of strategic import are matrixed against the objectives. An "x" in a cell indicates that the objective relates to the corresponding strategic area. Strategic areas with no checks should be reviewed. This check may be performed once objectives have been formulated.

- Business P's Check (Table 6.6)

  The business P's are the heart of a marketing mix. The traditional P's are:

  product—the product or service offered,

  price—the amount of money customers have to pay to obtain the product,

Table 6.5
Strategic Areas Check. What about strategic areas for which there are no objectives?

Objectives	Strategic Areas				
	Markets	Competition	Structure	Competencies	Etc.
Objective 1					
Objective 2					
Objective 3					
Objective 4					
Objective N					

Table 6.6
Business P's Check. Are there strategic moves covering all the Business P's?

Business P's	Strategic Moves				
	Strategic Move 1	Strategic Move 2	Strategic Move 3	Strategic Move 4	Strategic Move N
Product					
Promotion					
Place					
Price					
People					
Process					

place—the activities that make the product available to the marketplace, and

promotion—the activities that communicate the merits of the product to the marketplace.

Since the business P's summarize critical elements of market success, we check the plan to assure that they are covered. We extend the traditional business P's with two new P's equally important to market success:

people—human resource policies to promote a winning team, and

process—business processes that enable servicing the customer.

The business P's are matrixed against the strategic moves. An "x" in a cell indicates that the strategic move impacts the related business P. Business P's for which no strategic moves exist should be investigated. This check may be done once strategic moves have been formulated.

- 7 "S" Check (Table 6.7)

   The 7 "S" Model asserts that strategic alignment means developing a strategic fit between strategy and structure, style, systems, staff, skills, and shared values. The 7 "S" Model provides a check for alignment. As shown in Table 6.7, the strategic moves are matrixed with the 7 "S." An "x" in a cell indicates that the strategic move impacts that corresponding "S." The resulting matrix should be analyzed from the 7 "S" perspective. Are all the 7 "S" covered? Are they still in alignment? This check may be done once strategic moves have been formulated.

Table 6.7
7 "S" Check. Do strategic moves exist which cover all the 7 "S"?

7 "S"	Strategic Moves				
	Strategic Move 1	Strategic Move 2	Strategic Move 3	Strategic Move 4	Strategic Move N
Structure					
Style					
Systems					
Staff					
Skills					
Shared Values					

Table 6.8
Strategic Intent Check. Does each objective contribute to realization of the strategic intent?

Objectives	Strategic Intent
Objective 1	
Objective 2	
Objective 3	
Objective 4	
Objective N	

- Strategic Intent Check (Table 6.8)

    Objectives are matrixed against the strategic intent. The intersection is populated with an explanation of how the objective contributes to realization of the strategic intent. Objectives which don't contribute to this end should be carefully reviewed.

- Time-Line Check (Figure 6.3)

    Completion dates for objectives, goals, and strategic moves are plotted on a shared time-line. Are the completion dates doable? Do they distribute across the planning horizon? This check may be done once strategic moves have been formulated.

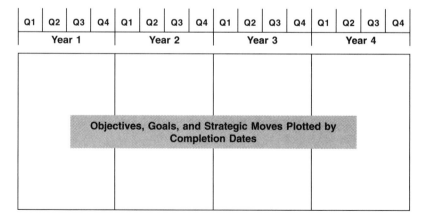

Figure 6.3   Time Line Check. Objectives and strategic moves should be validated from a time perspective to assure that the schedule is doable.

Table 6.9
Directives/Assumptions Check. Do any of the strategic moves violate the directives and assumptions?

Directives/ Assumptions (D/A)	Strategic Moves				
	Strategic Move 1	Strategic Move 2	Strategic Move 3	Strategic Move 4	Strategic Move N
D/A 1					
D/A 2					
D/A 3					
D/A 4					
D/A 5					
D/A N					

- Directives/Assumptions Check (Table 6.9)

  Directives and assumptions provided by the higher level organizational authority are matrixed with the strategic moves. An "x" in a cell indicates that the strategic move *violates* the directive.

- Key Findings Check

  As previously explained, key findings are information such as core competencies, critical success factors, five force drivers, capabilities, etc. These are items of strategic importance to success. One must ask questions such as:

  Have we taken actions to build SCA?

  Have we taken actions to reposition the five force drivers more favorably?

  Have we taken actions to nourish our strategic capabilities?

  Have we taken actions to nourish our core competencies?

  Have we taken actions to exploit our strengths, correct our weaknesses, deflect threats, and exploit opportunities?

  Have we taken actions to meet each critical success factor?

  Have we taken actions to address our value-chain drivers?

If not, why not? This check may be done once strategic moves have been formulated.

Completeness checks are beneficial because they view the strategic moves through multiple lenses. They identify possible shortcomings or incompleteness which may only be visible when viewed from a sectarian perspective.

6.3   Correctness Checks

Correctness checks are used as a means to assess the absolute value of the strategy. While logical checks assure that the format of the strategy is valid and the completeness checks assure that the strategy is comprehensive, correctness checks address the bottom-line question: Is this a good strategy for the business? If you achieve it, do you realize a noble cause or have you engaged in a community delusion and will you find yourself irrelevant to customers? Five approaches to be used in assessing correctness are as follows:

1. Devil's Advocacy

Devil's Advocacy is a method wherein a distinct and separate team is formed to aggressively critique the strategy. This devil's advocacy team has the mission to question all aspects of the plan and *propose alternatives*. Devil's advocacy results in heated debates and may get out of hand if people-sensitivity issues are not well managed. Nevertheless, many of the stakeholders may only review the strategy superficially (time constraints, immediate crises, etc.). A focused devil's advocacy team may discover errors which can be corrected prior to execution. Devil's advocacy may be done at the completion of assessment or the strategy step.

2. Expert Review

Expert review is the hiring of independent and outside experts to review the strategy and planning process. This technique works best when a long-term relationship has been established with the expert so that she has extensive familiarity with your business. To be both effective and efficient in reviewing the strategy the expert should:

- be familiar with your business,

- be familiar with the IM&M industry,
- be familiar with your customers,
- be familiar with your competitors, and
- have entry and access to industry benchmarking.

When used, expert review is often done in the form of an expert panel of at least three experts. Of particular importance, is the review of the commitment plan and the change management plan. A strategy is of little value unless it can be successfully implemented. The change management plan and the commitment plan are critical enablers to successful execution. This technique may be applied at the completion of the assessment or the strategy steps.

3. External Perspectives Check

The purpose of an *external perspectives check* is to test the strategy from the perspectives of key external constituencies. Typical external perspectives would include questions such as:

- Would stockholders want to own a company with this strategy?
- Will competitors be afraid of a company with this strategy?
- Will employees be excited by a company with this strategy?
- Will your customers find a compelling reason to do business with a company with this strategy?
- Will other companies wish to form alliances with a company with this strategy?
- Will suppliers want to develop preferred cooperation relationships with a company with this strategy?

For each of these questions, a convincing argument in the affirmative should be developed. If such an argument cannot be developed, the strategy's shortcomings need to be corrected.

4. Simulations

Simulations are computerized executions, or simulations, of the strategy. By building a software business model, the strategy may be "tested." This approach permits trail and error practice, what-if analysis, and learning—

when it is still easy and painless to learn and improve. A good simulation has the following attributes:

- It is played by decision makers.
- It is built on a realistic model of how the competitive market operates.
- It includes "game theory" algorithms to develop player moves.
- It includes strategy frameworks to help analyze actions.
- It includes a competitor team in role.
- It mimics real-world options.
- It has a rigorously defined set of measurable outputs by which to judge results.

Simulation playing offers the following benefits:

- iterative learning,
- trial and error improvement of strategy,
- understanding of the dynamic interplay of strategies,
- improved tuning of strategies,
- all the benefits of prototyping,
- along with scenarios, it is one of the best methods to prepare the management team for vigilance, and
- team building.

Sun Tzu says: "Be prepared and you will be lucky."[1] Simulations are one of the few methods available that let you test the strategy for correctness by executing it without the possibilities of harm but with the possibilities of great improvement.

5. Valuation Check

Financial performance remains the premier measure of business success. It is therefore mandatory that financial performance be one of the key measures of strategy correctness. A strategy cannot be correct if it does not meet the financial goals of the business. Consistent with whatever measures (payback, ROI, net present value, cash flow, shareholder value, IM&M as percent of sales, etc.) are used to evaluate IM&M performance, the strategy should be evaluated financially to see that it meets or, better yet, exceeds whatever financial hurdles have been established. Market success as measured by financial success is the reward for an excellent strategy. It is through financial measures that the clinical outcome of efforts are assessed.

A caveat is required. While financial valuation is important, strategic actions remain difficult to quantify. There is a continuing debate in the strategic planning community on how best to determine the financial value of a strategic plan. A commonsense way to address this problem is to make a simple value assessment. Given your current business scope and set of strategic positions, are you sure that if you invest in this strategy to achieve the proposed business scope and positions that you will get your money's worth? Will you receive value for your investment? Will you have nourished and created a set of sustainable competitive advantages that will generate the accident of success? Isn't this the central question?

Summary

These five techniques provide assistance in judging the correctness of the strategy. Perhaps one more that should be added is extensive draft read-outs throughout the organization. By engaging in extensive communications with staff members and their wide range of views, both improvements can be made and buy-in can be promoted concurrently.

6.4 Summary

Being involved in an industry that has enjoyed such continual growth and technological innovation, many members of the IM&M community forget that the IM&M industry is littered with business failures. Many seemingly successful companies have enjoyed, in retrospect, only temporary success. Unable to change with the times, their success was passing. Their failures were failures of strategy.

The following are a few of the more visible cases:

- Cullinet and Applied Data Research (ADR), which challenged IBM's supremacy in the mainframe DBMS market in the 1980s, failed to make the shifts to relational DBMS, open systems, and the ascendancy of the workstation/LAN environment. Both companies, pioneers and very respected technological companies in their day, were purchased by Computer Associates.

- Ashton-Tate, which owned the PC DBMS market with DBASE, was unable to upgrade the product and maintain quality. It was purchased by the smaller and more aggressive Borland Inc.

- Wang, on 18 August 1992, became the largest computer company ever to file for Chapter 11 Bankruptcy. Wang, whose revenue peaked at $2.9 billion in 1988, was once number 146 among the Fortune 500. On revenue of $1.896 billion for the fiscal year ending in September 1992, Wang lost $356.6 million. Having been a pioneer and extremely successful in word processing and office automation, Wang failed to understand the impact of the general purpose PC, standardization, and the substitution of LANS for proprietary minicomputers.

As is illustrated in Figures 6.4, 6.5, and 6.6, the ability of most IM&M vendors, our suppliers, to consistently increase wealth for their stockholders is, at best, erratic. They have experienced, only too well, the problems of continuously satisfying changing customer needs, managing the orderly integration of new technologies, and the ferocity of avid competition. This is the playing field on which you will have to compete.

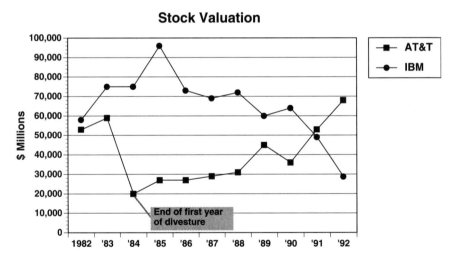

Figure 6.4   Stock Market Valuation I. IBM has been in decline since 1985, but AT&T has demonstrated consistent improvement since divestiture.

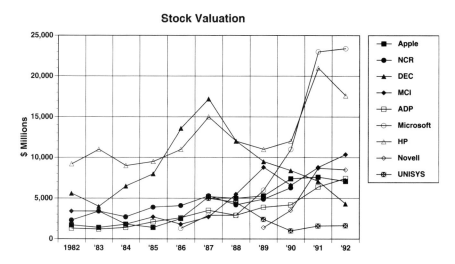

Figure 6.5   Stock Market Valuation II. DEC peaked in 1987, but look at Microsoft.

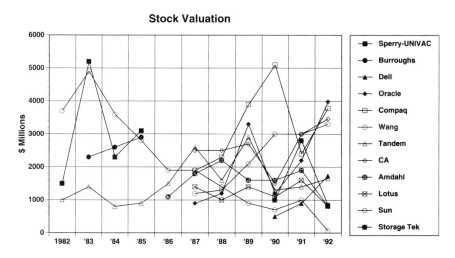

Figure 6.6   Stock Market Valuation III. Notice the decline of Wang, the roller coasters of Compaq and Oracle, and the rise and fall of Amdahl.

Table 6.10
Quality Methods Sixteen methods are available to test the strategy for quality.

Quality Methods		Applicable Strategic Planning Step	
Classification	Technique	Assessment	Strategy
Logical Relationship Checks	Conclusion/Objec-tive Check		X
	Objectives/Strategic Moves Check		X
	Owner/Strategic Moves Check		X
	Champion/Strategic Moves Check		X
Completeness Checks	Strategic Areas Check		X
	Business "P"S Check		X
	7 "S" Check		X
	Strategic Intent Check		X
	Time-line Check		X
	Directives/Assump-tions Check		X
	Key Findings Check		X
Correctness Checks	Devils Advocacy	X	X
	Expert Review	X	X
	External Perspec-tives Check		X
	Simulations		X
	Valuation Check		X

While these examples are vendors, the continued success of internal IM&M organizations is also being challenged. As was presented in Chapter 2, the outsourcers are driving more and more internal IM&M shops out of business. The August 1992 announcement of the creation of

Advantis (owned by IBM and Sears) to provide voice and data transmission, outsourcing, EDI, network integration services, and professional services on a global basis, will provide another outsourcing threat to the internal IM&M organization. IBM followed that move in October 1992 announcing the formation of the 1500 member IBM Consulting Group. High walls and deep moats will no longer provide the internal IM&M organization with any security.

Table 6.10 summarizes the techniques which were explained in this chapter. It is strongly recommended that they be used to assure the quality of the strategy. A strategy without quality is useless. If you are not willing to invest in quality, you are not prepared to invest in strategic planning. Sun Tzu says:

> So it is said that good warriors take their stand on ground where they cannot lose. Ground where one cannot lose means invincible strategy that makes it impossible for opponents to defeat you.[2]

An "invincible strategy" is a strategy infused with quality.

Footnotes

1. Sun Tzu, *The Art of War.*
2. Sun Tzu, *The Art of War.*

7

Administration

The purpose of this chapter is to understand the issues involved in administrating the strategic planning process. Strategic planning is a process. One can argue that it is the most important capability of an organization because it provides the direction and context for all other business activities. It therefore must be implemented and managed with concern for quality, speed, participation, and clarity.

Strategic Planning Method Critique

The strategic planning method which has been explained in Chapters 3–6 is not without its critics. The "totality" of the approach subjects it to criticisms of being bureaucratic and painstakingly slow, preventing "learning by doing," promoting a bias for thinking rather than a bias for action, not being action-oriented, and, perhaps worst of all, it is fatally flawed because it is fundamentally based on attempting to plan for an uncertain future with reasonable certainty.

Alternative methods of strategy development are proposed which emphasize hustle, accelerated decision making, a "do something and do it quickly" attitude, attack each and every opportunity, strategy in real-time, and act-do-learn-refine. The alternative approaches are action-oriented and are based on two premises:

1. The future is not foreseeable, and
2. The only way to learn is to do.

While these arguments are attractive and appealing, the defense of the presented method is based on the view that the business is one system and strategy must operate comprehensively at the system level or dysfunction will be inevitable. A business provides only a superficial delusion of consisting of parts; it has a clearly knit unity. Just as one cannot touch any part of a bowl of Jell-O without the whole thing quivering, one cannot change parts of a business without the other parts being impacted. The challenges of obtaining and maintaining commitment, achieving alignment, developing core competencies, capabilities, and sustainable competitive advantages, and stimulating winning behaviors are long-term endeavors. These arguments also miss an important point. The most critical benefit of strategic planning is not the plan but the process of focused thinking about the business. By learning the planning methods and becoming strategy literate, the management team internalizes strategy and acts strategically on a daily basis. So while strategic planning does not itself qualify as the basis of sustainable competitive advantage, its consequences do.

It is an interesting paradox that the impeccable logic of the strategic planning process, the rule of reason, also serves as the basis for its most severe criticism, most clearly stated: What benefit is derived from investing in time consuming perfect logic when dealing with an ever faster changing and unknowable future? This argument also misses the point. It is not the case that rationalist-based strategic planning is perfect, it's just that it's the best of the available alternatives. While the "ready-aim-fire," "hustle," and "empowerment" promoters provide appealing arguments, after the rhetoric ends there is little substance to build upon. How do they suggest that you create sustainable competitive advantage, core competencies, leverage, etc.? They don't provide any prescription, somehow they are just supposed to occur. So it is not the case that rationalist-based strategic planning should be embraced because of its state of perfection, it should be embraced because of its relative superiority.

Sun Tzu, while encouraging speed, adaption, and surprise, envisioned them occurring within the context of an overall guiding plan. Sun Tzu says:

> If you have no ulterior scheme and no forethought, but just rely on your individual bravery, flippantly taking opponents lightly and giving no consideration to the situation, you will surely be taken prisoner.[1]

Ad-hoc actions without forethought, design, and an integrative purpose are nonsense.

The kernel problem with the non-rationalist schools of strategy is that at their foundation is a hidden unstated belief that business is not craftable. In Section 1.3 you read that time is an accident of motion and sustainable business success is an accident of strategy. Accident, again, in this context, meaning a "consequence of." It was also asserted that it is only meaningful to take actions against primary objects; one cannot take affecting actions against accidents. The motion of the cosmos, the primary object, is beyond mortal manipulation, so time, its accident, is also not alterable. Strategy (at least rationalist strategy) is subject to mortal design, so business success, its accident, is influenceable. At the foundation of the arguments of the non-rationalist is a chain of accidents wherein business success is an accident of strategy, but strategy is an accident of serendipity, and serendipity is an accident of chance, but chance is an accident of providence. Since accidents are not influenceable, the non-rationalist school leaves us at the beginning of the chain with the primary object of providence which, like the motion of the cosmos, is also beyond our ability to influence. So one must choose to proceed rationally or irrationally. Rationality defines a notion of strategy that offers hope and methods for influencing the future. Irrationality offers a notion of strategy where strategic management is equated to prayer. The Divine stopped the sun in the sky (and thereby stopped time) to aid Joshua in his battle with the Canaanites. If not too busy with more pressing business, perhaps the Divine will show equal favor with us and bless our skunk works. The core problem with the non-rationalist school of strategy is that beneath its superficial appeal as a strategy of action, it is, correctly understood, a philosophy of hopelessness and impotency. The days of decision are at hand, and you must surface your *weltanschaug:* What is your outlook, your world view of strategy? Do you believe that "their victories were not flukes" or do you believe that "their victories were flukes?" Do you embrace the Nietzschean philosophy that "He who considers more deeply knows that, whatever his acts and judgments may be, he is always wrong," or do you believe positive change can be a consequence of premeditated planning? This is the pivotal question.

In reality, the conflict is often artificial; the disagreement is one of degree of formality. Even the most ardent proponent of hustle must, even if only done dynamically in her cerebellum, perform a situation analysis, reach a conclusion, decide on an objective, and define actions. Her actions do not arise spontaneously out of nothing as did the universe in Genesis. This person also must get resources allocated (commitment) and overcome obstacles (change management). Whether one believes in rigorous formal strategy formulation or *ad-hoc* dynamic formulation, the methods described in this book are of equal utility. What varies is the degree of formality, documentation, research, and reflection.

Nevertheless, the critique further emphasizes the need to implement strategic planning in a world class manner. This is not easily done. Barriers such as:

- Translating analysis into succinct and precise conclusions, objectives, and moves,
- Organizational skepticism of a process which is future-oriented,
- Organizational preoccupation with tactical survival,
- Cultural defense of "what is" currently being done,
- Lack of competency in strategic planning methods at all levels of the organization,

- A culture that equates strategy to IM&M strategy only, and
- Politics, politics, and more politics of implementing a new process.

To minimize the pain, here are some guidelines on designing the strategy process.

The Players

Figure 7.1 illustrates the major participants in the strategy process. The executive strategy team, lead by the CIO, is responsible for developing the strategy. Successful strategists think holistically and abstractly, accept ambiguity, work well with models, think in metaphors, are open-minded, unbiased, humble, research-oriented, curious, and worried. They are worried because they understand the ephemeral nature of success and the need to constantly change. Sun Tzu says:

If you can always remember danger when you are secure and remember chaos in times of order, watch out for danger and chaos while they are still formless and prevent them before they happen, this is best of all.[2]

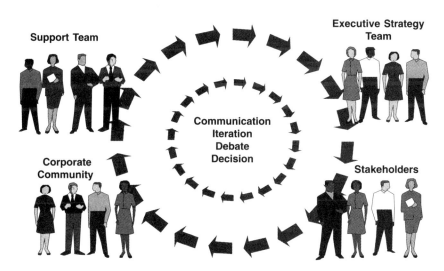

Figure 7.1   The Players. The key players in the strategy process are the strategist, the support team, the stakeholders, and the corporate community.

Strategists, unlike most, understand that the time to plan for major innovations is at the high points of success when time and resources are abundant; not at the point of crisis when time and options are limited.

A newspaper article commenting on the continued success of Intel identified this exact point:

> Intel has never relaxed, retaining to today the anxious mood that prevailed in 1968, when the company began with eight engineers and $3 million in capital. As chief executive Andrew Grove likes to say, "Only the paranoid survive." Intel came to recognize that if it didn't bring out products that would make the older ones obsolete, someone else would. It is Intel's goal to be the best possible cannibal in the world and eat their children as fast as they can.

The strategist understands that the prosperity and bounty that the organization enjoys is under constant attack. The jungle always stands ready to reclaim civilization. The strategist is never content with "what is." "What is" is the legacy of those who have come before, and it must be continually refreshed to remain vital. The bounty and prosperity of "what is" buys but fleeting time against fortune. The strategist is never self-satisfied. So while accountants count revenue, programmers count function points, marketers count accounts, and operations count outages, strategists count advantages.

A strategy team of "Art of War" strategists has three attributes:

1. It creates unique analytical frameworks to understand the current situation.

2. Its members have internalized strategy—their thoughts, actions, and perspectives are strategy-centric.

3. Its members have achieved a strategy state of being—strategy is not superimposed on them, they emanate strategy.

They achieve a state of heightened involvement with the business wherein their personal destiny and the fate of the business are intertwined.

In *The Divine Comedy*, Dante explains that the Inferno, Purgatory (Hell), and Paradise (Heaven) are not geographical places to which the immortal soul migrates after earthly death. Instead, they are "the state" of the soul after death. The soul does not go to its afterlife; it becomes, takes on the condition of its afterlife. This must also be the notion of strategic thinking; a notion of unity. Strategic thinking is not something appended or superadded to the strategist's intellect; it is the condition of the intellect.

The distinction between strategic thinking and a strategic plan is therefore evident. Strategic thinking is the real-time analysis, understanding, and reaction to events through dynamic mental invocation of strategic frameworks. All is seen, understood, interpreted, and reacted to through strategic frameworks. A strategic plan is a point in time summary, a bookmark, of strategic thought. Since strategic understanding is continual, a strategic plan as a reflection of strategic thought is always subject to revision based on events.

Sun Tzu says:

> The multitudes know when you win but they do not know the basis. Everyone knows the form by which I am victorious, but no one knows the form by which I ensure victory. The science of ensuring victory is a mysterious secret. Victory is not repetitious, but adapts its form endlessly.[3]

Other Players

The support team provides the support function to the strategy team. They are responsible for managing the process, maintaining the process documentation, providing expertise in methods, preparing strawpersons and drafts for strategy team review, coordinating meetings and read-outs, quality control, education, and guiding and facilitating debate. A competent support team is a critical success factor for the process.

Stakeholders represent key middle and lower level members of the organization hierarchy who provide input and advice and are the primary implementers of the strategy. Stakeholder buy-in is critical to success. One cannot expect middle and lower management to implement what they have had absolutely no say in and do not understand.

Data Collection (Figure 7.2)

Strategic planning is a data-intensive activity. Processes must be developed to provide recurrent data that provides intimate knowledge of the actual situation. For each business area of interest, a data collection process must be designed and implemented which identifies:

- Exactly what data is required,
- Who owns the data,
- The frequency of collection, and
- The format of collection.

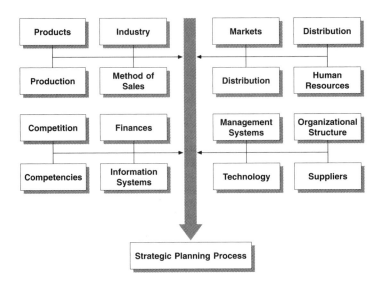

Figure 7.2   Data Collection. Processes have to be developed to collect accurate data in a scheduled and repeatable manner.

Data collection must occur on a scheduled basis. Obviously, without quality data, the entire planning process is compromised.

The methods of data collection used should encourage direct participation by as many people as possible. Focus groups, informal discussions, presentations, and open e-mail can be used effectively to gather information as well as formal and scheduled processes. While broad participation should be encouraged and all ideas entertained, all ideas should only be incorporated into the planning in proportion to their wisdom. Some people reason fallaciously that "since all people are equal in some things," that all "people are equal in all things." This is the fallacy of composition (see Table 3.31). When personal opinion is equated *a priori* to reason and vision based on a fallacious view of organizational democracy, pseudo-equality dilutes reason and vison and yields mediocrity.

What is of interest to our research is not what anyone thinks, opinions are of minimum strategic value, it is what someone knows. The ante to participate in the strategy debate is reason (convincing arguments) and vision (insight or imagination). If we abrogate insistence on basing debate on intellectual faculties (reason and vision), then equal consideration must be given to revelation, superstition, provincialism, or any other irrational criteria. Perhaps then we should add a seance to the planning process and improve the perfection of our efforts by conjuring up Sun Tzu and Machiavelli (how wonderful!) as our advisors. We could also burn at the stake as heretics any witches or warlocks who disagree with our findings; how convenient and permanent a method for forcing alignment. One can quickly see where admittance of irrationality leads.

Calendar of Events

The strategy process is best managed and communicated by publishing a master calendar of events. More detailed schedules of events may also be published to amplify the details for the items on the master schedule. Figure 7.3 illustrates a running 12 month calendar which is published monthly. Key items on the calendar are as follows:

- *Mid-June through October*—The yearly strategic planning steps of assessment and strategy are performed.
- *Mid-January*—A process improvement review is held to review the previous years activities and propose improvements in the overall strategic planning process.
- *Quarterly*—A strategy conference is held where action owners read-out plans and progress.
- *Mid-April*—A "Looking Back at Looking Forward" conference is held to review the accuracy of historical forecasts and assess ways to improve forecasting.

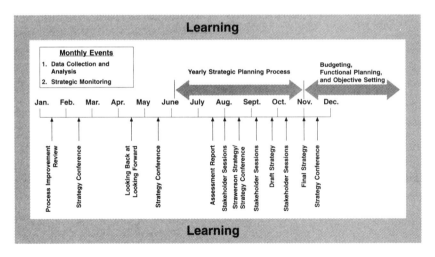

Figure 7.3 Calendar of Events. A master 12 month calendar should control the overall scheduling of the strategic planning process.

- *Monthly*—Data is collected and strategy is monitored.

The entire strategy process takes place against a background of continuous learning, both formal and informal, to support the maintenance of fresh, open, and fluid mental models in accord with times and circumstances.

Extendibility and Process Linkage

The proposed strategic planning process is highly modular with well-defined interfaces (conclusions, positions, business scope, etc.) The process can therefore be easily extended to interlock multiple strategy processes. While being extendible, the process must also be designed to feed and direct downstream dependent processes. Strategy should direct organizational objective setting, capital investments, budgeting, customer service plans, and yearly operational plans. Feedback loops and monitoring processes must be developed to assure that the downstream processes are proceeding in symmetry with the strategic plan.

Deliverables

There are four key outputs of the assessment and strategy steps of strategic planning. These outputs are as follows (see Table 7.1).

- The *assessment report* is generated at the conclusion of the assessment step.
- A *strawperson strategy* is generated as the initial output of the strategy step. Its purpose is to accumulate the ideas to date into a structured format to facilitate plan development.
- A *draft strategy* is a complete strategy being circulated for comment.
- After the draft strategy comments are collected and analyzed, a *final strategy* is developed. This document then becomes the basis and reference for all downstream planning activities.

Execution outputs consist of normal project management reports.

IM&M and Strategic Planning

Strategic planning is a process that lends itself to improvement through the intelligent use of IM&M. IM&M support can vastly improve the quality, efficiency, effectiveness, and timeliness of the effort. Figure 7.4 pro-

Deliverable Step	Assessment Report	Strawperson Strategy	Draft Strategy	Final Strategy
Business Scope	Current	Future	Future	Future
Strategic Positions	Current	Future	Future	Future
Conclusions	Complete Set			
Objectives		Complete Set	Complete Set	Complete Set
Strategic Moves		Complete Set	Complete Set	Complete Set
Logical Quality Control Checks		x	x	
Commitment Plan			Complete Set	Complete Set
Change Management Plan			Complete Set	Complete Set
Completeness Quality Control Check			Complete Set	
Strategy Valuation Statement			x	x

Table 7.1

Deliverables. Outputs are generated consistently with the strategic planning step and its state of iteration.

Business Practices							
The Business Applications				About the Business Applications			
Online Transaction Processing (OLTP)	Operational Support Systems (OSS)	Business Process Automation (BPA)	Time-Shared	Modeling	Information Retrieval	Ad hoc Reporting	Decision Support
Transaction Processing				Information Sharing			

Figure 7.4   Application Classification. Business applications can be partitioned into those that run the business and those that analyze the business.

vides a taxonomy for business applications. Strategic planning would fall into the "about the business" class of applications. Table 7.2 summarizes the types of IM&M technology which are most opportunistic to deploy in support of strategy work.

Getting Started

Implementing a strategic planning process within an IM&M organization is a four step process consisting of:

1. *Assessment*—Understanding how strategic plans are currently formulated and executed. What is the process used, who participates, and what analytical methods are favored? Does a business scope exist? Are there managed positions? What type of execution monitoring and vigilance are used? At the completion of this step, the analyst should have a complete answer to the question: "What are they doing and how are they doing it?"

2. *Design*—The design of a customized strategic planning process to meet the needs of this IM&M organization. Research must be done to determine how the process described in this book is to be modified to meet the particular culture and style of your organization. Gap analysis can then be done to understand the chasm between where the organization is currently and where it should be in the future. At the completion of this, the analyst should have a model of the three step strategic planning process that the organization will adopt and the necessary steps to transition it there from its current processes.

3. *Preparation*—Doing the necessary one time "startup" activities of education, data collection processes, initial business scope definition, consultant briefings, initial positioning, kickoff strategy studies, etc., to enable an orderly first execution of the strategic planning process. At the completion of this step, the organization is postured to execute the new strategic planning process.

4. *Execution*—Execution of the new strategic planning process of assessment, strategy, and execution per your design and preparation.

Table 7.2
IM&M and Strategic Planning. There are numerous ways to infuse the strategic planning process with IM&M support.

IM&M Technology	Strategic Planning Application
Word processing software	Preparation of documentation
Project management software	1. Management of strategic planning process 2. Evaluation of strategic plan
Presentation graphics	Presentations
E-mail	Announcements, communications, meeting notices, reminders, distribution, solicitations, etc.
Imaging	Collection of information about external business environment (market forecasts, articles, financial statements, etc .)
Groupware	Collaboration, information sharing
Video conferencing	Meeting facilitation
Financial and simulation software	Forecasting, modeling, and spreadsheets
Artificial intelligence	Rule-based models
Database access (remote terminal emulation access)	1. Industry newsletters, 2. Library access, 3. Competitor and financial databases, 4. Clipping services, and 5. Internal databases.
Strategic planning application software	Process automation through software products which have packaged the various strategic planning models

As has been strongly suggested before, the biggest hurdles in implementing change will be resistance to change and a shortage of commitment. It is therefore incumbent for the successful strategic planning process implementer to carefully include in her design a well thought out change plan and commitment plan to support her efforts. Strategic business planning is a radical departure from the way in which most IM&M organizations have traditionally planned. One must anticipate frozen mental models, overt resistance, and passive resistance. Be of strong courage and always remember, "...It is best to win without fighting." Use indirect means to facilitate change and acceptance.

In priming the management team for the strategic planning process, it is essential to impress upon them the importance of what they have chosen to undertake. The desired end state of strategy, deep and far reaching strategies that position you for assured success, cannot be achieved without proper preparation, process, and commitment. If you do not master strategy but pretend to manage through strategy, you create a fraud. A charlatan, you will create problems even greater than those from which you had hoped to escape. Your actions will be in vain. The choice of mastery is the only valid alternative.

Communication

The strategy team cannot be omnipresent. Omnipresence is an impossibility; absence of it is therefore not a fault, but the cause for the requirement of a communication plan. The strategic plan is not a secret. While certain details of it may be restrictive, the strategy cannot serve as the context for push-down empowered decision making if it is only known to a select few. So the empowered masses can either become the "aimless empowered" who without guidance do their best and accidentally align in actions, or they can be the "focus empowered" who share a common strategic agenda. Should they wander about in awe of a great but hidden purpose without fathoming it? What advantage is accrued by a stealth strategy?

Administration is responsible for developing a communication program which assures the strategy is communicated throughout the organization in detail appropriate for each job function. What is not known nor understood cannot be implemented. Since you want the strategy implemented, you must insure wide pollination of the strategy message.

Summary

Strategic business planning is the highest level of decision making for the business. It provides direction, focus, and purpose as a business continually strives to move closer to its strategic intent. Being such a crucial business process, the administration of the effort is important to overall business success.

Successful implementation of strategic business planning hinges on the following critical success factors:

- *Education*—The impacted community must be educated in the process, strategic planning methods, and roles and responsibilities.
- *Stakeholder commitment*—The strategy team must be committed to strategic business planning as the vehicle of strategic business management.
- *Linkage*—Downstream processes must be linked with and measured by their support and execution of the strategic plan.
- *Competency*—The support team must be competent in the strategic planning process and methods to develop organizational respect and credibility.
- *IM&M*—The use of IM&M to infuse the process with quality, speed, effectiveness, and efficiency.
- Learning system—The design of both a formal and informal learning system to continually challenge and update the mental models of the strategy team.

These items must be done to insure success.

Footnotes

1. Sun Tzu, *The Art of War.*
2. Sun Tzu, *The Art of War.*
3. Sun Tzu, *The Art of War.*

8

Understanding Contemporary IM&M

The purpose of this chapter is to apply the skills you have learned to strategically understand the major contemporary IM&M issues impacting your business. Few professions are inundated with as much change, technological wizardry, hype, opinions, information, and misinformation as the IM&M profession. Information technology magazines, managerial consultants, books, seminars, gurus, pundits, oracles, and academics all scream for our attention to lecture us about the issue or technology of the moment. We are forewarned that this technology is the Holy Grail of computing, the mystical silver bullet has finally arrived, and we better rapidly adopt it, or, conversely, we are lectured on the dangers and pitfalls of adopting a different technology. There are plenty of advice givers and opinions but few convincing arguments.

Unfortunately, the arguments and analysis routinely provided are shallow and simplistic. Whether the reason for the simplicity of the debate is lack of strategic framing skills on the part of the presenter or an assumption of strategic planning ignorance on the part of the audience or both, almost all arguments presented to strategically promote or denigrate IM&M technologies reduce to cost reduction, improved productivity, or improved decision making. While these are valid rationales, those who are strategically literate can and should do better, much better, to appreciate the deeper strategic significance and opportunities that new technologies offer.

This chapter will address this issue as follows:

* Section 8.1: Understanding Contemporary IM&M Issues Strategically

   This section will analyze 16 contemporary IM&M issues and technologies from a strategic perspective. Using the frameworks and analytical methods learned in this book, the issues will be evaluated to determine their deeper strategic significance.

- Section 8.2: Understanding Contemporary IM&M News Strategically

  This section will analyze contemporary IM&M news items from a strategic perspective. Using the frameworks and analytical methods learned in this book, the news items will be evaluated to determine their deeper strategic significance. This will also demonstrate the power and advantage of being able to analyze IM&M events strategically on a daily basis

- Section 8.3: Reprise

  This section will do a broad review of what you have learned in this book and will present some final thoughts on the integration of strategic business planning and IM&M.

It is our general contention that the family of strategic concepts, frameworks, methods, and theories that have been presented, as a group, provide a comprehensive explanatory schema of strategic action. IM&M issues and news of strategic import should, consequently, be explainable as instances of this overall schema.

Sun Tzu says:

A general must see alone and know alone, meaning that he must see what others do not see and know what others do not know. Seeing what others do not see is called brilliance, knowing what others do not know is called genius.[1]

Let us see if we can build advantage by better understanding the contemporary issues which confront us.

8.1 Understanding Contemporary IM&M Issues Strategically

The purpose of this section is to analyze 16 major IM&M issues to assess their strategic significance. By understanding the issues strategically, plans for their implementation can be made which maximize benefits, and wasteful time can be avoided on high hype but low payoff ideas. Each issue will be analyzed using the following format:

- *Definition*: A short definition of the issue,
- *Analysis*: A strategic analysis of the issue, and
- *Conclusion*: Strategic assessment.

Many of the technologies reviewed in this section were discussed in Section 2.2 and you may wish to review that material in concert with reading this analysis.

1. Outsourcing

Definition: Outsourcing is the use of external service providers to provide IM&M services which had been traditionally provided by internal IM&M organizations. Two of the primary types of outsourcing are facilities management and systems integration discussed in Section 2.3.

Analysis: You are confronted with a glaring paradox. If IM&M is as strategically important to the business for all the reasons that have been argued, i.e., IM&M is competitiveness, IM&M provides the basis for improving the value chain, IM&M provides the basis for building superior capabilities, IM&M provides the basis for breaking bottlenecks, IM&M provides the basis for repositioning against the Five Forces, etc., why would you outsource such a fundamentally critical resource? Won't the investment in meeting customer satisfaction, especially the management of excitement attributes, require extensive use of IM&M?

Machiavelli understood this issue best:

> ...The arms on which a prince bases the defense of his state are either his own, or mercenary, or auxiliary. Mercenaries and auxiliaries are useless and dangerous. If a prince bases the defense of his state on mercenaries, he will never achieve stability or security...the reason for this is that there is no loyalty or inducement to keep them on the field apart from the little they are paid and that is not enough to make them want to die for you.... I conclude, therefore, that unless it commands its own arms, no principality is secure, rather it is dependent on fortune since there is no valor and no loyalty to defend it when adversity comes.[2]

Only the most "factoryish," pure operational aspects of IM&M should be outsourced. Expertise may be purchased for critical functions to allow the learning curve to be accelerated.

Conclusion: Outsourcing of other than the most routine and non-valued added IM&M services doesn't even qualify as good nonsense. Outsourcing is essentially a question of whether you view your information technology as a core business competency. If you do, outsourcing compromises the viability of the business because you turn control of a basic core competency over to a mercenary. While this perspective is contrarian and heretical to the actions of many well-respected companies and runs counter to the anticipated growth of the outsourcing industry, you must separate the action of outsourcing from judgment of the action (see Table 2.17 and Figures 2.49 and 2.50).

Time and benchmarking will tell whether the companies that chose outsourcing have made a superior or inferior strategic decision. I would suggest that many of the decisions to outsource are driven not by strategic vision but by tactical savings, a view that IM&M is not strategic (it's a "glorified mailroom") and fad-surfing. With apologies to Machiavelli, his admonition, applied to outsourcing, could be restated as follows:

> …The assets on which a CIO bases the IM&M of his business are either his own or outsourcers. Outsourcers are useless and dangerous. If a CIO bases the IM&M of his business on outsourcers, he will never achieve stability or security…the reason for this is that there is no loyalty or inducement to keep them on the field apart from the little they are paid and that is not enough to make them want to die for you…. I conclude, therefore, that unless it commands its own IM&M assets, no business is secure, rather it is dependent on fortune since there is no valor and no loyalty to defend it when adversity comes.

A humble tribute to the timelessness of Machiavelli's insight and the advantage of looking at the world through timeless lenses.

2. Open Systems/Standards

Definition: Open systems and standards refers to the movement within the IM&M industry to use products based on standards. These open standards promote interoperability and portability between heterogeneous vendor environments. The standards are defined by an assortment of government, user, vendor, and standards groups.

Analysis: Open systems and standards are of the highest strategic importance to the IM&M user community. The reason for this is that openness fundamentally alters the balance of the Five Forces to a position more favorable to the buyers of IM&M services at the expense of the suppliers. Figures 8.1 through 8.5 illustrate the change in the Five Force balance of power due to the imposition of open systems on an environment previously dominated by proprietary systems. There is a clear and material shift in the Five Forces in favor of the buyer.

Conclusion: A strategic thrust of any organization is to maximize its position within the Five Forces. Open systems with the benefits of portability, interoperability, scalability, and competition should be adopted as quickly as possible, consistent with the state of open systems technology and the care and feeding of the embedded systems base.

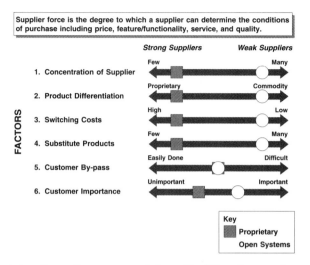

Figure 8.1   Open Systems and Supplier Five Force. Open systems re-
defines industry competitive structure in favor of the customer. *Source*
"Implementing Client/Server Computing: A Strategic Perspective,"
Bernard H. Boar, McGraw-Hill, 1993 with permission of publisher.

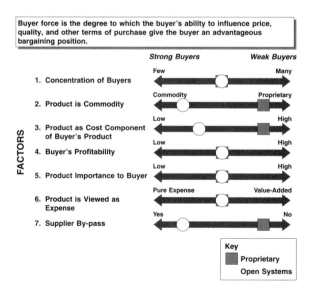

Figure 8.2   Open Systems and Buyer Five Force. Open systems re-
defines industry competitive structure in favor of the customer. *Source*
"Implementing Client/Server Computing: A Strategic Perspective,"
Bernard H. Boar, McGraw-Hill, 1993 with permission of publisher.

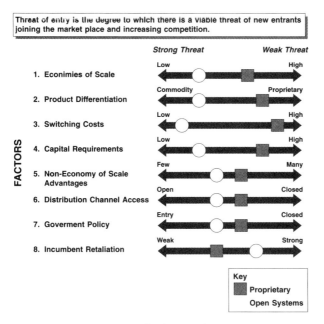

Figure 8.3   Open Systems and Threat of Entry Five Force. Open systems re-defines industry competitive structure in favor of the customer. *Source* "Implementing Client/Server Computing: A Strategic Perspective," Bernard H. Boar, McGraw-Hill, 1993 with permission of publisher.

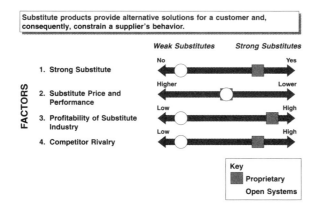

Figure 8.4   Open Systems and Substitute Product Five Force. Open systems re-defines industry competitive structure in favor of the customer. *Source* "Implementing Client/Server Computing: A Strategic Perspective," Bernard H. Boar, McGraw-Hill, 1993 with permission of publisher.

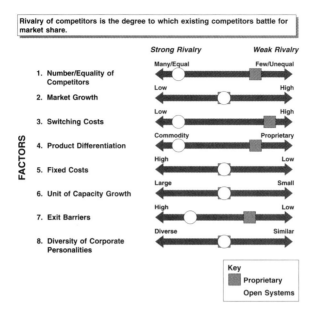

Figure 8.5   Open Systems and Rivalry Five Force. Open systems re-defines industry competitive structure in favor of the customer. *Source* **"Implementing Client/Server Computing: A Strategic Perspective," Bernard H. Boar, McGraw-Hill, 1993 with permission of publisher.**

3. Distributed Database Management Systems (DDBMS)

Definition: DDBMS refers to emerging database technology which permits multiple physically distinct databases (homogeneous and heterogeneous) both locally and dispersed to be viewed by a user as a single logical database.

Analysis: DDBMS is strategically important because it increases the "range" of the desired reach/range/maneuverability architecture illustrated in Figure 2.2. IM&M reaches its maximum potential for competitiveness when it permits users to share information (range). DDBMS is the critical emerging technology to allow transparent access to traditional and new information objects.

Conclusion: DDBMS is a range-extender technology and should be implemented as quickly as possible, consistent with its life cycle evolution.

4. Objected-Oriented Technologies

Definition: Object-oriented technologies refers to a family of technologies built on the key object-oriented concepts of encapsulation, messaging, inheritance, and the unit of manipulation being an object.

Analysis: The strategic importance of object-oriented technologies is best understood by the strategic notion of leverage. Object-oriented technologies are multipliers. They promote reusability, modularity, and sharing and, consequently, accelerate the software life cycle process.

Conclusion: Object-oriented technologies provide the greatest software leverage availability.

5. Wireless Communication Technologies

Definition: Wireless communication technologies refers to a family of both local and wide areas communication technologies which permit communication without the use of wires.

Analysis: Wireless communication technologies are important because they increase the "reach" of information. As illustrated in Figure 2.2, part of the composition of a competitiveness architecture is maximum reach, the ability of anyone, anywhere, at anytime to access information. Wireless communications contributes to this strategic goal.

Conclusion: Wireless communication is a reach-extender technology.

6. Client/Server Computing[3]

Definition: Client/Server computing is a processing model in which a single application is partitioned between multiple processors (front-end and back-end) and the processors cooperate (transparent to the end-user) to complete the processing as a single unified task. A client/server bond product (middleware) ties the processors together to create the illusion of a single system image. Client/Server computing is synonymous with the labels of network computing, requestor/server architecture, workstation/server architecture, user-centered computing, and client/server computing architecture.

Analysis: Client/server computing is strategically important because it provides the maneuverability foundation for the Reach/Range/Maneuverability architecture. Table 2.2 defines the attributes of a maneuverable architecture. Client/server computing meets these requirements as follows:[4]

    Maintainability—The decomposition of monolithic, rigid systems into discrete interlocking parts enhances maintainability. As happens with most engineered products, it is easier to fix, replace, and service by constraining repairs to components with well-defined interfaces rather than having to fix, replace, and service a single monolithic entity.

    Modularity—The client/server architecture is constructed on the notion of connectable modules. Each client and server is a system module, independently (subject to interfacing constraints) replaceable. New system functions are added by scaling existing modules or adding new modules. New clients are added by scaling existing clients or adding new clients.

Adaptability—Figure 8.6 illustrates the various ways that client/server solutions can distribute presentation, processing, and data services between clients and servers to achieve an initial optimum solution. As circumstances evolve, the partitioning can be evolved to meet the new requirements. *Recursion* (not illustrated) permits endless architectures to be cut and pasted together as solutions. The best mix and match set of partitions is driven by the application-dependent dimensions of data volume, transaction volume, data manipulation intensity, geographical demographics of users, and attributes of each client/server component.

Adaptability is further enhanced by the recursive character of client/server computing that permits the creation of logical services. A client can request a service of a server that is only a logical service, i.e., through recursion it calls on other servers to do the real work. Highly functional servers can be developed but packaged in endless combinations for simple use by applications. Logical services are the

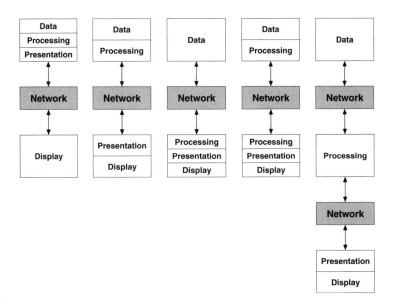

Figure 8.6   Alternative Client/Server Partitioning. Clients and servers may have services partitioned in multiple ways. *Source* **"Implementing Client/Server Computing: A Strategic Perspective," Bernard H. Boar, McGraw-Hill, 1993 with permission of publisher.**

processing equivalent to distributed DBMS which creates logicaldatabases. By combing the two concepts together, one can create an architecture that is incredibly adaptable since users only see logical services and logical data. The physical services and databases are only accessible through indirection and consequently can be re-configured as required without disturbing the user's view and access to the IM&M world.

Scalability—Together with the attributes of modularity, openness, standards, and adaptability, client/server solutions can be scaled to meet the changing needs of the business.

Portability—Processing power comes in many sizes, including palmtop, notebook, laptop, pentop, desktop, deskside, mainframe, super-mainframe. Building client/server solutions based on standards permits applications to be placed and replaced where it is most advantageous.

Openness/Standards—The emergence of IM&M standards was an enabling event to permit the emergence of client/server solutions. Client/server architectures are built on standard application program interfaces (API's) which serve as the window to the network of services.

Autonomy—Clients may have minimum capability, as happens with diskless PCs and x-window terminals, or they can be fully configured. Appropriately configured, each client can work both independently and as part of the bonded corporation.

Flexibility—The client/server architecture is a fundamentally stronger architecture to model the real world complexities of user and computer relationships than the host-centered model. Figure 8.7 can be used to explain this by referencing basic data modeling constructs. A "one-to-many" data modeling structure permits the modeling of one-to-many relationships (for example, a hotel has many rooms). This equates architecturally to the host-centered computing architecture.

A stronger data modeling construct is the "many-to-many" construct that permits the modeling of many-to-many relationships (for example, a program is composed of many modules, but a module is included in many programs). This equates to the client/server architecture.

Just as the "many-to-many" data modeling construct is more powerful than the "one-to-many" construct (because it can better model the complexities of real world relationships), so a "many-to-many" architecture (client/server) is more powerful than a "one-to-many" architecture (host-centered) for the same reason. The "one-to-many" construct is, in reality, a simple subcase of the "many-to-

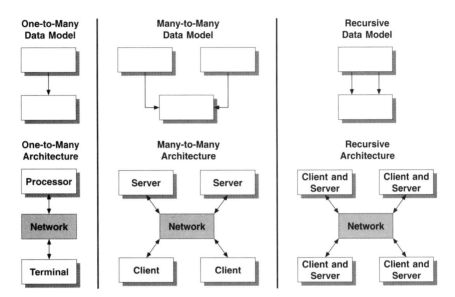

**Figure 8.7   Many-To-Many Architecture. CSC can model more compli-
cated user-processor relationships than host-based processing. *Source*
"Implementing Client/Server Computing: A Strategic Perspective,"
Bernard H. Boar, McGraw-Hill, 1993 with permission of publisher.**

many" construct. The "many-to-many" is the more general case
and, consequently, the more flexible one for modeling and revising
the system reflection of the real world.

A "many-to-many" construct can model recursive structures (for
example, a program calls other programs and a program is called by
many programs). The recursive capability of client/server computing can analogously model recursive processing structures that the
"one-to-many" architecture cannot.

Data Accessibility—Client/Server computing enables both "The
Business" and "The about the Business" databases to be positioned
as high-accessibility servers.

Interoperability—Client/Server computing consists of, by definition, clients and servers that are connected over networks. Interoperability is a definition attribute of the architecture.

Appliance Connectivity—Information collection, presentation, and
preparation devices are clients. As long as they meet the bonding
requirements, they can be appended to the architecture in the same
manner as any other client module.

Client/Server computing meets the requirement of a maneuverable architecture. In doing so, it broadens the reach and range of the IM&M

resource and positions the IM&M resource for maximum competitiveness (see Figure 2.2).

Conclusion—Client/Server computing is the foundation for a maneuverable IM&M architecture; it promotes the IM&M architecture to the status of a pivot position.

7. Pen-Based Computing

Definition: Pen-based computing refers to a user interface wherein an electronic stylus is used as the input mechanism, mimicking a pen or pencil as opposed to a character or graphical user interface. The screen essentially serves the role of electronic paper.

Analysis: Pen-based computing is of strategic significance because it extends the traditional and prevalent human interface metaphor of pen and pencil. Pen-based computers provide a more familiar and natural interface which can expand the scope of computing to a wider audience. By adding pen-based computers to the technology arsenal, the IM&M organization expands the ability to provide more enriched technology clusters to meet customer needs.

Conclusion: Pen-based computing provides a more powerful and natural human interface for the user community. Its absorption into the technology portfolio facilitates the construction of products and services with better fitting technology clusters.

8. Electronic Commerce

Definition: Electronic commerce refers to electronic interchange technologies which replace traditional paper-based transactions with electronic transactions.

Analysis: The strategic significance of electronic commerce is that it provides a mechanism to use IM&M to interlock value chains. Through electronic bonding and improved timeliness, productivity and value-added can be appended to your value chain and that of your supplier, distributor, or customer. Electronic commerce also raises new barriers to market entry since it raises the "ante" of capability that must exist to compete in the market.

Conclusion: Electronic bonding technologies, EDI, electronic funds transfer, e-mail, etc., are value chain interlocking technologies.

9. Multimedia

Definition: Multimedia refers to user interface technologies which encompass all forms of information (sound, text, video, image, and data).

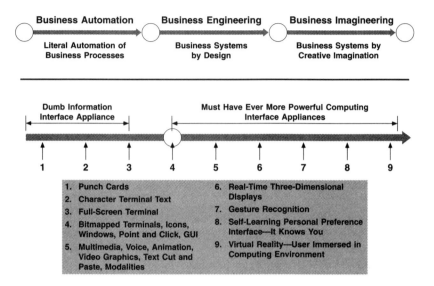

Figure 8.8   Human Interface Evolution. Multimedia interfaces will be increasingly important as the human interface metaphor evolves to permit "Imagineering" the Business.

Analysis: The strategic significance of multimedia is tautological. IM&M, by definition, is the preparation, collection, transport, retrieval, storage, and presentation of information in *all* its forms." The emergence of multimedia technologies is simply delivering on the definitional promise of IM&M. As was the case with pen-based computing, multimedia richly expands the technology portfolio to enable the creation of technology clusters which provide better solutions for the functions needed to meet user requirements. As illustrated in Figure 8.8, multimedia is key to continued improvement in the functionality of the human interface.

Conclusion: Multimedia revolutionizes the user interfaces, permitting much richer solutions.

10. Chargeback

Definition: Chargeback is the mechanism used by the internal IM&M organization to charge users for products and services.

Analysis: Chargeback is the most visible component of the evolution of the internal economic system between the IM&M organization and the user community. Any economic system has to solve three fundamental questions:

1. What products or services will be produced and in what quantities?

2. How will economic resources be used in producing these products or services?

3. For whom will the products or services be produced?

The internal processes which govern these decisions are budgeting, chargeback, and priority setting. What is happening is that as a result of the issues discussed in prior Chapters, many businesses are moving their internal IM&M economies from a centrally planned socialist economy to a free-market economy where the users are "free to choose." Users buy services in quantities that they determine (by virtue of the budgeting system) and the IM&M organization competes through pricing, service, and value-added to meet the needs of this free market. Priorities are set by demand as opposed to a traditional priority setting council. The tension of the free-market system solves the problem of resource allocation and backlog. The IM&M organization becomes demand driven and is no longer the throttle on the use of information technology (the customers do this). It lets the marketplace decide the right mix of products and services.

Conclusion—IM&M management must understand that the movement to a free economy from a centrally planned economy changes their Five Force position radically. While government (business policy) edict used to protect the IM&M hegemony over IM&M, business policy is now lowering barriers to entry and encouraging competition. The IM&M organization must therefore convert itself from a mainframe monopolist business to an IM&M service provider who wins based on competitive merit. Consistent with the view that the IM&M organization should function as a free-market provider. Of the three basic models for performing chargeback, straight cost allocation based on usage, resource optimization (influence users to maximize use of available resources), or market discipline pricing, it is suggested that over time, IM&M organizations will have no choice but to adopt market discipline pricing.

11. Groupware

Definition: Groupware is an application that allows groups of individuals, collocated and dispersed, to work concurrently on a common project in a shared environment. Goupware includes e-mail messaging systems, database e-mail enabled applications, message management applications, workgroup automation systems, calendaring, scheduling, and document management systems.

Analysis: Groupware is a technology of collaboration, and collaboration, is a form of alignment. Groupware permits work to be brought to individuals rather than individuals being brought to the work. In an increasingly global business world, technologies which enable far-flung operations to work together as one are increasingly important.

Conclusion: Groupware is a means to alignment.

12. CASE

Definition: Computer Assisted Software Engineering (CASE) technologies are applications which automate the business application of software development and maintenance.

Analysis: Business software development and maintenance, the entire software life cycle of analysis, design, construction, testing, implementation, maintainance, etc., is a business application; conceptually no different than order entry or inventory management. Rather than managing a database of orders and customers and transactions of "enter order" or "order status" which would exist in an order entry application, the business software application requires a repository of "record layouts" and modules and transactions of "create screen" and "compile code."

Viewed in this way, CASE is a product for the developer marketplace and competes with all other development products, including hand crafting methods, as a superior price and performance and value-added solution to the problem of application development. Developers, analogous to an order entry user, have to assess to what degree the existing and emerging CASE tools do, in fact, meet their needs.

Conclusion: CASE is an application composed of IM&M technologies to be used to build IM&M applications. As such, it competes on a life cycle price and performance and value-added basis against substitute approaches to optimizing the value chain of software development. Given the current state of CASE, decision makers should carefully assess to what degree the proposed CASE tools improve the value chain.

13. Artificial Intelligence

Definition: Artificial Intelligence is software which permits the encoding and sharing of decision logic.

Analysis: Artificial intelligence is a technology for sharing, duplicating, and cascading knowledge throughout the business. It permits business knowledge automation. It is a technology of leverage because it multiplies and amplifies pockets of scarce human expertise.

Conclusion: Artificial intelligence should be understood as a high-leverage technology.

14. Application Prototyping[5]

Definition: Application prototyping is the building of software models as the method of soliciting user business application requirements

Analysis: The building of quick software models as the means to solicit and validate user requirements has become even more important given the emerging user interfaces, i.e., animation, video, GUI, 3-D, gesture recognition, and virtual reality. It is difficult to imagine writing a rigorous prespecification document to communicate these types of interfaces to the user when the dynamics of the interface could only be demonstrated and appreciated by example.

Conclusion: Application prototyping can be understood from a number of strategic perspectives:

1. *Bottleneck*—Prototyping breaks the requirements definition bottleneck.
2. *Value chain*—Prototyping both reduces cost and adds value to the application development cycle.
3. *Critical success factors*—Prototyping meets the user CSF for an application that meets her needs.

Most importantly, prototyping should be understood as an "excitement" attribute per the Kano method.

15. The Death of the Mainframe

Definition: "The Death of the Mainframe" is an ambiguous phrase which to the most ardent mainframe haters means that the host-based computing model has peaked and is now in the decline stage of the product life cycle to be replaced in its entirety by network computing (in all its variations). Proponents of this view cite market research studies such as those illustrated in Figure 8.9 as evidence.

Analysis: There are a number of things that this ambiguous phrase could mean:

1. It could mean the end of all processing services, presentation, process, and data manipulation occurring only together within a single large processor, i.e., the host-centered computing model which has dominated business computing since the 1960s.
2. It could mean the end of proprietary dominance of mainframe-class processors, i.e., microprocessor-based systems running open system software provide mainframe-class performance but at microprocessor price and performance through parallelism.

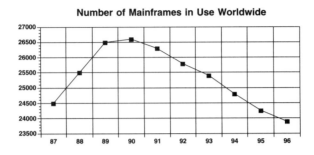

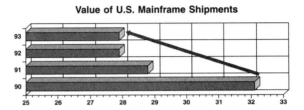

Figure 8.9   Mainframe Decline. The number of mainframes world-wide is anticipated to decline by 11% by 1996. *Source* IDC.

3. It could mean the end of the centrally operated data center, i.e., the network computing world is a world of inter-connected departmental servers in office environments with no need for specialization of labor or economies of scale which occur in a data center.

4. It could specifically mean the end of IBM's mainframe solutions, i.e., MVS and VM.

5. It could mean a price class of processors.

6. It could mean any combination of the above plus whatever else the speaker means it to mean.

My perspective on this is as follows:

1. The mainframe, defined as a proprietary software architecture which was the exclusive home for presentation processing and data manipulation services, is dying but is certainly not dead. As was illustrated in Figure 8.6, network computing offers superior maneuverability by permitting the placement of presentation, processing, and data manipulation in the most advantageous position. Likewise, recent announcements of microprocessor-based systems running open systems software such as those by Hewlett Packard

and NCR at one tenth the cost of traditional IBM class systems make these new mainframes (a mainframe being a performance class) attractive substitutes.

2. Because of the above, superior price and performance and maneuverability, it will only be prudent for decision makers to evolve new applications to the new environment. Nevertheless, there is a large embedded base of traditional mainframe applications which continues to grow, and market research reports indicate that while IBM class mainframe sales are flat in box numbers, they are increasing in total MIPS sold. The traditional mainframe is dying, but not in the sense of going away in the foreseeable future. It is dying in the sense of becoming a smaller and smaller part of the overall IM&M marketplace and losing its historical position of dominance and arrogance. This is illustrated in Table 8.1 that shows while mainframe class MIPS will grow by a respectable factor of ten in the 90s, this will clearly be overshadowed by the growth of micro-based MIPS which are anticipated to grow by a factor of 100 so that by the turn of the century, PC MIP demand will be 10000 times the mainframe MIP demand. Even if one chooses an apologist argument such as ten PC MIPS equals one mainframe MIP, the conclusion is overwhelming.

3. The role of the traditional data center in the network computing world needs to be redefined. There are many functions whose value chain is best accomplished through specialization of labor and economies of scale. Network computing does not change this.

Conclusion: A strategic view of this phrase is that both what is a mainframe and what functions are placed on it are in evolution. Given the

Table 8.1
MIPS Forecast. By the turn of the century, PC MIP demand will exceed mainframe MIP demand by a factor of 10000. *Source*: Meta Group

Demand for MIPS (000s)			
Year	Mainframes	Minis	Micros
1960–1969	2	<1	
1970–1979	17	2	
1980–1989	440	110	400,000
1990–1999	4,000	2,800	40,000,000

huge embedded base of traditional mainframe applications, and their growth in resource needs and the continuing need of certain applications for MIP concentration or central services (such as shared corporate databases), one should see through the shallowness of this phrase in light of the system legacy and act prudently.

Most of the people who say the mainframe is dead make the fallacy of suppressed evidence. In 1992 there were 23000 mainframes sites and worldwide mainframe sales revenue was about $28 billion. If IBM broke itself into separate autonomous companies, as has been suggested, the Enterprise Systems Group (mainframes) would have been about a $14 billion business in 1992 (#31, 1992 Fortune 500). Assuming a continued sales decline at 10% *per annum* (market researcher Dataquest has estimated a compounded annual decline in mainframe sales of 3.5% through 1996) in five years it would be a $7 billion business, and in eight years it would be a $2.08 billion business. According to the 1992 Fortune 500 list, the Enterprise Systems Group would be the 73rd and 164th Fortune 500 company, respectively. Assuming that a rational IBM management will take appropriate actions to get their costs in line, find new applications, and deliver much more economical parallel processing versions, these dead mainframes will be generating quite a bit of revenue for a number of years to come. Most companies would die to achieve these positions.

16. The Decline of IBM

Definition: This issue is the recognition that IBM's historical dominance of the computing industry is in decline.

Analysis: This issue is closely related to the advent of open systems, "the death of the mainframe," and the emergence of the compelling re-engineering IM&M technologies (Section 2.2). There has been a clear shift in the marketplace from IBM's traditional strengths, and this is reflected in IBM's flat financial performance, lost of industry influence, and poor positions in high growth IM&M technologies (see Figure 8.9). IBM has taken actions such as selling cheap PC clones, entering the OEM business in a major way (1993 goal of $3 billion), creating partnerships with former rivals Apple and Toshiba, reorganizing the business into semi-autonomous companies, and announcing the evolution of SNA from a hierarchical networking architecture to a peer-to-peer networking architecture—not requiring a mainframe (March 1992 networking announcement). Industry analysts, in reaction to IBM problems, have made statements that even a few years ago were unthinkable:

- Referring to the December 1991 reorganization of IBM into semi-autonomous companies by Chairman Akers, "It's his last ditch effort to save the company from seemingly endless decline."

- Referring to the December 1991 reorganization of IBM into semi-autonomous companies, "What we're seeing here is the beginning of the dismantling of the IBM company."

- "IBM is a dinosaur. IBM's bread and butter business is mainframes, and it focused too much on that business while it ignored or came late to areas of the computer business that are fastest growing. So IBM's cash cow is already obsolete."

- Suggesting that IBM would be better off broken up after its stock hit the mid $60s in the fall of 1992 (down from a 1987 high of $160+), an analyst said, "IBM might have a lot more value broken up.... IBM is worth more dead than alive.... The train called IBM is headed towards the junkyard, unless the parts of it get off and go their own way."

- A mutual fund manager explaining why she was divesting her holdings in IBM. "We've made the basic conclusion that this is a company in a long-term decline."

To many peoples' astonishment, the credit rating services of both Phelps-Dodge and Moody lowered IBM's credit rating because of "Deterioration in IBM's competitive position and reduced influence over its customer base."

IBM's problems can be explained by a number of strategic failings:

- A glacial frozen mental model. IBM had convinced itself that the host-centered model of computing was forever—it would never change.

- IBM had a poor market perspective. It tried to lead its customers where they didn't need to go through concepts such as Systems Application Architecture (SAA) and a mainframe-centric repository.

- IBM failed to understand the power of the five forces. The price and performance and feature and functionality advantages of open systems and the new microprocessor-based solutions offers an attractive substitute that overwhelms the barriers to switching.

- The drive for business competitiveness overcame the need for making the safe decision. While IBM might always be the safe decision, it is not a reach, range, and maneuverability decision.

- The insistence on maintaining a mainframe-centric view of IM&M that created a solutions bottleneck for customers which created a gap for network solutions based competitors. The IBM cachet could not constrain emigration to more attractive solutions.

- The victory of politics over marketplace needs.

IBM executed the worst strategy of all; complacency.

As an aside, a similar analysis could be performed with regard to DEC. For fiscal 1992, DEC announced a net loss of $2.8 billion; this followed a 1991 net loss of $600 million. For the first quarter of 1993, DEC announced a loss of $260.5 million coupled with a 5% staff downsizing and followed this with a second quarter 1993 loss of $73.9 million. Its founder and chairman, Mr. Kenneth Olsen, under pressure from the board of directors, has resigned, and the company's future is bet on an unproven RISC processor, Alpha. At the end of 1992, DEC dropped to third place behind IBM and Hewlett-Packard in the US mid-range market. Like IBM, DEC did not wish to see or understand the transitions to open systems, personal computers, and workstations on LANs from minicomputers. On 15 October 1992, five years after the great 19 October 1987 stock market crash, DEC sold at $35 a share; down 73% from the October 1987 closing price (IBM sold at $73 a share; down 30%).

Microsoft serves as an interesting counter example to these companies. While one fifth the size of DEC and one twentieth the size of IBM, Microsoft had profits of $463 million and $708 million on sales of $1.8 billion and $2.8 billion for 1991 and 1992, respectively. Microsoft's revenue per employee is 2.18 times that of DEC and 1.41 times that of IBM. So while DEC announced its first quarter 1993 loss of $260.5 million and IBM announced its third quarter 1993 loss of $2.7 billion, Microsoft announced its first quarter 1993 profits of $209 million on $818 million of revenue yielding an outstanding margin of 26%.

Conclusion—IBM is taking actions designed to allow it to effectively compete in an open network-based computing environment coupled with a decline in host-based computing. Time will tell to what degree IBM can reassert itself as a dominant leader, if at all, and to what degree it can play the game on equal footing as just another competitor. IBM's "dismal" third quarter 1992 loss of $2.78 billion did not bode well for the future, and the "free fall" continued when on 16 December 1992, IBM announced:

- It was taking an additional $6 billion charge in the fourth quarter of 1992.
- There would be an additional 25000 staff reduction.
- The sacrosanct no layoff policy would probably be revoked.
- R/D would be cut an additional $1 billion on top of the already $1 billion cut for 1992.
- The dividend may be cut.

Mainframe revenue will drop 10% this year and continue to drop next year. IBM's business continues to deteriorate much faster than expected with no end in sight.

IBM's stock closed at 56.125, a ten year low. The January 1992 board meeting should provide the next set of announcements on how IBM intends to change itself back to "Big Blue" from "Big Black and Blue."

Preventing frozen mental models is a continuing challenge for any successful company because the terms of success are subject to continual redefinition. Both IBM's and DEC's failures to change with the times, unfortunately, provide stunning examples of strategic failure.

17. CIO Critical Issues of Information Systems Management

Definition: The issues itemized in Figure 2.3 are a consensus view of the most critical strategic issues confronting the IM&M function.

Analysis: Table 8.2 provides a strategic framework explanation for each of the 20 issues. This is important because the explanation of the current ills as fundamental strategic shortcomings confirms the thesis that IM&M organizations will benefit tremendously by adopting strategic planning methods. One needs to attack strategic problems through strategic methods.

A review of the 20 issues indicates that:

- Every issue that has been rated in the top eight positions since 1988 is still an issue in 1992.

- Of the top ten 1992 issues, seven of them have been on the list since 1988 and one since 1989.

- The 1992 top issue, "Aligning I/S and Corporate Goals," has been among the top four issues every year (four years as item one or two) and represents the most fundamental strategic objective of alignment.

- Three items which were rated in 1988/89 and then left the list, have returned.

- The problems cover the full spectrum of strategy. Failings of alignment, maneuverability, competencies, capabilities, bottlenecks, value chain, sustainable competitive advantage, and positioning are all included.

Table 8.3 illustrates that the same issues have again been reshuffled on the 1993 list. The strategic problems are chronic, pervasive, and pandemic.

Table 8.4[6] provides a view of strategic IM&M problems which focuses on the development process. Again, one sees a set of strategic problems

Table 8.2
Explaining the Top 20 I/T Issues. The top 20 issues all reflect failings in
the basics of strategy development and execution. *Source of Issues*:
CSC/Index.

Position	Strategic Issue	Explanatory Strategy Framework
1	Aligning I/S and corporate goals	Alignment
2	Re-engineering business functions through I/T	Capabilities and/or value chain
3	Creating an information architecture	Reach, range, maneuverability
4	Utilizing data	Leverage
5	Improving the I/S human resource	Core competencies
6	Instituting cross-functional systems	Alignment
7	Improving software development quality	Bottleneck
8	Improving leadership skills in I/S (tie)	Change management
9	Boosting software development productivity (tie)	Bottleneck
10	Develop an I/S strategic plan	Alignment
11	Cutting I/S costs	Value chain—Productivity
12	Instituting total quality management in I/S	Critical success factors
13	Integrating information systems	Reach, range, and maneuverability
14	Using I/S for competitive break-throughs	Sustainable competitive advantage
15	Managing dispersed systems	Reach, range, maneuverability
16	Educating management in I/S	Leverage
17	Promoting the I/S function	Change management—Politics
18	Updating obsolete systems	Reach, range, maneuverability
19	Capitalizing on advances in I/T	Product Positioning—Technology clusters
20	Connecting to customers and suppliers	Interlock value chains

Table 8.3
1993: Top 10 I/T Issues. The top ten I/T challenges remain essentially the same. *Source of Issues*: CSC/Index.

1993 Position	1992 Position	Strategic Issue	Explanatory Strategy Framework
2	1	Aligning I/S and corporate goals	Alignment
1	2	Re-engineering business functions through I/T	Capabilities and/or value chain
7	3	Creating an information architecture	Reach, range, maneuverability
4	4	Utilizing data	Leverage
4	6	Instituting cross-functional systems	Alignment
3	8	Boosting software development productivity (tie)	Bottleneck
9	10	Develop an I/S strategic plan	Alignment
6	11	Cutting I/S costs	Value chain—Productivity
8	18	Updating obsolete systems	Reach, range, maneuverability
10	N/R	Changing technology platforms	Product positioning—Technology clusters

that are enduring (every issue has been present for every year except one issue in one year), and the problems cover a wide set of strategic topics. These problems are, likewise, chronic and pervasive.

Conclusion: Table 8.5 suggests that all these problems are but florid symptoms and the underlying root cause is the absence of strategic management of the IM&M resource. The problems confronting the IM&M organization are not due to the mischief of Satan or his servant Beelzebub; your spirituality is not being tested as in the case of the biblical Job. The hiring of an exorcist will not purge you of your inflictions and sorrows. The roots of the problem lie in the absence of strategy. Recall the admonition of Sun Tzu:

> Those who are good at taking care of problems, take care of them before they arise.[7]

The solution to the problem lies in the adoption of strategic planning methods to manage the IM&M function. Unlike the alchemist of the medieval ages, you can transmute your situation from that of endless decline to that of endless possibilities, the only constraint being your strategic imagination. The problems summarized in Tables 8.2 through 8.4 need not be endlessly refractory.

It is not necessary for IM&M management to be a modern day Sisyphus, the Greek mythological figure who was condemned to eternally push a rock up a steep hill in Hades; only to see it endlessly plunge back to the bottom of the hill just as it reached the top. The CIO shouldn't surrender to these seemingly intractable issues and place at the portal to her office the same words that are inscribed over the gates to Dante's hell; "Abandon hope; all ye who enter here."[8] The problems belong to the sweep of strategy and the solutions can be found through the use of strategic methods. It need not be our fate to endure an external existence of strategic absurdity as did Sisyphus.

Table 8.4
1992: Top Ten System Development Issues. The top ten issues all reflect failings in the basics of strategy development and execution. *Source of Issues*: CSC/Index.

Position	Strategic Issue	Explanatory Strategy Framework
1	Rapidly responding to systems requests	Bottleneck
2	Increasing developer productivity	Bottleneck
3	Identifying and developing strategic information systems	Alignment
4	Developing an information architecture	Reach, range, maneuverability
5	Dealing with maintenance, systems obsolescence, migration to new systems	Reach, range, maneuverability
6	Demonstrating the value of development projects to senior executives	Change management—Politics
7	Instituting a formal total quality management program in systems development	Critical success factors
8	Achieving support for cross-functional systems	Alignment
9	Developing and implementing metrics for systems	Objectives—Measurements
10	Managing end-user systems development	Reach, range, maneuverability

Table 8.5
Root Cause Analysis of Critical I/T Issues. The root cause of the problems confronting the IM&M organization is the failure to manage IM&M strategically.

Symptoms ————->	Top 20 I/T Issues and Top 10 System Development Issues Figure 2.3, Table 8.2, Table 8.3, Table 8.4
Problem ————->	IM&M Pincer: Business need for competitiveness from IM&M technology, technology change, competition
Root Cause ————->	Absence of strategic management of the IM&M resource

Summary

It is interesting that this analysis of contemporary strategic issues is in general agreement with conventional wisdom about each topic, but for fundamentally different reasons. This difference results in dramatically different actions. A strategist is interested in object-oriented technology because of long-term positioning for leverage; not because of a project's productivity improvement. A strategist is interested in wireless communications because it expands reach by a dimension; not because a person can get e-mail easier. A strategist is interested in open systems because it fundamentally improves her Five-Force position, not because she can hold a threat over her vendor's head for the next project. A strategist is excited about client/server computing because it fundamentally positions her for maximum IM&M maneuverability, not because it gives the next project a cheaper solution. A strategist does not confuse instances of benefit with the infrastructure of benefit.

This is the big difference and value of understanding IM&M strategically. When you understand IM&M strategically, technologies are the means to multiplying benefit. They are understood, implemented, and interwoven to weave a quilt of leverage for the business. When you don't understand IM&M strategically, each technology solves an instance of a problem. When you don't understand IM&M strategically, the best you can do is muddle through.

8.2   Understanding Contemporary IM&M News Strategically

The purpose of this section is to analyze IM&M news events using the strategic frameworks learned as the vehicle for framing the analysis. The news events are selected from what appeared in the industry press in the late summer and fall of 1992. The objective of this exercise is not to high-light these events as unusually important, but to demonstrate the advantage accrued to the IM&M strategist who reads the IM&M news through strategic lenses. Since events of strategic significance can be related to strategic frameworks, classifying the event with the defining framework brings all the understanding of the framework to bear on the analysis and allows for more in-depth appreciation of the event and the actions that need to be taken to respond.

Each news event will be analyzed using the following presentation structure:

- *News item*—the title of the news item,
- *Description*—a brief description of the news item, and
- *Explanatory Strategic Framework*—the identification of the strategic analytical method which best explains the event.

It is clear that the IM&M industry is not an exotic business immune to the laws and explanations of strategic planning and that the weekly news is readily explainable through the established strategy frameworks.

1. *News item*—Wang declares Chapter 11 bankruptcy

Description: Wang, formerly a Fortune 500 company, after four years of losses and a revenue decline of $1 billion, declared chapter 11 bankruptcy. Wang is the largest IM&M industry player to ever file for bankruptcy.

Explanatory Strategic Framework: Misalignment—Wang's business scope did not evolve in accord with the industry trends of open systems, downsizing, and the movement to LAN-based PCs as the locus of computing.

2. *News item*—IBM announces PC company

Description: IBM announced the formation of a new semiautonomous PC company to compete in the personal computer segment of the industry.

Explanatory Strategic Framework: Structure follows strategy—this was the inevitable restructuring following the December 1991 IBM announcement that it would become more competitive by dividing itself into more nimble and focused business units with reduced corporate control.

3. *News item*—PC price wars continue

Description: Prices of both x386 and x486 microprocessor-based PCs continue a downward spiral in a viciously competitive market.

Explanatory Strategic Framework: Five Forces shift to buyer power—Five Force factors of ease and cost of switching, commodization, and number of suppliers all have shifted to move market power to the customer.

4. *News item—CIO Magazine* announces annual survey of key I/T priority items

Description: *CIO Magazine* published its annual list of the top concerns of America's CIO community.

Explanatory Strategic Framework: See Table 8.6.

5. *News item*—Microsoft concedes that its developers used undocumented APIs

Description: After publication of a book, Microsoft conceded that its application developers used undocumented Windows APIs but denied that it provided any competitive advantage and that it is a common industry practice of no consequence.

Explanatory Strategic Framework: Sustainable Competitive Advantage—the struggle of business is the struggle for advantage. By logical deduction, either Microsoft used undocumented APIs to accrue disadvantage, to accrue parity, or to accrue advantage. It would be wholly illogical for Microsoft's developers to use undocumented APIs to purposefully disadvantage themselves. If the objective was competitive parity, why not use the documented APIs? This leaves the only logical alternative to be either current advantage or positioning for future advantage.

6. *News item*—Lotus announces that future version of Notes will include SQL

Description: Lotus announced that a future version of Notes will include an open SQL interface, enabling Notes to access relational databases.

Explanatory Strategic Framework: Reach/Range/Maneuverability—improves the range of data that Notes can access.

7. *News item*— IBM announces repositioning of AD/Cycle

Description: IBM announced that AD/Cycle will be migrated to a LAN-based architecture from the original host-centered architecture.

Explanatory Strategic Framework: Market Leader—IBM tried to take customers where they didn't want to go (more mainframe-centric solutions) and based on poor market response has decided to reposition the product in alignment with customer demands.

Table 8.6
CIO Magazine I/T Priority Items. The *CIO Magazine* priority items
cross a wide range of strategic actions.

CIO Priority Item	Explanatory Strategic Framework
1. Align technology with business strategy.	Alignment
2. Implement state of the art solutions.	Value chain—Use emerging I/T to improve productivity or add value.
3. Provide and improve information access.	Reach/Range/Maneuverability Architecture
4. Enhance customer service.	Critical success factors
5. Create links within the organization.	Change management—Politics
6. Train and empower employees.	Human resource architecture
7. Create links with external customers.	Interlocking value chains
8. Support business re-engineering.	Capabilities and value chain
9. Act as change agent and catalyst.	Change management—Frozen mental models
10. Educate business units about I/T.	Leverage—Multiply and amplify benefits of I/T.
11. Evaluate emerging technologies.	New product positioning—New technology clusters
12. Implement standard systems and architecture.	Reach/Range/Maneuverability Architecture

8. *News item*—Get ready for video e-mail

Description: By 1995, users should anticipate being able to get e-mail which moves beyond text only to full multimedia.

   Explanatory Strategic Framework: Product positioning (technology clusters)—convergence of high speed WANS/LANS, multimedia, and mail standards will enable evolution of mail technology.

9. *News item*—Oracle's sales revenue for application line more than doubles

Description: Oracle announced Release 9 of its application suite for human resources, manufacturing, and finance. Oracle is one of the few DBMS vendors to also sell applications.

Explanatory Strategic Framework: Bottleneck—as the unit costs of technologies continue to decline, the key bottleneck of the use of IM&M technology shifts to expediting the availability of applications.

10. News item— Sears PLC enters a five year contract with British Telecommunications for EDI

Description: Sears PLC will interlock its 3000 United Kingdom stores with more than 50000 suppliers through BT's EDInet Service. The objective is to maximize sales and minimize inventory.

Explanatory Strategic Framework: Interlocking value chains—the EDI network will be used to send orders, invoices, and shipping records between Sears PLC and its suppliers.

11. *News item*—The CASE bubble deflates

Description: Editorial asserts that CASE is a dismal failure and that user expectations have not even vaguely been met.

Explanatory Strategic Framework: Product Positioning (Function Cluster)—absence of integrated tools has failed to meet functional requirements to meet user (developer) needs.

12. *News item*—IBM brings CICS to AIX

Description: IBM will make a version of its populate mainframe TP monitor CICS available on the AIX platform. The product will conform to SQL-Access, Distributed Computing Environment (DCE), and XA interoperability standards.

Explanatory Strategic Framework: Reach/Range/Maneverability Architecture—CICS/AIX improves maneuverability.

13. *News item*—Tuxedo interoperability to be improved

Description: The Tuxedo on-line transaction monitor will be ported to the IBM ES/900 family of mainframes under the AIX/ESA operating system and will provide dynamic-link library access for OS/2 and Windows applications.

Explanatory Strategic Framework: Reach/Range/Maneuverability Architecture—all these items improve Tuxedo's maneuverability.

14. *News item*—HP-95LX Palmtop gets wireless e-mail capability

Description: The Viking Express, a portable radio modem from GE, allows wireless e-mail over the RAM Mobile Data radio network.

Explanatory Strategic Framework: Reach/Range/Maneuverability—the wireless modem improves reach.

15. *News item*—DEC announces new direction

Description: Mr. Palmer, the new CEO of DEC, announces a 14 point plan to revitalize DEC. This announcment is followed two months later by a restructuring of DEC's operations into nine business units ("structure follows strategy").

Explanatory Strategic Framework: See Table 8.7.

16. *News item*— CA commits to UNIX

Description: CA announced that it will port its operations management software, Unicenter, to the Sun platform. UNIX versions of CA-Datacom and CA-IDMS are also expected in the spring of 1993. Additional Unicenter products will be ported to Pyramid, Sequent, NCR, and Tandem (NonStop-UX)

Explanatory Strategic Framework: Commitment—reinforce commitment to open systems and downsizing as CA's strategic direction.

17. *News item*—Microsoft to sell "Windows" for Groups

Description: Microsoft demonstrated a new operating system to support workgroup computing and people who need to share information and work in teams.

Explanatory Strategic Framework: Windows for Groups is collaboration software which is a form of alignment.

18. *News item*—New entrants to shake up color scanner market

Description: Several new players have entered the growing color scanner market causing increased competition.

Explanatory Strategic Framework: Five Forces—Threat of Market Entry—low barriers to entry make it easy for new players to enter as the market starts to grow.

19. *News item*—EDS reorganizes

Description: EDS announced a reorganization to prepare to grow to a global $35 billion dollar company from the current $7 billion of revenue. EDS reported 1992 revenue of $8.2 billion, a 16% increase over 1991 and net profits of $635.5 million. The company has also diversified its revenue to the point that 59% is from other than its troubled parent, General Motors.

Table 8.7
DEC Initiatives. The 14 point new direction for DEC is built on the fundamental strategies of leverage, alignment, and focus.

DEC Initiative	Explanatory Strategic Framework
1. Focus on a small number of customer driven global business units where we can be #1 or #2.	Focus
2. We will have a components business unit.	Leverage
3. We will have a direct merchandising unit.	Leverage
4. Our primary dimension to address complex customer driven solutions is industry. We will have SI as a core capability.	Core competency
5. The primary focus of product development is to satisfy the business units.	Alignment
6. We will have a separate multivendor services unit.	Focus and Reach/Range/ Maneuverability
7. We need a small corporate marketing group to drive our corporate image and integration across business units.	Alignment
8. The account manager will make decisions related to satisfying the needs of the customer and will depend on si expertise for competitive SI quoting and pricing.	Focus
9. Business units own advertising, pricing, marketing strategy, etc.	Focus
10. Countries are to execute business plans and manage the sales and services organization.	Focus
11. There will be a worldwide sales manager responsible for developing the core capabilities of the sales organization.	Leverage
12. Functions will be responsible for best in class practices and achieving competitive benchmarks.	Benchmarking
13. We will have one hardware engineering group.	Leverage
14. We will have one network communications group.	Leverage

Explanatory Strategic Framework: Anticipatory Change Management—EDS re-organized in anticipation of needs rather than reacting to events. As illustrated in Figure 8.10, EDS provides an excellent antithesis to IBM and DEC. It will be interesting see whether the emerging superstars,

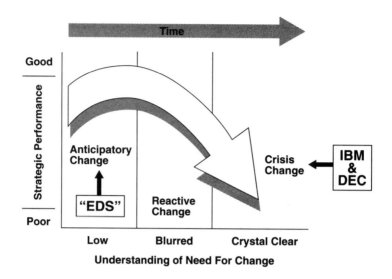

Figure 8.10   Anticapatory Change. EDS provides a stark contrast to
IBM and DEC.

Microsoft (approximately 90% of the PC OS market) and Intel (approximately 75% of the 32-bit microprocessor market) will follow in the ways
of EDS or IBM and DEC.

20. *News item*—Unisys to expand the number of platforms on which Mapper 4GL runs

Description: Unisys announced that it will make available ports of its Map-
per 4GL for IBM RS600, SCO UNIX, and Novell's Univel environments to
complement existing ports to Sun, Microsoft Windows, and OS/2.

Explanatory Strategic Framework: Reach/Range/Maneuverability framework—improvement in maneuverability through portability

21. *News item*—Microsoft and Lotus step up consulting programs

Description: Both Lotus and Microsoft are aggressively stepping up their
direct consulting capabilities to assist customers in the building of applications using their respective technologies.

Explanatory Strategic Framework: Bottleneck—both Lotus and Microsoft
are trying to eliminate the bottleneck of building finished applications.

22. *News item*—IBM launches client/server customization unit

Description: IBM has renewed its Client/Server Computing Group by adding 500 programmers to it. A work force of over 900 will now be dedicated to supporting customer client/server needs on both IBM and non-IBM equipment.

Explanatory Strategic Framework: Reach/Range/Maneuverability Framework—IBM has accepted that the marketplace wants maneuverability and client/server is maneuverability. Client/Server computing is now officially part of the IBM catechism. The faithful may rest assured that if they adopt client/server solutions that there will be a place for them in the computing world to come, and they will not be sentenced to eternal computing purgatory. This action coupled with a separate announcement of a new "Open Systems Center" which provides a customer laboratory for "proof of concept" of multivendor systems, demonstrates a welcome thaw in the mainframe frozen model.

23. *News item*—Novell to buy UNIX System Laboratory

Description: Novell has agreed to buy UNIX System Laboratory from AT&T. The deal will give Novell a superior position in influencing and controlling the evolution of the UNIX operating system.

Explanatory Strategic Framework: SWOT and Strategic Competitor Analysis—Microsoft's new product, Windows-NT, is a direct threat to Novell's leadership in network operating systems. By further integrating UNIX with Netwrare, Novell can provide a counter balance to the Microsoft juggernaut.

24. *News item*—FTC to seek action on Microsoft

Description: The FTC has completed its 30 month investigation of Microsoft's licensing practices and is rumored to be preparing recommendations on how to sanction Microsoft. The report alleges various monopolistic practices by Microsoft.

Explanatory Strategic Framework: Five Forces—Threat of Entry Force—Government Policy Factor—The government intervention in the marketplace will change the balance of competitiveness by forcing a change in how Microsoft does business.

25. *News item*—IBI's EDA/SQL software leads the data access pack

Description: Information Builders Inc. (IBI) Enterprise Data Access (EDA)/SQL tool has become the standard for enterprise data access. The product provides access to 50 different databases (relational and non-relational) running on 35 different hardware platforms. EDA/SQL server software runs on 14 different platforms.

Explanatory Strategic Framework: Reach/Range/Maneuverability Architecture—Extension of Range

While the news items included in this analysis are quite varied, they all lend themselves to strategic explanations. Table 8.8 summarizes the strategic explanations of these news items. It is clear that the IM&M strategist who reads the industry press or listens to industry pundits or attends vendor briefings has a significant advantage by bringing this type of capability to the analysis. Mastering and applying strategic business planning methods is therefore not an abstract academic exercise but has daily application in understanding the motion of the IM&M industry.

The question requiring resolution, then, is not whether to adopt strategic business planning or not; you will do that. The question is whether you will do it now or wait. By understanding the question this way, the consequences are clear. Waiting enables the continuity of the comforts of the *status quo* for some time but does so in the ever darkening shadow of the closing IM&M pincer. Doing it now requires vision and commitment to massive change. Adopt strategic business planning now and start the process of renewal and the journey to a new era of prosperity. If you do not, you will find yourself in a few years presiding over a moribund organization in the death rattle of the enveloping IM&M pincer. The time has come to choose; choose wisely.

Table 8.8

News Item Summary. The day-to-day IM&M industry news is explainable by use of the various strategy frameworks.

IM&M News Item	Explanatory Strategic Framework
Wang declares Chapter 11 bankruptcy	Misalignment
IBM announces PC company	Structure follows strategy
PC price wars continue	Five Force shift to buyer power
CIO Magazine I/T priority items	See Table 8.5
Microsoft concedes that its developers used undocumented APIS	Sustainable competitive advantage
Lotus announces that notes will include SQL	Reach/Range/Maneuverability architecture—Improvement of range

Table 8.8 *continued*

IM&M News Item	Explanatory Strategic Framework
IBM to reposition AD/Cycle	Market leader
Get ready for video e-mail	Product positioning—Technology clusters
Oracle's sales revenues double for applications	Bottleneck
Sears PLC enters EDI agreement with British telecommunications	Interlocking value chains
Case bubble deflates	Product positioning—Function cluster
IBM brings CICS to AIX	Reach/Range/Maneuverability architecture—Improvement of maneuverability
Tuxedo interoperability to be improved	Reach/Range/Maneuverability architecture—Improvement of maneuverability
HP-95LX get wireless e-mail	Reach/Range/Maneuverability Architecture—Improvement of reach
DEC initiatives	See Table 8.6
CA commmits to UNIX	Commitment
Microsoft to sell Windows for Groups	Alignment
New entrants shake up color scanner market	Five Forces—Threat of entry
EDS reorganizes	Change management
Unisys to increase platforms that Mapper 4GL runs on	Reach/Range/Maneuverability Architecture: Improvement of maneuverability (portability)
Microsoft and Lotus step up consulting programs	Bottleneck—Application development
IBM launches client/server customization unit	Reach/Range/Maneuverability Architecture—Improvement in maneuverability
Novell to buy UNIX system laboratories	SWOT and Strategic competitor analysis
FTC to seek action on Microsoft	Five Forces—Threat of entry force—Government policy factor
IBI's EDA/SQL leads the data access pack	Reach/Range/Maneuverability Architecture: Improvement of range

8.3 Reprise

We have now concluded our exploration of the strategic planning methodology. Strategic planning provides the most advanced way to plan and position for the future. IM&M provides the most powerful resource (except for the human resource) to build, sustain, and compound competitive advantage. The marriage of the two yields the optimum formula for winning in the 1990s.

Throughout this book, the strategic importance of IM&M to the business has been emphasized. IM&M is strategically important because when used intelligently with forethought, design, and purpose, it can provide the means to alter strategic positions and dramatically improve competitiveness. IM&M can serve as the primary mover of strategic change by:

- Creating a highly leveraged set of core competencies which can infuse multiple products with irresistible functionality,
- Creating capabilities which create outstanding service and value for customers,
- Providing the means to alter the balance of the Five Forces and associated factors in your favor,
- Providing the means to meet critical success factors,
- Providing the means to engineer and interlock value chains with superior price and performance and value-added,
- Providing the ability to create excitement attributes and strategic distance between you and your closest competitor,
- Providing the means to break value chain bottlenecks,
- Providing the means to create cross organization systems which enable collaboration and alignment of efforts, and
- Providing the means to alter the "rules of the game" and break a competitor's game plan.

IM&M can be a tool of continual strategic renewal. This is why IM&M is a strategic resource and must be managed through strategic planning methods.

Inevitably, students of a discipline request that the essence of a teaching be condensed into a compact set of principles. What are the universal truths? Which ideas transcend the rest in importance? Can the complexity of assessment, strategy, and execution be encapsulated into a few enduring principles?

I believe that a dozen fundamental ideas emerge from an assay of strategic planning. These ideas need to be focused on one overriding objective for the IM&M resource. The essential notions of strategic planning are as follows:

1. *Strategic intent*—an ambitious and stable long-term objective,
2. *Sustainable competitive advantage*—the definition and nourishing of the basis of winning,
3. *Driving force*—the primary determiner of future markets and products,
4. *Alignment*—a shared competitive agenda,
5. *Focus*—concentration of effort and resources,
6. *Core competencies and capabilities*—the skills and processes that enable successful competition,
7. *Leverage*—the multiplication, acceleration, and amplification of advantage,
8. *Vigilance*—continual observation of the environment for threats and opportunities,
9. *Maneuverability*—the ability to swiftly change to be in accord with events or to cause events,
10. *Position*—the understanding of the state of a resource,
11. *Commitment*—perseverance in the face of obstacles and hurdles, and
12. *Mental models*—the way that both individuals and the organization view the world.

These 12 concepts need to be concentrated on the primary objective of continuously increasing the reach, range, and maneuverability of the IM&M asset. The sole purpose of IM&M is competitiveness. This objective is only realized by:

- Maximizing the reach of IM&M so that anyone, anywhere, at anytime can access all IM&M resources,
- Maximizing the range of IM&M so that all information objects can be shared by authorized users, and
- Maximizing the maneuverability of IM&M so that applications can be constantly revised in harmony with dynamic business requirements.

All IM&M strategies are subservient to this primary and compelling objective. This objective is not self serving, nor is its purpose to achieve an abstract technical elegance for technical elegance sake. Its purpose is to provide the structure required to enable vast improvement in the ability of IM&M solutions to ever better service dynamic business needs.

It is instructive to compare this primary objective with the primary objective of military strategy presented in Section 4.5. The essence of military strategy is "concentration of force against weakness." This is accomplished by using the associated eight principles of military strategy to cause a "dislocation" of the enemy which permits "exploitation" (see Figure 4.8). Dislocation means paralysis, confusion, misalignment, internal conflict, dispersion of resources, etc. Exploitation means making oneself strong so to be able to take advantage of the dislocation. How does a business in the 1990s create dislocations and the associated exploitation?

A reach/range/maneuverability IM&M architecture provides the strategic lever to accomplish dislocation and exploitation on the business battlefield. By using IM&M to maneuver the business, the management team can define the competitive agenda. Rather than being a victim of events, the business can use IM&M to create windows of opportunity. IM&M can be both the means of creating dislocation and the methods of exploitation.

Strategic planning is a discipline of the intellect. IM&M is a tool of action. By focusing the essential 12 concepts of strategic planning on maximizing IM&M reach/range/maneuverability, IM&M becomes the means of conducting the competitive battle. This is the path of escape from the IM&M pincer (see Figure 1.3). The business demand for competitiveness from IM&M can be fully met, the ability to absorb and integrate emerging opportunistic IM&M technologies can be accomplished, and the advance of the outsourcing competitors can be parried by a three step plan:

1. Tactically continue, as always, delivering day-to-day value and service to your IM&M customers.

2. Put in-place a reach/range/maneuverability IM&M architecture; the means to infusing the IM&M resource with tremendous value-added.

3. Partner with your clients to use the resulting IM&M resource to design dislocations and exploitation in the marketplace. Win and grow by enabling your clients to win and grow.

There is no need to wander any longer in a fog. There is a way out of the labyrinth. The objective of IM&M is competitiveness; it can be realized by applying strategic planing methods to optimize the reach/range/maneuverability of the IM&M asset. IM&M is then repositioned from being merely an administrative and record keeping tool to being the power tool of business strategy and execution. As shown in Figure 8.11, IM&M can be used to achieve perfect business and IM&M alignment, a

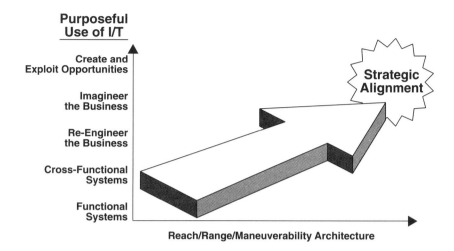

Figure 8.11   Strategic alignment is achieved between the business and information technology when IM&M can be used to create, design, and exploit business opportunities.

state of fusion, when a reach/range/maneuverability architecture permits business to go beyond using information technology to merely build systems and permits the business to use information technology to create, design, and exploit business opportunities. It is at this point that IM&M becomes a source of sustainable competitive advantage for the business.

The strategic intent of the IM&M organization is therefore obvious; it must be to achieve a perfect state of strategic alignment with the business. This will permit the business to create opportunites for itself and problems and dislocations for its competitiors; it will permit the continuance of good fortune for the business and the preemption of misfortune. It, IM&M, will become a basis of sustainable competitive advantage; it will permit the business to innovate through information technology. It is at this point through mastery of IM&M and strategy that you can escape the eternal treadmill of being the victim of changing time and circumstances and be the creator of extended good fortune for the enterprise and extended misfortune for your competitors.

The logic of IM&M strategy for the 1990s, illustrated in Figure 8.12, is therefore as follows:

> If you invest your energy in developing a powerful reach/range/ maneuverability architecture, then you will be able to achieve a perfect state of strategic alignment where IM&M can be used to create dislocations and opportunities in the marketplace for the business.

If you can use IM&M to create dislocations and opportunities, then you can escape the eternal challenge as understood by Machiavelli. Rather than being the hapless victim of time and circumstances, you can be the designer of time and circumstances. If you can craft time and circumstances, then surely your strategy must be deep and far reaching. If your strategy is deep and far reaching, then you will surely win by virtue of your superior positions over others whose strategy is shallow and near sighted.

This is a strategy worthy of those who have mastered the disciplines of strategy and IM&M and the disciples of Sun Tzu and Machiavelli, our teachers. It is a strategy that makes the stretch for perfection.

Bertrand Russell, the foremost philosopher of the 20th century, said (paraphrased):

The good is inspired by loving kindness and guided by knowledge.

Loving kindness provides motivation and knowledge provides the means. Since loving kindness and knowledge are both infinitely extensible, an ever better "good" can be imagined for humanity. If we copy this idea, then strategy must be inspired by vision and guided by reason. Vision defines both the ends for strategy and the sandbox for reason. *Reason* provides the means of realization. And, as loving kindness and knowledge are limitless, so are vision and reason. Therefore, a perfect strategy is also imaginable.

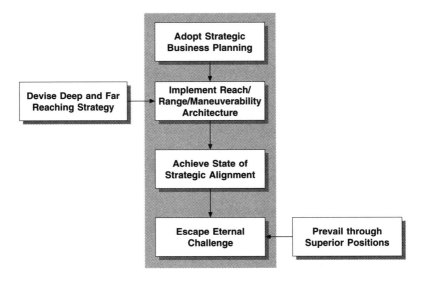

Figure 8.12   The Logic of IM&M Strategy. How much the better that time and circumstances should be a product of strategy than strategy being a product of times and circumstances.

Footnotes

1. Sun Tzu, *The Art of War.*
2. Machiavelli, *The Prince.*
3. Boar, *Implementing Client/Server Computing: A Strategic Perspective.*
4. Boar, *Implementing Client/Server Computing: A Strategic Perspective.*
5. Boar, *Application Prototyping: A Requirements Strategy for the 80s.*
6. *CSC/Index.*
7. Sun Tzu, *The Art of War.*
8. Dante, *Divine Comedy: Inferno.*

9

Epilogue

Unfortunately, business schools do not routinely graduate the greatest entrepreneurs; neither do the most pious monasteries regularly serve as the spiritual birthplace for saints. Likewise, neither this book nor any other can instantly provide sufficient tutoring and insight to transform you into a "great IM&M strategist." It would have been very satisfying to commence this paragraph with the phrase "Now that we are learned strategists...," but such is simply not the case. At best, we are aware of the possibilities, we understand the approaches, and we are energized to increase our proficiencies.

We are aware that the future can be planned for, influenced, and shaped. It is understood that there exists a rich and robust set of frameworks, models, and analytical tools through which we can discover and develop the possibilities. We are energized to master the merging of strategic planning and IM&M through doing. We have a new clarity of the importance and purpose of IM&M and fully appreciate that its contributions are too critical to be left to the novice prowess of those who can't understand and those who won't understand what lies before us, however unclear.

The therapy prescribed in this book, the marriage of strategic planning methods and IM&M, is cause for optimism. IM&M is not some exotic and unique business resource. The rich techniques of strategic management can be applied to use it effectively and efficiently. Some, however, are not optimistic. They believe that the root problems with IM&M lies not in the arena of strategy but in the immaturity of IM&M. They believe both IM&M as an engineering discipline and the level of hardware, software, and communications sophistication is simply too immature to serve as the foundation of business advantage. I believe that they are wrong. They are wrong because the fundamental problem is not one of immature technology but one of the absence of strategy.

On reflection, the strategy problem is not so much that the IM&M community continues to be a poor strategist, but that it never was required to bother with strategic thinking. The first 30 years of commercial IM&M

supported a monopoly hegemony over centralized and mystique-oriented IM&M technologies. What was required was functional expertise, efficient operations of expensive MIPS, storage and memory to maximize utilization of resources, nursing the IM&M mystique of being "special and different (sorcerers)," and showing up. All of that is now in massive transition. We are subject to competition, the internal business and IM&M economy requires us to be market-oriented, the new and emerging technologies of IM&M both obsolete our skills and move IM&M technology away from the data center, and users have an ever growing understanding of IM&M; the sorcerer's apprentices are becoming quite capable themselves. So in the absence of continued good fortune, like all others subject to the stress of competition, we must adopt and proceed with strategy as our guide. We must learn to observe, think, interpret, analyze, plan, and act strategically.

The need for strategic planning thus originates in the dynamics of three variables: *change, uncertainty,* and *complexity.* If change was minimal, the future was highly predictable, and the complexity level of IM&M technology was declining, then strategic planning would not be necesssary. Conversely, when change is rampant, uncertainty is prevalent, and complexity is growing exponentially, strategic planning is required to provide direction, guidance, and flexibility to the organization. It is this latter situation which confronts the IM&M organization of today.

But where are we to focus our attention? Given limited time and resources, should we focus on capabilities? Or should it be core competencies? Or perhaps commitment or maybe the human resource architecture? What should be the soul of strategy? The answer is obvious; it must be all of them. While different strategic frameworks take on temporary preeminence at a particular time in accord with events, strategy is the discipline of aligning the whole towards a unified purpose. Neglect creates dysfunction. Sun Tzu says:

> When you can attack anywhere and defend everywhere, then your strategy is complete.[1]

Time and circumstances have not abridged, abrogated, or nullified this requirement; the heart of strategy is completeness. "But we can't, we have neither the time, resources, or concentration to create such an exhaustive strategic plan; it is too great a burden" you protest. You are in error and still do not grasp the deeper truth. It is just the opposite. It is when you manage the business in a day-to-day tactical manner that you carry the burden of Atlas. When you manage the business strategically, the burden lifts and you can ascend to ever greater accomplishments. As your strategic prowess grows and matures in completeness, winning becomes ever easier, yielding more time and energy to even greater stratagems. This is the promise of strategy.

So what have you learned; what is strategy? Strategy is choice; making choices in the present to position for the future. Strategy is change; moving the organization from where it is to where it needs to be. Strategy is leadership and leadership is strategy. Sun Tzu says:

> The lives of the people and the order of the nation are in the charge of the generals.... When their assistance is complete, the country is strong. When their assistance is defective, the country is weak.[2]

Strategy is foresight; the deep intellectual challenge of trying to see and understand when the future is still "formless," communicating that foresight, and mobilizing the organization to act. Strategy is a process in motion, unending and never complete, constantly adapting to be in accord with events. Strategy is holistic understanding of all the functions of the business; including all, neglecting none. Strategy is alignment; creating a shared competitive agenda and preempting misalignment. Strategy is leverage, multiplying, and amplifying each benefit. Strategy is an art, assembling a plan from a puzzle of missing and irregular pieces. Strategy is commitment, perseverance in the face of obstacles and hurdles. Strategy is qualitative over quantitative; all can add and subtract but few can see before existence. Strategy is the means of *fairly* creating and maintaining an *unfair* marketplace advantage. Strategy is the Quixote quest to command (or at least bend) fortune rather than be a timeless victim of it. Strategy is learning; maintaining a fluid mental model in accord with ever changing times and circumstances. Strategy is seeding many experiments now to cull the best ideas for commitment later. Strategy is confronting the hard issues of change; the problem of leadership is not acknowledging the need for change, the challenge of leadership is choosing, from the endless permutations, when to change, how to change, and, most importantly, what to change to. Strategy is following reason (and vision) to wherever they lead; incremental change for times of stability and radical change for times of discontinuity. Strategy is preparing yourself to win the endless race; the race between the organization's speed of adaptability and the swiftness of change in the marketplace.

While strategy is all these things, these definitions are incomplete. Strategy transcends them all. Perhaps Sun Tzu best captures the true meaning of strategy:

> Strategy is important to the nation—it is the ground of death and life, the path of survival and destruction, so it is imperative to examine it. There is a way of survival which helps and strengthens you; there is a way of destruction, which pushes you into oblivion.[3]

Such is the essence of strategy.

Footnotes

1. Sun Tzu, *The Art of War.*
2. Sun Tzu, *The Art of War.*
3. Sun Tzu, *The Art of War.*

Appendix A

Aphorisms of Strategy

The teachings of Sun Tzu and Machiavelli provide an enduring set of fundamental principles of strategy. These teachings provide a broad schema of strategy upon which one can build specific strategies consistent with the times. A philosophy of strategy would be more akin to theology than the traditions of science. It is for this reason that the insights of the greatest strategists maintain their integrity, constancy, and relevancy over time. While adhering to these teachings does not guarantee success, violating them almost certainly assures failure. When the advice of a current pundit or guru contradicts these maxims, one should proceed with caution. The continuing validity of these insights have been demonstrated over 2000 and 500 years, respectively. While the details of implementation have changed radically, the generic principles have remained remarkably constant. Sun Tzu and Machiavelli have stood the test of time. Most of the advice and counsel given by modern day pundits is forgotten by the end of the seminar coffee break. This may be exaggerated, but only slightly so. Those who give advice which violate the teachings of these masters indict and convict themselves of being false prophets by their own words.

The majority of aspiring strategists would be much better off studying the teachings of Sun Tzu and Machiavelli than most teachers of business or IM&M strategy. The teachings of Sun Tzu and Machiavelli provide an holistic mental framework from which to master and manage the strategy problem. Their teachings provide a deep and far reaching philosophy of strategy. Relatively, most contemporary strategists are but temporaries who provide partial insights and procedural mechanics. Time will demonstrate whether or not they provide persistent value. There is more to be learned in the classics section of the library than the business section.

As we approach the 21st century, information technology will assume a position of preeminence among the engineering sciences. It will assume such a position because the vast majority of worldwide commerce and personal communications and entertainment will be information technology centric. As stated before, information technology success will first demand success as a strategist. Information technology success will be an accident of your strategic wisdom. One day you should expect to find in the classics section of your library a volume entitled *Philosophia Strategiea (A Philosophy of Strategy)*. On that day, strategy will take its rightful place among the philosophical issue of life. In the interim, we proceed with the best advice available, the superb and timeless advice of Sun Tzu and Machiavelli.

Advantage

"Struggle means struggle for advantage; those who get the advantage are victorious."

"…It is best to win without fighting."

Alignment

"Those whose upper and lower ranks have the same desire are victorious…. Those skilled in strategy achieve cooperation in a group so that directing the group is like directing a single individual with no other choice…. Employ the entire force like employing a single individual."

"Strategy is a problem of coordination, not of masses."

Alliances

"If you carry on alliances with strong countries, your enemies won't dare plot against you…. Make informed alliances…compete for alliances…. If you do not compete for alliances and helpers, then you will be isolated with little help."

Assessment

"Compare the strength of the enemy with your own and you will know whether there is sufficiency or lacking. After that, you can assess the advisory of attack or defense."

"The one with many strategic factors in his favor wins, the one with few strategic factors in his favor loses…. Observing the matter in this way, I can foresee who will win and who will lose."

"If you know others and know yourself, you will not be imperiled in a hundred battles; if you do not know others but know yourself, you will win one and lose one; if you do not know others and do not know yourself, you will be imperiled in every single battle."

"The considerations of the intelligent always include both harm and benefit. As they consider benefit, their work can expand; as they consider harm their troubles can be resolved."

"Attack what can be overcome, do not attack what cannot be overcome.... To advance irresistibly, push through their gaps.... So when the front is prepared, the rear is lacking, and when the rear is prepared the front is lacking. Preparedness on the left means lack on the right, preparedness on the right means lack on the left. Preparedness everywhere means lack everywhere.... Attack where there is no defense."

Benchmarking

"Men nearly always follow the tracks made by others and proceed in their affairs by imitation, even though they cannot entirely keep to the tracks of others or emulate the prowess of their models. So a prudent man must always follow in the footsteps of great men and imitate those who have been outstanding. If his own prowess fails to compare with theirs, at least it has an air of greatness about it."

Change

"It should be borne in mind that there is nothing more difficult to handle nor more doubtful of success, and more dangerous to carry through than initiating change. The innovator makes enemies of all those who prospered under the old order, and only lukewarm support is forthcoming from those who would prosper under the new. Their support is lukewarm partly from fear of their adversaries; who have the existing laws on their side, and partly because men are generally incredulous, never really trusting new things unless they have tested them by experience. In consequence, those who oppose the changes attack vigorously and the defense made by the others is only lukewarm."

"Time sweeps everything along and can bring good as well as evil, evil as well as good."

"Confront them with annihilation, and they will then survive; plunge them into a deadly situation, and they will then live. When people fall into danger, they are then able to strive for victory. ...When they have fallen into dire straits, they obey completely."

Commitment

"When an army goes forth and crosses a border, it should burn its boats and bridges to show the populace that it has not intent of looking back."

Competition

"What causes opponents to come of their own accord is the prospect of gain. What discourages opponents from coming is the prospect of harm."

"So the rule is not to count on opponents not coming; but to rely on having ways of dealing with them; not to count on opponents not attacking; but to rely on having what can't be attacked."

"What motivates competitors is profit . . . what restrains competitors is harm.... Wear enemies out by keeping them busy and not letting them rest...make them rush about trying to cover themselves, they will not have time to formulate plans.... To keep them from getting to you, attack where they will surely go to the rescue."

Execution

"Some rulers are fond of words but do not transfer them into deeds."

"...One must never allow disorder to continue so as to escape a war. Anyhow, one does not escape; the war is merely postponed top one's disadvantage."

Foresight

"What the aware individual knows has not yet taken shape. If you see the subtle and notice the hidden when there is no form, this is really good. What everyone knows is not called wisdom. A leader of wisdom and ability lays deep plans for what others do not figure on."

"The multitudes know when you win but they do not know the basis. Everyone knows the form by which I am victorious, but no one knows the form by which I ensure victory. The science of ensuring victory is a mysterious secret. Victory is not repetitious, but adapts its form endlessly."

"A general must see alone and know alone, meaning that he must see what others do not see and know what others do not know. Seeing what others do not see is called brilliance, knowing what others do not know is called genius."

"If you can always remember danger when you are secure and remember chaos in times of order, watch out for danger and chaos while they are still formless and prevent them before they happen, this is best of all."

"All wise rulers must cope not only with present troubles but also with ones likely to arise in the future and assiduously forestall them. When trouble is sensed well in advance it can easily be remedied; if you wait for it to show itself any medicine will be too late because the disease will have become incurable.... Disorders can be quickly healed if they are seen well in advance (and only a prudent ruler has such foresight); when, for lack of a diagnosis, they are allowed to grow in such away that everyone can recognize them, remedies are too late."

Leadership

"The lives of the people and the order of the nation are in the charge of the generals.... When their assistance is complete, the country is strong. When their assistance is defective, the country is weak."

"Act when it is beneficial, desist if it is not. Anger can revert to joy, wrath can revert to delight; but a nation destroyed cannot be restored to existence, and the dead cannot be restored to life. Therefore an enlightened government is careful about this. This is the way to secure the nation."

Learning

"Test them to find out where they are sufficient and where they are lacking. Do something for or against them, making opponents turn their attention to it, so that you can find out their patterns of aggressive and defensive behavior."

Market Research

"What enables an intelligent leader to overcome others and achieve extraordinary accomplishments is foreknowledge. All matters require foreknowledge."

Maneuverability

"Adaptation means not clinging to fixed methods, but changing appropriately to events...those who can face the unprepared with preparation are victorious. The ability to gain victory by changing and adapting to the opponent is called genius."

"Some win through speed.... Use swiftness to wear them out.... Get the upper hand though extraordinary swiftness...be as fast as the lightning that flickers before you can blink your eyes."

Organization Design

"Structure depends on strategy. Forces are to be structured strategically based on what is advantageous."

"There is simply no comparison between a man who is armed and one who is not. It is unreasonable to expect the armed man should obey the one who is unarmed.... This is how we can distinguish between innovators who stand alone and those who depend on others; that is between those who to achieve their purpose can force the issue and those who must use persuasion. In the second case, they always come to grief having achieved nothing. Whenever they depend on their own resources and can force the issue, then they are seldom endangered."

Outsourcing

"...The arms on which a prince bases the defense of his state are either his own, or mercenary or auxiliary. Mercenaries and auxiliaries are useless and dangerous. If a prince bases the defense of his state on mercenaries, he will never achieve stability or security...the reason for this is that there is no loyalty or inducement to keep them on the field apart from the little they are paid and that is not enough to make them want to die for you...I conclude, therefore, that unless it commands its own arms, no principality is secure, rather it is dependent on fortune since there is no valor and no loyalty to defend it when adversity comes."

Planning

"In ancient times, skillful warriors first made themselves invincible."

"It is easy to take over from those who do not plan ahead."

"Those who are good at getting rid of trouble are those who take care of it before it arises."

"Those who face the unprepared with preparation are victorious."

"…A victorious army first wins and then seeks battle, a defeated army first battles and then seeks victory."

"Be prepared and you will be lucky."

"If you have no ulterior scheme and no forethought, but just rely on your individual bravery, flippantly taking opponents lightly and giving no consideration to the situation, you will surely be taken prisoner."

Positioning

"In ancient times, those known as good warriors prevailed when it was easy to prevail. Their victories are not flukes. Their victories are not flukes because they *position* themselves where they will surely win, prevailing over those who have already lost."

Quality

"So it is said that good warriors take their stand on ground where they cannot lose. Ground where one cannot lose means invincible strategy that makes it impossible for opponents to defeat you."

Strategist

"They do not wander when they move. They act in accord with events. Their actions and inactions are matters of strategy."

Strategy

"There are only five notes in the musical scale but the variations are so many that they all can't be heard. There are only five basic colors but their variations are so many, that they all can't be seen. There are only five basic flavors, but the varieties are so many that they can't all be tasted. There are only two basic charges in battle, the unorthodox surprise attack and the orthodox direct attack but the variations of the orthodox and the unorthodox are endless. The unorthodox and the orthodox give raise to each other like a beginningless circle—who can exhaust them."

"Go forth without having determined strategy and you will destroy yourself in battle."

"When your strategy is deep and far-reaching, then what you gain by your calculations is much, so you can win before you even fight. When your strategic thinking is shallow and nearsighted, then what you gain by your calculations is little, so you lose before you do battle. Much strategy prevails over little strategy, so those with no strategy cannot but be defeated. Therefore it is said that victorious warriors win first and then go to war, while defeated warriors go to war first and then seek to win."

"Strategy is important to the nation—it is the ground of death and life, the path of survival and destruction, so it is imperative to examine it. There is a way of survival, which helps and strengthens you; there is a way of destruction, which pushes you into oblivion."

Success

"...Some princes flourish one day and come to grief the next without appearing to have changed in character or in any way. This I believe arises because those princes who are utterly dependent on fortune come to grief when their fortune changes. I also believe that those who adapt their policy to the times prosper and, that those whose policies clash with the times do not. This explains why prosperity is ephemeral.... If time and circumstances change, he will be ruined if he does not change his policy. If he changed his character to the times and circumstances, then his fortune would not change."

Surprise

"In battle, confrontation is done directly, victory is gained by surprise."

Vision

"What everyone knows is what has already happened. What everyone knows is not called wisdom. What the aware individual knows is what has not yet taken shape; what has not yet occurred. If you see the subtle and notice the hidden so as to seize victory when there is no form, this is really good."

The frustrating challenge confronting all of us who seek strategic wisdom is that there is a chronic surplus of Solieris and an ever acute shortage of Mozarts. Solieri was a highly successful and celebrated court composer in the time of Mozart. While honored and acclaimed in his day, time judged him mediocre and sentenced him to obscurity. Mozart, his antagonist, was controversial but brilliant, and time promoted him to the status of musical genius. Solieri was but a run-of-the-mill composer who offered fleeting value while Mozart, less honored in his day, offered persistent value. I am fearful that many who present themselves as oracles of strategic advice are but modern day Solieris. Few have known strategy as deeply and in the manner as have Sun Tzu and Machiavelli, the Mozarts of strategic thinking. All strategic wisdom starts with them.

Appendix B

Glossary

Alignment   Coordination, collaboration, and perseverance towards a shared set of objectives

Argument   An inductive or deductive method of reasoning

Assessment   The activity of developing a clear and thorough understanding of the business situation from both an internal and external perspective

Benchmarking   Measuring and comparing against the recognized best

Bottleneck analysis   The analysis of value chains for bottlenecks

Business model   Answers to the basic questions of what a business will sell, how it will relate to its customers, and how it will make money

Business "p"s   Product, position, promotion, price, people, and process

Business scope   Defines the essential characteristics of a business

Capabilities   The business practices and processes which deliver value and satisfaction to the customer

Champion   The executive responsible for assisting an owner

Change management plan   Planned actions to preempt resistance to change

Commitment plan   A set of actions taken to establish credibility

Competitor analysis   Strategic analysis of a competitor

Conclusions   Explicit statements describing the state of the business

Contingency plan   A plan to deal with a low probability event whose occurrence would prevent achieving an objective

Core competency   The collective learning of the organization

Critical success factors   Specific competencies, capabilities, processes, etc. which an organization must do well to succeed

Delphi technique   A process to develop a consensus forecast about the future

Devil's advocacy   A quality control method where a subteam critiques the strategy

Directives and assumptions   Givens that govern the strategic planning decision making

Driving force   Primary determiner of products and services and markets

Dynamic issues management   Process used to mange unforeseen events of strategic importance

Economy   The processes used to govern the production and exchange of goods and services

Emergent strategy   Realized strategies that were not intended. They emerged from the dynamics of the situation.

Execution   Putting the strategic plan into motion

Expert review   A quality control method where external experts review the strategy

Five forces   A framework which asserts that the competitive position of an industry can be understood by the relationships between five forces of supplier power, buyer power, threat of entry, substitute products, and rivalry.

Fortune   Serendipity or good luck

Fragmentation   The partitioning of a marketplace into groups of customers with extremely distinct needs

Frozen mental models   A view of the world which is not subject to change

Gap analysis   The difference between a current state or position and a desired state or position

Goals   An interim objective

Human resource architecture   A framework for translating values into behaviors

Implementation program parameters   Rules, guidelines, etc. which are to be followed in implementing a strategic move.

Implementation programs and projects Specific projects to execute the strategy

Information form, function, and movement A way of understanding IM&M as the relationships between information form (sound, data, image and text), information functions (presentation, processing, storage, transport and OAM), and information movement (people to people, people to machines, and machines to machines)

Intended strategy The explicit product of the strategic planning process

Kano methodology A methodology for causing marketplace dislocations by mastering excitement customer satisfaction attributes and driving them to threshold attributes

Key findings Knowledge learned during the assessment step of particular value

Kondratiev waves A theory developed by Dr. N. Kondratiev which asserted that productivity in Western societies was fueled by a dominant era technology

Learning Continued improvement of process by feedback from actual experiences

Leverage The multiplication of the benefit of a strategic move

Market leader The manner in which a business follows or leads its customers

Matrix analysis Analyzing through matrices the intersection of two strategic business areas

Market opportunity analysis The use of a set of analytical methods to determine the attractiveness of a market opportunity

Mental model How both an individual and an organization views and understands the world

Mission The purpose of the business

Monitoring Periodic review of implementation programs for corrective actions

Objectives Specific measurable and dated states to be achieved

Owner The person responsible for making a strategic move happen

Payoff matrix A diagramming technique to illustrate the "payoff" for different actions

Pivot positiion   A position from which many alternative actions may be taken

Politics   The divisions of an organization into special interest groups

Position   An illustration of a strategic area along one or more strategic dimensions

Product map   A set of graphs and matrices which together illustrate the position of a product

Rationalist school of strategy   Strategy is the product of rational, purposeful, conscious, and deliberate acts.

Reach/Range/Maneuverability architecture   The IM&M architecture of the business which permits anyone, anywhere, at anytime to access (reach) any shareable information object (range) or service

Realized strategy   Those intended and emergent strategies that worked in practice

Re-engineering   Radical redesign of business processes with the employment of IM&M

Root cause analysis   Decomposition of a problem into the segments of symptoms, problem, and etiology

"S" curves   A life-cycle growth and decline pattern common among technologies

Scenarios   The definition of possible futures

Segmentation   Partitioning a market based on common needs

Simulations   Computerized simulations of a strategy to test it

Situational analysis   The collection and analysis of information about the business for the purpose of developing conclusions about the state of the business

Strategic alignment   A state of coordination, perseverance, coordination of effort, and commitment

Strategic business unit   A collection of related businesses with a distinct mission, a market, a set of competitors, a set of products, profit and loss responsibility, and a dedicated management team

Strategic intent   Long-term ambition of the business

Strategic move   An action to achieve an objective

Strategic planning   A plan to provide direction, concentration of effort, consistency of purpose, and flexibility as a business moves to continually improve its competitive position

Strategic thinking   Dynamically analyzing and understanding events in terms of strategic frameworks

Strategic thrust   A repositioning goal for a product

Strategy (a.k.a. Strategic plan)   Identifying the desired future state of the business in terms of a business scope and future positions, objectives, strategic moves, a commitment plan, and a change management plan

Strategy coherence   A method to force alignment across strategic moves

Structure follows strategy   Organizational design follows the definition of a strategy and enables that strategy

Sustainable competitive advantage   The distinct asset, skill, capability, resource, process, etc. which creates a capability gap between the company and its competitors

SWOT analysis   Analysis of the business from the perspectives of strengths, weaknesses, opportunities, and threats

Tactics   Detailed actions taken to implement a strategic move

Theory/Hypothesis   A theory is a systematically related set of statements, including some law-like generalizations that both explain and predict phenomena. An hypothesis is a predictive assumption derived from a theory which is testable for validity.

Unrealized strategy   Intended strategies that fail

Value chain analysis   A method for understanding the translation of resources through processes into final products

Values   What the business believes in

Vigilance   Continual proactive scanning of the environment for events requiring strategic responses

Vision   A guiding theme that articulates the nature of the business and its intent for the future

7 "S" model   An analytical model which views strategy as a strategic fit between the strategy and structure, style, systems, staff, skills, and shared values.

Appendix C

The Structure and Process of Strategy

People naturally feel more comfortable with a new subject when they can experience it in a familiar context. Figure C.1 shows a data entity diagram of the entities which compose a strategic plan. Figure C.2 provides a high level data flow diagram of the assessment and strategy steps of the strategic planning process.

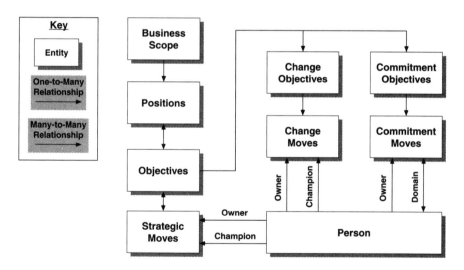

Figure C.1   The Structure of Strategy. This data entity diagram shows the structural data relationships between the entities that compose a business strategy.

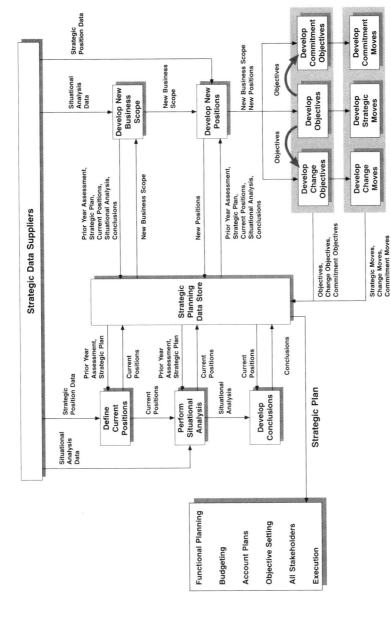

Figure C.2   The Process of Strategy. This data flow diagram shows the steady state process flow of the strategic planning process.

345

Appendix D

IBM: January/February 1993

IBM's sorrows continued to mount in January 1993 with no relief in sight. The events were as follows:

- January 14,1993: Debt Rating

    Standard & Poors lowered IBM's credit rating from AAA to AA-. The other major debt rating services, Phelps-Dodge and Moodys, had taken similar action earlier in 1992. Nineteen billion dollars of debt issued from IBM Credit Corp., IBM International Finance NV, and IBM Japan Ltd. were impacted.

- January 19,1993: 1992 Results:

    IBM announced its 1992 fiscal year results with the following "low-lights:"

    1. Revenue declined .4% from $64,766 billion to $64,523 billion.
    2. Fourth quarter revenue declined 11% from $21,968 billion to $19,560 billion.
    3. A loss of $4.97 billion for the year; a 74% greater loss than the previous year's loss of $2.86 billion. The loss of $4.97 billion was the highest loss ever reported for a US business.
    4. Without an accounting rules change of $1.9 billion, the loss for 1992 would have been $6.87 billion.
    5. IBM experienced its first ever operating loss for the year of $45 million.
    6. Headcount was reduced by 40,000 employees. Since 1986, staffing has declined by 100,000 employees and an additional 25,000 jobs are expected to be shed in 1993.

An analyst referred to these results as "the most wanton squandering of corporate wealth in history."

- January 26,1993: Board of Directors Meeting

    The board of directors meeting culminated with the following actions:

    1. John Akers agreed to step down as IBM CEO.
    2. The chief financial officer, Frank Metz, would retire.
    3. President Jack Kuehler will become vice-chariman.
    4. The quarterly dividend was cut 55% from $1.21 to $.54 per share.
    5. A board committee of outsiders would select a new chairman within 90 days.

Perhaps what was most telling, however, was what didn't, but almost, occurred. As illustrated in Figure D.1, both Intel and Microsoft rapidly approached IBM in stock valuation. This event, when it occurs, is highly symbolic as it represents the passing of the torch from one vision of computing to a very different vision of computing. It also clearly illustrates that no colossus, even one as once great and strong as IBM, is immune to changes in times and circumstance. It will be interesting to observe in the years to come how long the new Goliath will reign and what weapon the inevitable David will use to defeat it.

On February 10, 1993, IBM Enterprise Systems, the mainframe business unit, held a new product press conference. A set of bigger and better than ever traditional mainframes were announced. Mr. Nicholas Donofrio, General Manager of Enterprise Systems, candidly but optimistically addressed the audience about both IBM's and Enterprise System's futures. After the announcements concluded, the media rounded up the usual gang of pundits who provided the requisite number of pithy remarks. They debated whether Enterprise Systems' revenues were down 8% for 1992 as Mr. Donofrio stated or closer to the 12% estimated by a leading market research firm. Some forecasted years of difficulty ahead, which would not end until IBM shrunk by a third to $40 billion in revenue (this would drop them from fourth on the Fortune 500 to eighth), while others were confident that IBM management had gotten the message and a turnaround would be forthcoming. Two weeks later, IBM ended its no layoff policy and announced that 500 headquarters employess would be released.

If one stops and reflects on the last 12–24 months of IBM news, one cannot but surmise that IBM's worse nightmare is yet to unfold. The Israelites suffered an extended period of misfortune when time and circumstances changed in Egypt and "there arose a Pharaoh who knew not Joseph." Likewise, it appears that there will now arise a generation of information technology decision makers who will not know that real business computing could only be done on IBM mainframes. IBM has forfeited its distinguishing sustainable competitive advantage; the tautology that business computing equates to IBM mainframe computing. How will they replace it?

Now, God was benevolent and remembered his commitment and covenant with Abraham and sent a deliverer in Moses to rescue the Israelites. We'll have to wait and see if the IBM Board of Directors selects a savior for IBM of proportional merit. We can be sure, however, of three things: the new CEO will not have the advantage of being able to perform miracles, he or she won't be afforded the luxury of 70 years of wandering to complete the turnaround, and "it ain't going to be pretty."

Final Note: As this book drew to completion, Mr. Louis Gerstner, Jr. was named CEO of IBM. The reaction of the pundit community was mixed. If anything, it was tilted toward the negative because Mr. Gerstner was not a computer expert. I believe Mr. Gerstner was an excellent choice. IBM is rich in technology. Its problems, as discussed in the body of this book, were failures of management to deal directly with the changing realities of the marketplace. IBM had more than enough technology to compete— had it chosen to compete rather than defend the *status quo*. Mr. Gerstner will hopefully bring to IBM what it needs most, management and strategy to exploit its technology horde in alignment with a fundamentally altered marketplace.

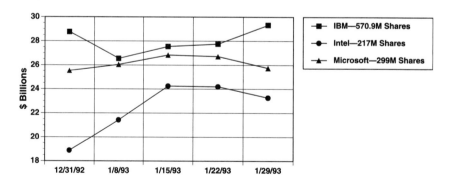

Figure D.1   The New Goliath. Both Microsoft and Intel are threatening to surpass IBM in stock valuation.

Appendix E

Paradise Lost

An interesting, though admittedly unorthodox example of using Liddell-Hart's eight principles for strategy formulation as the basis for evaluating a set of strategic moves is provided by the character Satan in John Milton's "Paradise Lost" (see Section 4.3). The scene is as follows: Satan, a former archangel, has lead an ill-fated rebellion against God. After two days of indecisive combat, Satan and his host are overwhelmingly routed by extraordinary superior force and driven out of Heaven, through the abyss, into Hell. Beaten, defiant, proud, and revengeful, Satan devises the following strategy to settle accounts with God:

Objective: Destroy the good that God does by perverting good to evil.
Strategic Moves:

1. Do not provoke a direct battle with God—do not engage in direct confrontation.

2. Carry on war with Heaven by leading Man away from God; replace God in the hearts and minds of people by evil.

3. Achieve all ends by fraud—appear desirable but in actuality be evil.

4. Investigate the suitability of God's rumored creation, Man, for the first attack. Man being "less in glory" than angels should be vulnerable.

5. Attack Man on earth, an outpost away from Heaven.

6. After reconnaissance, choose any of the following options:

   Lay waste to earth with hellfire.

   Take possession of earth; make earth a more pleasant refuge then hell.

   Drive inhabitants to hell.

   Seduce inhabitants into alliance.

Satan, through his second in command, Beelzebub, convinces the other fallen angels to follow his plan in a meeting in Pandemonium (the capital of Hell). This meeting is an interesting study in organizational politics as Satan has to overcome three alternative positions which include a peace plank, a war plank, and a wait-and-see plank.

Satan's strategic moves by be evaluated against the eight principles as follows:

1. *Adjust your ends to your means*—Satan acknowledges that his powers are grossly inferior to God and chooses to compete through guile rather than force.

2. *Keep your object in mind*—Satan's object is revenge. He will accomplish this by corrupting and perverting God's creations

3. *Choose the line of least expectation*—Satan chooses a target, Man, who he is not sure exists, does not know where he is, and must escape Hell to attack.

4. *Choose the line of least resistance*—Man is made "inferior in glory" and will be lightly guarded.

5. *Choose a line of operations offering alternative objectives*—Satan will decide whether to lay waste to earth, take it over, drive the inhabitants to Hell, or make allies of the inhabitants after his assessment of the actual situation.

6. *Ensure that dispositions are flexible and adaptable to circumstances*—Satan will take actions based on his analysis of the situation on earth.

7. *Do not throw your weight into a stroke while your opponent is on guard*—Satan will not attack Heaven.

8. *Do not renew an attack along the same line or in the same form once it has failed*—Satan will not again engage in direct combat with God.

Satan's strategic moves were very well developed. His problem was in choosing a competitor who is omnipresent, omniscient, and omnipotent. God has perfect sustainable competitive advantage.

Appendix F

Customer Satisfaction Measurements

In the competitive business environment that more and more internal IM&M organization will find themselves, customer satisfaction is one of the most important, if not the most important, dimension of strategic success. Table F.1 provides an example of the types of measures that need to be implemented. A level of measurement granularity must be selected. For example, for production transaction processing systems, performance measurement may be done by transaction within time of day (peak/non-peak) or within time of month (critical/non-critical). These measures must then be linked to the Kano methodology to direct investment. Table F.2 provides a more detailed expansion of customer service measurements for fault management.

Table F.1
Strawperson Customer Satisfaction Measurements. A robust customer satisfaction measurement system is required to be a successful competitor.

Customer View of Product		Internal Process View of Product	
Customer satisfier	Satisfier Driver (product attributes)	Value chain process	Correlated measurements
Quality	Availability	Fault management	1. (Total, average, median) number of outages per unit of time 2. Mean time to repair by problem severity level 3. Mean time between failures 4. (Total, average, median) time unavailable per unit of time
	Performance	Service delivery	1. (Average, median, 90% <, 95% <) interactive response time (end to end, internal host) 2. Percent of batch jobs completed on time 3. Percent of input and output delivered on time
Price	Cost	Asset management	1. By asset category, percent utilized 2. By asset category, percent utilized and billable 3. By asset category, forecast to actual
		Vendor management	1. Percent of key vendors with best price agreements 2. Percent of key vendors delivering components ready to integrate
		Cost management	1. Value chain function cost per billable unit 2. Value chain function head count per billable unit
Pre-sales service	Order management	Product provisioning	1. Percent of orders completed on time 2. Percent of orders backlogged 3. Percent of orders revised
Post sales service	Billing accuracy	Billing	1. Percent of debit/credit corrections 2. Percent of customers notified of billing errors 3. Percent of billing inquires closed with one call 4. Percent of billing entries late billed

Table F.2
Detailed Fault Management Metrices. This table illustrates an explosion of fault management metrices to support a customer satisfaction measurement system.

Domain: All Systems Images
Time Period: All Scheduled Hours
Period: Calendar Month

Fault Management Metrics

Measurement Type	Measure	Development and Test Environments				Production Environments							
		Prime Shift		All Scheduled Hours		Prime Shift				All Scheduled Hours			
						Critical Monthly Processing Periods		All Periods		Critical Monthly Processing Periods		All Periods	
		Result	Target	Result	Target	Result	Target	Result	Target	Result	Target	Result	Target
System time between failures	Mean												
	50%<												
	80%<												
	95%<												
	100%<												
System time to repair	Mean												
	50%<												
	80%<												
	95%<												
	100%<												
System outages	Number												

Appendix G

Object-Oriented Organization Design

It is common to hear consultants lobby for the application of excellent management principles to the administration of information technology. Less advocated but equally valid, is the use of excellent I/T concepts as frameworks for performing various management functions. A particularly interesting example of this idea is the use of object-oriented design principles as the basis for performing organization design.

Object-oriented design is a concept in which entities are viewed as "black boxes." An object has one or more attributes that define the object and a set of internal methods or procedures that operates on those attributes. The object is encapsulated in the sense that the details of how the object behaves is hidden (internalized). Client objects send "messages" to server objects identifying the object procedure (service) to be performed and any required parameters. A very well defined message interface between clients and servers, a named service with understood behavior and functionality and a set of parameters, insures high reuse (leverage) of server objects. Logical objects are easily created which front for multiple physical object servers, i.e., the logical object receives a named service message and input parameters and invokes numerous objects to complete the task. The client, however, only sees the logical intermediary.

Object-oriented design, consequently, offers a number of benefits:

1. *Reusability*—Object-oriented design strongly encourages and enables cut and paste solutions.

2. *Leverage*—Objects can advertise their services and be used numerous times.

3. *Complexity hiding*—Clients only have to know the interface, not the procedural details.

4. *A many to many relationship between client and servers*—A client may invoke multiple object servers and an object server may be used by multiple clients.

5. *Logical services*—Servers may provide robust functionality to a client but in practice invoke multiple other logical and physical object servers.

6. *Recursiveness*—Objects may, in turn, become clients and request services from other objects. When one combines this notion with the above notion of logical services, one can create a "layered" environment where everyone builds on each other.

In Section 4.3, when organization structure and design are discussed, it is suggested that "…functional organizations, analogous to object servers…" should advertise and provide services to process owners. What we are suggesting is that while one may (must) organize functionally for various reasons, functional units should behave just like objects. They should have a set of services they can perform for customers. Functional units grow, in the free IM&M economy, by advertising and ever improving their services for clients. Since the services are well defined at the interface points, it becomes easier and easier for clients to string services together and create logical services to be re-used by other clients. The client's view of the organization unit is "Don't tell me what your hierarchial functions are, tell me what services you can provide, how I invoke them, and what they will cost me."

Figures 4.13 and 4.14 illustrate this concept. In the first case, a product manager buys a logical service from a process owner. The process owner builds her service by stringing together services from the object-oriented functional units. Those units who behave most consistently with free market economics and customer satisfaction will thrive as process owners are ever more inclined to include their services in their horizontal end-to-end processes. In Figure 4.14, a core systems integration group invokes specialist servers to append to their core network computing platform specific OAM, applications support, and application enabling capabilities. In both cases, the object server does research into advances in their field of specialty and can multiply advances by updating the solutions for all their clients.

When one views organizational design from an object-oriented perspective, one accomplishes two great benefits. First, it richly supports the strategic notion of leverage. An object-oriented organization is an organization of multipliers. Recursiveness, further, encourages service reusability. Service providers who do not reuse other object services will have to duplicate them which will raise their unit cost and make their services less attractive. Second, it richly supports a free market internal IM&M

economy. To remain viable, object servers need to be customer focused, to continually upgrade their services and find expanding clients for their services. Leverage plus free-market economics yields customer-focused productivity for an organization.

An algorithm for performing object-oriented organizational design would execute the following:

1. The object-oriented design ideas which we have discussed are established as the conceptual framework and background for design.
2. Divide the organization into two mega-service providers, the value chain and support services.
3. Repetitively decompose each service into further levels of detail. Increasingly elaborate the definitions of what services are provided and the parameters of the interface. Figure 4.12 illustrates the first decomposition.
4. In parallel and recursively, mold this purely service decomposed design by the following influencers:
   - IM&M economy,
   - Capabilities and process execution,
   - Geography,
   - Core competencies,
   - Customer focus,
   - Technology focus,
   - Supplier focus, and
   - Management levels.

While organizational design clearly remains an art, the object-oriented focus provides a novel way to liberate oneself from the traditional functional hierarchy and think more in terms of horizontal services. The IM&M organization can then be both big and small at the same time; big in the sense that it can offer a huge range of services and small in the sense that each server unit is an entrepreneurial business.

Appendix H

Not Even Good Nonsense

There is an old story about the US Senate. After a particularly long and bombastic speech, the next Senator rose, turned to his colleague and, to the enthusiastic applause of the gallery said, "Sir, that doesn't even qualify as good nonsense." Apparently, the good Senator had had enough of listening to muddle-headed arguments.

The following is another excellent example of the muddle-headed thinking that is, unfortunately, only too common in the IM&M debate. It is because of such reasoning that a reasonable mastery of the rules of logic, as presented in Section 3, is required. The term "good nonsense" refers to fallacious arguments which convince. People who believe fallacious arguments or create fallacious arguments and continue to defend them when confronted with the fallacies committed are "muddle-headed."

- *Muddle-Headed Thinker:* A Network Computing Zealot
- *Muddle-Headed Conclusion:* Mainframes are dead.
- *Muddle-Headed Thoughts:* The mainframe is dead. Is the mainframe really dead? Well, not exactly. There are quite a few mainframes in use—but they are tolerated, not loved. Mainframes persevere because the client/server world has not caught on to some of the existing benefits that mainframes offer, such as data integrity, security, manageability, and system reliability.... New technology will eventually make client/server computing superior to mainframe features....

This argument demonstrates that muddle-headed thinking is not controlled by mainframe zealots—the network computing crowd also has its share of muddle heads. This argument suffers from two fallacies:

1. *Denying the Antecedent:* The phrase "But they are tolerated not loved" is built from the following unstated logic:

If users love an information technology, then it is a good technology.

Users do not love mainframes.

Therefore: Mainframes are not good technology (they are tolerated due to need).

The form of this argument symbolically is:

a→ b

~a

→~b

(The arrow should be read as "therefore" and the "~" as "not.")

We demonstrate this argument to be of a fallacious form by the following counter-example:

If you are a Cardasian, you are a Federation enemy. (True)

Romulans are not Cardasians. (True)

Therefore: Romulans are not enemies of the Federation. (False)

What we demonstrate by counter-example is that there exists at least one case where, for an argument of the stated form, that the premise is true and the conclusion is false. This is sufficient to demonstrate that the form of argument is invalid and that no general inference of validity may be made by any argument of that form. This particular fallacious form is known as the "Fallacy of Denying the Antecedent."

2. *Contradiction:* The phrase "the mainframe is dead…well not exactly…" is an example of contradiction. Most people intuitively accept the illogic of contradiction but do not know why it is so bad. Contradiction is unacceptable in an argument because if you accept contradiction, you can prove any false statement to be true. Consider the following example:

The mainframe is dead.	True (contradiction of below)
The mainframe is not dead.	True (contradiction of above)
The mainframe is dead.	True (from above)

or

All consultants are Klignons.	False (all consultants are Romulans)

(Since the above statement is an "or" statement and one of the statements is true, the truth value of the statement is true.)

The mainframe is not dead.   True (from above)

Therefore: All consultants are Klignons.   True (but it is false)

Nothing is more muddle-headed then permitting contradiction.

We therefore conclude that this argument is fallacious. Just to assure clarity, what we mean is that no meaningful inference can be made between the premise and the conclusion. It may be true that mainframes are dead, but this argument does not convince a rational person of such.

Though not a fallacy, this argument also violates the rules of debate by refuting itself. The logic that begins with "Mainframes persevere because..." may be sketched as follows:

> If client/server computing is to replace mainframe computing then client/server computing must offer greater feature/functionality than mainframe computing.
>
> Client/server computing does not offer greater feature/functionality.
>
> *Therefore:* Client/server computing cannot replace mainframe computing.

This argument is of the valid form "Denying the Conclusion" and convincingly refutes the assertion of the argument that mainframes are dead—why would you do that? Saying that someday when client/server computing has greater feature/functionality it will replace mainframe computing doesn't tell us anything very novel. After all, by that logic, someday "urangi-dokwa" computing which has superior feature/functionality will replace "unloved" client/server computing. If a technology is dead if it will someday be replaced, then all technologies are always dead; hardly an illuminating argument.

When you suspect an argument is fallacious but just don't know why, a useful approach is to try to reduce the argument to absurdity. To do this, you do the following:

- Assume the premise in question to be true.
- Generate an argument from the premise with a valid form which either:

> reaches a conclusion which contradicts the premise,
>
> creates a contradiction of some other statement, or
>
> reaches a false conclusion. (This is a contradiction also; a true premise and valid form should not yield a false conclusion).

By this approach, from an assumed true premise and valid form, we create a contradiction. For this to happen, either the form must be invalid or the premise false. Since we know the form is valid, the premise must be false.

Fallacies, whether intentional or not, meet the needs of certain people to make a point.. Since needs are often a function of role, one would expect fallacies to be a function of role. We would suggest the following relationship between roles and common fallacies (reference Table 3:31):

Vendor	Guru	Consultant	Academic
Suppressed evidence	False dilemma	Hasty conclusion	Contrary to fact
Doubtful evidence	Equivocation	Appeal to authority	Provincialism
Tokenism	Contrary to fact	Genetic error	Strawperson
Ambiguity	Compound question	Slippery slope	Questionable analogy

You should carefully consider which fallacies you routinely employ to build arguments and why your arguments require fallacies to seem convincing. You should insist that these people (vendor, guru, consultant, academic) present convincing arguments. The old maxim "The one who asserts, must prove" applies here. If they wish to play the advice game, they must be prepared to demonstrate a valid argument and a truthful premise.

It is important to always remember that persuasiveness is not a term of logic. Arguments which are quite persuasive are often fallacious. These arguments are called "good nonsense." Arguments which are sound, often do not persuade. Persuasiveness has to do with the receptiveness (psychology) of an audience to an argument. We would hope that rational people will accept convincing arguments and reject fallacious ones. This, however, is often not the case for two reasons:

1.   The fallacy is hidden.
2.   The audience wishes to have its prejudices feed and is really not interested in increasing knowledge.

The purpose of reason is to increase knowledge, but it is only a tool. Convincing arguments are not less convincing because of popular displeasure nor are fallacious arguments less fallacious because of broad concurrence. As a practical reality, however, convincing arguments which do not persuade are futile arguments since we are unable to act on our knowledge. It is an ethical obligation of leadership to insist on rationality and to go where rationality leads.

Hopefully you have had some fun reading this section. Its point, however, is extremely serious. There are many advice givers, but not necessarily an abundance of good advice. It is your responsibility to insist on receiving convincing arguments and having the personal integrity to only present convincing arguments.

Reason is the pursuit of knowledge. You may proceed based on one of the following three options: You may proceed based on rational arguments. In this case, you must understand the rules of logic and ignore muddle-headed thinking.

You may proceed based on irrationality. In this case, you accept irrationality (fallacious arguments) as a basis of decision making. If you do, you might as well admit seances, sorcery, palm reading, etc. to your decision making practices. They are no worse then irrationality and much more fun.

You may proceed based on non-rational criteria such as emotion, prophecy, faith and pure will. This is left to the individual to decide.

There is no shortage of "good nonsense" in the I/T literature, seminar presentations, books, and vendor handouts. It is your obligation to be a logical consumer.

Figure H.1 summarizes the critical relationship between reason and strategy. Business success is an accident of strategy. Strategy, as taught by Sun Tzu, is to be deep and far reaching. If you are to accomplish that, you require convincing arguments which are valid and persuasive. Reason is a necessary precursor to a winning strategy. The consequences of proceeding based on nonsense are obvious and need not be recounted. For those who follow the teachings of Sun Tzu, there is no praise of folly.

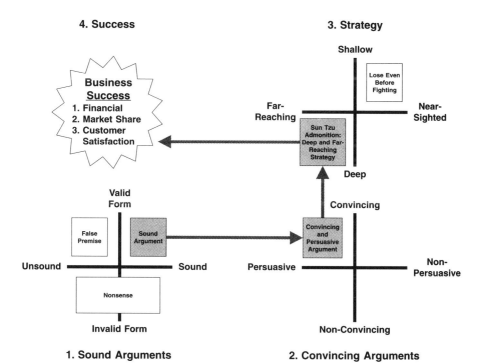

Figure H.1 Reason and Strategy. Convincing arguments which persuade are a necessary prerequisite to developing deep and far reaching strategy.

Index